MPLS VPN Security

Michael H. Behringer

Monique J. Morrow

Cisco Press

800 East 96th Street
Indianapolis, Indiana 46240 USA

MPLS VPN Security

Michael H. Behringer

Monique J. Morrow

Copyright © 2005 Cisco Systems, Inc.

Published by:
Cisco Press
800 East 96th Street
Indianapolis, IN 46240 USA

Printed in the United States of America 1 2 3 4 5 6 7 8 9 0

First Printing June 2005

Library of Congress Cataloging-in-Publication Number: 2003116565

ISBN: 1-58705-183-4

Warning and Disclaimer

This book is designed to provide information about **MPLS VPN security**. Every effort has been made to make this book as complete and accurate as possible, but no warranty or fitness is implied.

The information is provided on an "as is" basis. The author, Cisco Press, and Cisco Systems, Inc. shall have neither liability nor responsibility to any person or entity with respect to any loss or damages arising from the information contained in this book or from the use of the discs or programs that may accompany it.

The opinions expressed in this book belong to the author and are not necessarily those of Cisco Systems, Inc.

Trademark Acknowledgments

All terms mentioned in this book that are known to be trademarks or service marks have been appropriately capitalized. Cisco Press or Cisco Systems, Inc. cannot attest to the accuracy of this information. Use of a term in this book should not be regarded as affecting the validity of any trademark or service mark.

Corporate and Government Sales

Cisco Press offers excellent discounts on this book when ordered in quantity for bulk purchases or special sales.

For more information, please contact: **U.S. Corporate and Government Sales** 1-800-382-3419 (corpsales@pearsontechgroup.com).

For sales outside the U.S., please contact: **International Sales** international@pearsoned.com.

Feedback Information

At Cisco Press, our goal is to create in-depth technical books of the highest quality and value. Each book is crafted with care and precision, undergoing rigorous development that involves the unique expertise of members from the professional technical community.

Readers' feedback is a natural continuation of this process. If you have any comments regarding how we could improve the quality of this book or otherwise alter it to better suit your needs, you can contact us by e-mail at feedback@ciscopress.com. Please make sure to include the book title and ISBN in your message.

We greatly appreciate your assistance.

Publisher	John Wait
Editor-in-Chief	John Kane
Executive Editor	Brett Bartow
Cisco Representative	Anthony Wolfenden
Cisco Press Program Manager	Jeff Brady
Production Manager	Patrick Kanouse
Development Editor	Sheri Cain
Project Editor	Sheila Schroeder
Copy Editor	Emily Rader
Technical Editors	Saul Adler
	Raymond Zhang
	Marc Binderberger
	Reina Wang
Editorial Assistant	Tammi Barnett
Cover Designer	Louisa Adair
Composition	Interactive Composition Corporation
Indexer	Christine Karpeles
Proofreader	Melissa Pluta

CISCO SYSTEMS

Corporate Headquarters
Cisco Systems, Inc.
170 West Tasman Drive
San Jose, CA 95134-1706
USA
www.cisco.com
Tel: 408 526-4000
      800 553-NETS (6387)
Fax: 408 526-4100

European Headquarters
Cisco Systems International BV
Haarlerbergpark
Haarlerbergweg 13-19
1101 CH Amsterdam
The Netherlands
www-europe.cisco.com
Tel: 31 0 20 357 1000
Fax: 31 0 20 357 1100

Americas Headquarters
Cisco Systems, Inc.
170 West Tasman Drive
San Jose, CA 95134-1706
USA
www.cisco.com
Tel: 408 526-7660
Fax: 408 527-0883

Asia Pacific Headquarters
Cisco Systems, Inc.
Capital Tower
168 Robinson Road
#22-01 to #29-01
Singapore 068912
www.cisco.com
Tel: +65 6317 7777
Fax: +65 6317 7799

Cisco Systems has more than 200 offices in the following countries and regions. Addresses, phone numbers, and fax numbers are listed on the
Cisco.com Web site at www.cisco.com/go/offices.

Argentina • Australia • Austria • Belgium • Brazil • Bulgaria • Canada • Chile • China PRC • Colombia • Costa Rica • Croatia • Czech Republic
Denmark • Dubai, UAE • Finland • France • Germany • Greece • Hong Kong SAR • Hungary • India • Indonesia • Ireland • Israel • Italy
Japan • Korea • Luxembourg • Malaysia • Mexico • The Netherlands • New Zealand • Norway • Peru • Philippines • Poland • Portugal
Puerto Rico • Romania • Russia • Saudi Arabia • Scotland • Singapore • Slovakia • Slovenia • South Africa • Spain • Sweden
Switzerland • Taiwan • Thailand • Turkey • Ukraine • United Kingdom • United States • Venezuela • Vietnam • Zimbabwe

About the Authors

Michael H. Behringer obtained his diploma in computer science at the Technical University of Munich. For five years, he worked at the European Internet service provider DANTE, based in Cambridge, UK, where he last held the position of senior network engineer, responsible for the design and implementation of DANTE's pan-European networks. In 1998, Michael joined Cisco Systems and is now based in Nice. As a senior distinguished engineer, he focuses on service provider security issues such as MPLS security and denial-of-service attack prevention.

Michael is an active member of the IETF, where he started publishing work on MPLS VPN security in 2001. He is the author of "Analysis of the Security of BGP/MPLS IP VPNs" (draft-behringer-mpls-security) and coauthor of "Security Framework for Provider Provisioned Virtual Private Networks" (draft-ietf-l3vpn-security-framework). Michael is a frequent speaker at security and networking conferences and has published a number of articles.

Monique J. Morrow is currently a CTO consulting engineer at Cisco Systems, Inc. She has more than 20 years' experience in IP internetworking, including design, implementation of complex customer projects, and service development for service providers. Monique has been involved in developing managed network services such as remote access and LAN switching in a service provider environment. She has worked for both enterprise and service provider companies in the United States and in Europe. Monique led the Engineering Project team for one of the first European MPLS VPN deployments in 1999 for a European service provider.

Monique has been a speaker at the following conferences: MPLS Congress-Paris, 2000; MPLSCon 2000, London; MPLS Japan, 2002; APRICOT, Taipei, Taiwan, 2003; MPLScon 2003; Supercomm 2003; MPLS Japan 2003, MPLS Japan 2004; IEEE IPOM in Beijing, 2004; MPLS Conference 2003; The 16th Communication Systems Workshop (CSWS) on Information, Communication, and Signal Processing ("Verification of Broadband Services and Its Future," Nov. 12–13, 2003) by Communications System Engineers in IEICE, Japan; APRICOT 2004 in Kuala Lumpur; and has spoken at several Cisco Networker conferences.

Monique is coauthor of the book *Developing IP-Based Services: Solutions for Service Providers and Vendors* (Morgan-Kaufmann, 2002). Monique was a technical reviewer for the book *Internet QoS: Architectures and Mechanisms for Quality of Service*, by Zheng Wang (Morgan-Kaufmann, 2001). She contributed a chapter on MPLS to the book *Networks: Internet, Telephony, Multimedia: Convergences and Complementarities*, by Daniel Hardy, et al (De Boeck Diffusion, 2002; France Telecom Lead) and was content reviewer for the book *MPLS and VPN Architectures*, Volume II, by Ivan Pepelnjak, et al (Cisco Press, 2003).

Monique is currently working on three books—one exploring business aspects of MPLS, another discussing MPLS VPN security, and a third presenting enterprise drivers and concerns for IP-based service delivery.

Monique is active in both the IETF and ITU-T SG 13, with a focus on OAM. She has an M.S. in telecommunications management and an M.B.A. Monique is also a Cisco Certified Engineering Expert (#1711).

Monique is currently engaged in MPLS OAM standards development and has been engaged in carrier discussions internationally on the topic. Monique is co-guest editor of a special issue of the *IEEE Communications Magazine* on the topic "OAM in MPLS-Based Networks," published in October 2004 (http://www.comsoc.org/ci1/Public/ 2004/oct/index.html).

Monique is co-guest editor of a special issue of the *IEEE Communications Magazine* on the topic "Inter-Provider Service Quality on the Internet," with publication scheduled for June 2005 (http://www.metanoia-inc.com/ IEEECommMag_InterProviderQoS_CFP.htm).

Additionally, Monique is working on GMPLS, GRiD, and next-generation network topics pertinent to both carriers and NRENs, where delivery between providers is a key. In the area of GMPLS, Monique is co-guest editor of the *IEEE Communications Magazine* on the topic "GMPLS: The Promise of the Next Generation Optical Control Plane," with publication scheduled for July 2005.

About the Technical Reviewers

Saul Adler is a systems architect at Cisco Systems, focusing on network infrastructure security. He is currently focused on service provider network security with a focus on MPLS security requirements. As a former vice president and network architecture manager for both Bankers Trust and Deutsche Bank, Saul has more than 15 years' experience in designing, deploying, and supporting global enterprise networks. This includes solutions for supporting the data center, trading floor, branch office, Internet DMZ, and telecommuters. Saul obtained an MSEE from Polytechnic University in Brooklyn, New York.

Marc Binderberger is an IP architect at COLT Telecom Plc. His focus is backbone technologies such as routing protocols and MPLS, design and implementation of Internet and VPN networks, and related security aspects. Marc holds a Ph.D. in physics and has eight years' experience in telecommunication and networking technologies.

Y. Reina Wang has more than 10 years' experience in the packet switching network industry as a networking engineer for Bell Labs and AT&T Labs. Her area of expertise aligns on new network feature implementation and realization in the service provider network scope. Her profound and up-to-date knowledge in IP Multicast, MPLS VPN, MPLS Inter-AS VPN, and Multicast VPN, coupled with hands-on and practical experience, prepared her as a lead engineer in enabling these network features in large and complex network environments. Currently working in the IP Network Certification Organization at AT&T Labs, leading for AT&T global IP network feature enablement testing. Reina graduated from the Georgia Institute of Technology and earned master's degrees in physics and electrical engineering.

Raymond Zhang is a senior network architect for INFONET in the areas of global IP backbone infrastructure, routing and service architecture planning, and their evolutions. Current main areas of interest are large-scale backbone routing, traffic engineering, performance and statistical analysis, MPLS-related technologies (including PPVPN, interdomain traffic engineering, multiprovider QoS and security, and so on), and multicast.

Dedications

To my parents: Ihr habt mich zu dem gemacht was ich bin.

—Michael Behringer

I dedicate this book to family and dear friends who have been passionate in supporting this effort; my parents, Sam and Odette Morrow; and a super friend in life, Veronique Thevenaz.

—Monique Morrow

To all of our customers and colleagues who continue to ask hard questions.

Acknowledgments

We wish to acknowledge a number of people who have made this book possible, namely our employer, Cisco Systems, and our managers, Christine Hemrick, Steven Steinhilber, Chip Sharp, and Axel Clauberg. Without their support, this book would not have been written. We are grateful to our technical reviewers who have assured that the content is of quality and relevant to the industry: Y. Reina Wang, AT&T; Marc Binderberger, COLT Telecom; Raymond Zhang, INFONET; and Saul Adler, Cisco Systems. We would like to thank these reviewers for their time and effort. Additionally, we would like to acknowledge the following individuals at Cisco Systems who have contributed to this effort (unknowingly): Azhar Sayeed, Sangita Pandiya, Jim Guichard, Mark Townsley, Gery Czirjak, Thomas Nadeau, George Swallow, Alexander Renner, Laure Andrieux, Eric Vyncke, Jeff Apcar, and Barry Greene. It has truly been a team effort! We also thank Jayshree Ullal, senior vice president of Security at Cisco Systems, for taking the time out of her very busy schedule to write the foreword to our book. Finally, we are most grateful to our editors and the Cisco Press team—Raina Han, Brett Bartow, Jim Schachterle, Sheri Cain, and Tammi Barnett—for working diligently with us on this book and keeping it on schedule for publication.

This Book Is Safari Enabled

The Safari® Enabled icon on the cover of your favorite technology book means the book is available through Safari Bookshelf. When you buy this book, you get free access to the online edition for 45 days.

Safari Bookshelf is an electronic reference library that lets you easily search thousands of technical books, find code samples, download chapters, and access technical information whenever and wherever you need it.

To gain 45-day Safari Enabled access to this book:

- Go to http://www.ciscopress.com/safarienabled
- Complete the brief registration form
- Enter the coupon code PCKR-VECJ-JXK8-I9JG-UYYF

If you have difficulty registering on Safari Bookshelf or accessing the online edition, please e-mail customer-service@safaribooksonline.com.

Contents at a Glance

Table of Contents

Foreword

In 1996, Cisco pioneered a concept called *tag switching* to establish efficient tags and protocols across a connection-oriented ATM network. A decade later, tag switching has permeated into the core of large-scale internetworks using MPLS (Multiprotocol Label Switching) to become the mainstream standard. In parallel, network security has also evolved from simple access lists and perimeter firewalls to the creation of remote secure access and tunnels across thousands of users and subscribers using VPNs (virtual private networks). This powerful combination of security and scale has generated one of the most versatile solutions for the Internet of the 21st century.

At Cisco, the innovations of MPLS VPNs with built-in Cisco IOS services deliver versatile voice, video, and data access at multigigabit line rates to achieve successful enterprise and service provider networks. The software code base has grown from several thousand lines to an excess of a million lines, and the engineering staff has grown from a handful of engineers to more than 1000 engineers.

There are many components that comprise the Cisco Self-Defending Networks including foundational IP protection, threat defense, trust and identity, effective transport connectivity, and secure management. Large service provider and enterprise customers are wrestling with the threat models and network scalability as the adoption of MPLS permeates widely. This book offers a unique guide to technology aspects of MPLS VPN security, providing deployment guidelines for building Internet-class security with real-world case studies. It addresses the key priority for customers: securing and managing services with high network availability.

Over the past decade, internetworks have evolved from adjunct security to integrated and holistic capabilities, tightly interwoven into the fabric of Cisco switches, routers, and appliances. The authors of this book, Michael Behringer and Monique Morrow, have a deep and rich understanding of security issues such as denial-of-service attack prevention and infrastructure protection from network vulnerabilities. They offer a very practical perspective on the deployment scenarios, thereby demystifying a complex topic. I hope you enjoy their insights into the design of self-defending networks.

Jayshree V Ullal

Senior VP/GM Security Tech Group
Cisco Systems, Inc.

Icons Used in This Book

 PC

 Sun Workstation

 Terminal

 File Server

 Laptop

 Gateway

 Router/CE/RR

 Bridge

 VPN

 Catalyst Switch

 Multilayer Switch

 ATM Switch

 Cache

 PE/ASBR

 P

 Network Cloud

Line: Ethernet

Line: Serial

Line: Switched Serial

 Optical Services Router

 PIX Firewall

 Route/Switch Processor

Command Syntax Conventions

The conventions used in this book to present command syntax are the same conventions used in the IOS Command Reference. The Command Reference describes these conventions as follows:

- **Boldface** indicates commands and keywords that are entered literally as shown.
- *Italics* indicate arguments for which you supply actual values.
- Vertical bars (|) separate alternative, mutually exclusive elements.
- Square brackets ([ ]) indicate optional elements.
- Braces ({ }) indicate a required choice.
- Braces within brackets ([{ }]) indicate a required choice within an optional element.

Introduction

Much has been written about MPLS as a technology and service enabler—and certainly, for the past several years, both service providers and enterprises have been deploying MPLS in their networks. This book focuses on the security aspects of MPLS VPNs for implementation, and it goes further to discuss not only MPLS architectural security, but security overall and its impact on deployment. Security, when implemented correctly, enables networks to run business-critical applications, even on a shared infrastructure or on the Internet. Therefore, we have written this book in order to provide best practice guidelines and to discuss security principles as companies deploy MPLS in their networks. Bear in mind that any network, whether it is a voice, Frame Relay, or ATM network, can be attacked and has been. Having an awareness of security and the security requirements for networks and services is the first step toward mitigating against such attacks.

Who Should Read This Book

This book is intended for network managers, engineers, and network operations and security staff of organizations that deploy MPLS or are subscribers of a service based on MPLS. We have provided configuration examples for the operations team to balance theory with practical examples of the security principles.

How This Book Is Organized

Part I, "MPLS VPN and Security Fundamentals," gives the foundations for MPLS VPN security work:

- Chapter 1, "MPLS VPN Security: An Overview," gives a short introduction to the fundamental principles of security and how MPLS VPNs work, and provides comparison to other VPN technologies. It also defines "zones of trust" for an MPLS VPN environment.

- Every security project should first define the threats against each trusted zone. Chapter 2, "A Threat Model for MPLS VPNs," builds a threat model with specific attack points.

Overall security is determined by the security of three components: the architecture, the design, and the operation. Part II, "Advanced MPLS VPN Security Issues," discusses these three components separately:

- Chapter 3, "MPLS Security Analysis," analyzes the MPLS VPN *architecture* on its security properties. It explains which level of security can be reached using this architecture and how the architecture can be secured adequately against the threats defined in Chapter 2.

- Chapter 4, "Secure MPLS VPN Designs," explains how to *design* secure MPLS VPN networks. It gives recommendations on how to implement various network topologies securely.

- Chapter 5, "Security Recommendations," suggests how to *operate* the network securely. Best practices in securing routers are explained here, and many examples are given.

Part III, "Practical Guidelines to MPLS VPN Security," discusses special cases:

- Chapter 6, "How IPsec Complements MPLS," discusses applications of IPsec in MPLS VPN environments.

- Chapter 7, "Security of MPLS Layer 2 VPNs," explains special security issues in Layer 2 VPNs.
- Chapter 8, "Secure Operation and Maintenance of an MPLS Core," explains how to manage an MPLS VPN network securely.

The book is rounded up by some practical case studies, a configuration example, and resources in Part IV, "Case Studies and Appendixes":

- Chapter 9, "Case Studies," encompasses details from all the previous chapters to provide examples for overall secure solutions.
- Appendix A, "Detailed Configuration Example for a PE," provides an example of a number of security features configured on a single router.
- Appendix B, "Reference List," provides a list of sources to which you can refer for more information on MPLS VPN security.

MPLS VPN and Security Fundamentals

In this chapter, you learn about the following:

- Key security concepts
- VPN technologies
- MPLS VPN fundamentals
- MPLS VPN security reference model

CHAPTER 1

MPLS VPN Security: An Overview

This chapter provides the basic building blocks for understanding MPLS VPN security by explaining security concepts and the fundamentals of VPN technologies, such as MPLS VPN. Further, it develops a security reference model for MPLS VPNs that serves as a foundation for terminology and key concepts in later chapters.

Key Security Concepts

To be able to analyze and evaluate the security of MPLS networks, it is important to understand some fundamental security concepts. This section specifically targets network engineers who normally do not work much with security. For security engineers, this section serves as a review of the fundamentals.

This section discusses these fundamental security concepts:

- Security differs from other technologies
- What is "secure"?
- There is no such thing as 100 percent security
- Three components of system security
- Principle of the weakest link
- Principle of the least privilege
- Other important security concepts

Security Differs from Other Technologies

This book targets both networking and security professionals not as separate groups, but as a joint engineering team. Together, both groups need to design, implement, and operate a network for it to be functional and secure. Security has to be planned into the network from the beginning because various functional networking solutions may have completely different security properties. This is also the reason why security cannot be easily retrofitted into an existing network: Some network design decisions might later complicate network security. For example, if the address plan of a network is disjoined with contiguous subnets distributed over different parts of the company, it is harder to define a consistent security policy. Therefore, a good network design and operation should always involve both the network engineers and the security engineers.

However, companies often have relatively strict separation between the networking group and the security group. Sometimes this separation is formalized in an organizational structure, but even when both types of engineers are part of the same group, the security engineers and the rest of the group frequently have communication issues. When both groups must jointly manage some parts of a network, frictions can regularly be observed between the groups.

The security group is often seen by the networking people as too restrictive, and networking people often have the reputation of being too permissive. The typical discussion centers on a new security measure, which requires network management changes. The network engineers do not acknowledge the added value of the new measure ("we have never had an issue with this"), while the security group deems it necessary. Often there is no objective way to prove the effectiveness of a security measure.

One of the main reasons that it is important for both network and security engineers to be involved in the network design is that security as a technology area is substantially different from other technology areas: To succeed in other areas, such as wide-area networking, one needs to find a single way among several options to implement a solution. For example, there are many ways to interconnect two sites, with a number of technologies such as MPLS, ATM, and so on, and with various routing protocols. Many of these options will lead to success, maybe with subtle differences. So an engineer can select one of several options and implement it. Proving that this solution works is relatively simple and can be done by simulating user behavior and tools. Even if some aspects of a technology do not work as expected, the solution can often be used anyway. Maybe one routing protocol converges faster than another in the case of an outage of connections; but in most cases, both protocols will be sufficient for the solution. So in most technologies, there are many possible solutions, and only one is required for an implementation.

In security, this logic is reversed: a security engineer is successful if no security breaches occur. This cannot be fully tested, so there is never a full guarantee that all security mechanisms are configured correctly. An intrusion into a VPN, for example, can occur in many different ways: through a vulnerability in a company web server, a configuration mistake on the firewall, or an unsecured modem in somebody's office. So while a network engineer can quite easily prove that his network is still working correctly, a security engineer can only do this by testing all potentially vulnerable points of the network. However, one single security breach can uncover an engineering mistake.

In other words, the difference between security and other technologies lies in how one defines success: *A network engineer is successful when he finds one single way to implement a network. A security engineer is unsuccessful if there is one single way to break into the system.* It is very hard to prove that a security engineer is successful: only failures are clearly visible.

What Is "Secure"?

When talking about security concepts, the first question one needs to answer is, "What is meant by the term 'secure'"? In fact, there is no global definition for this concept. In a normal family household, for example, a good door lock is considered adequate security. In a jeweler's shop, a door has to be considerably more robust to be secure; and in a bank, there might be guards in addition to several strong doors. So in every scenario, the first step is to define "secure."

Early discussions on MPLS VPN security had exactly this problem: To some users, "secure" was equivalent to "encryption." Of course, with this definition, MPLS VPNs as such would be insecure. Many enterprises, however, do not necessarily require encryption, and for them "secure" meant essentially separation from other networks. These two viewpoints clashed because they were based on different definitions for "secure." Based on their respective definitions, both groups were actually right.

Both enterprises and service providers define corporate security in a security policy. A *security policy* defines the necessary technical measures and operational procedures to secure a network. The starting point is a *threat model*, which defines security exposure on different levels; for example, physical security (somebody carrying out a computer) or network security (hackers gaining illegitimate access to network resources). The threat model serves as a basis for defining security requirements.

In the MPLS VPN environment, security can be viewed from two different angles: from the VPN customer and from the service provider. Both possess different threat models: For a customer, it is important to safeguard against network intrusions from outside of the customer's VPN. Therefore, one of the main threats for a VPN customer is intrusions into his or her domain. For a service provider, one of the key issues is availability of the core network. Thus one of the main threats is prevention of denial of service (DoS) attacks. Both aspects are important in MPLS VPN scenarios, but each part of the network has a different emphasis in its threat model.

NOTE	Real or perceived threats may change over time, and the security policy might need to be updated to reflect such changes. Security is not static—it is an ongoing process in which the threat model periodically needs to be reviewed. The security policy and measures must then be updated.

The security reference model described later in this chapter in the section "A Security Reference Model for MPLS VPNs" allows the clear distinction of the different network zones in an MPLS VPN environment and defines the so-called "zones of trust." Each of these zones of trust has its own security policy and its own threat model.

So the formally correct way to define "secure" in a certain context is to start by defining the zones of trust in a given environment and then to develop a threat model for each zone and for the overall environment. "Secure" can then be defined using the requirements coming from the threat model.

This book follows this procedure as well: In this chapter, we define the zones of trust for an MPLS VPN environment, we define a threat model, and in Chapter 3 we define the security requirements. Thus, the first three chapters define the term "secure" for the context of MPLS VPNs and serve as a basis for the rest of the book.

No System Is 100 Percent Secure

There is no absolute, 100 percent system security despite the fact that single components of a given system may be 100 percent secure. Entire systems can never be 100 percent secure—often because of the human factor involved.

For example, the one-time pad (OTP) in cryptography is a 100 percent secure encryption algorithm. Every bit in the clear text is encrypted using a bit from a key string. If the key string is as long as the plain text and is never reused, and if the bits in the key string are entirely random, the encryption as such is 100 percent secure. However, of course, this key string has to be carried from the encrypting to the decrypting side. It may be intercepted, or the device used for writing the message may have a backdoor that allows sniffing the plain text. So the overall system will never be 100 percent secure.

When engineers are asked to work on new projects, they are often given sloppy guidelines such as "it must be secure," without any further explanation. One of the problems here is, as explained above, that the term "secure" needs to be defined. Second, even if there is a clear understanding of what is meant by the term "secure" in a certain context, security is not an absolute value and can never be achieved 100 percent. A more reasonable approach is to define a system as sufficiently secure against a list of perceived threats. This is one of the reasons why a security policy must contain a threat model. Security must always be measured against perceived threats.

Three Components of System Security

Many discussions about MPLS VPN security commenced with analysis of the architectural aspects of the solution. For example, the assertion was made that nobody can intrude from the outside of a customer network into a customer VPN. The technical reason for this was that the service provider core would not accept labeled packets from outside the service provider network.

Then the customer discovered that if an operator misconfigured a provider edge (PE) router, VPN separation would no longer be guaranteed. The customer concluded that MPLS is insecure, but this is an incorrect conclusion because the problem of the misconfiguration is an operational problem that can happen in any technology. Network operations must be strictly controlled to avoid such problems. These discussions confused the origin of the security problems by assuming they were architectural rather than operational.

This confusion became apparent when traditional VPN technologies, such as ATM, were looked at. People had to admit that those technologies had essentially the same problems, yet they were assumed to be secure. So what went wrong in these discussions?

The previous OTP example provides an explanation: even if an algorithm is proven to be 100 percent secure, the overall system might still have weaknesses in other areas.

Therefore, when classifying the overall security of a system such as an MPLS VPN network, one has to analyze separately the three fundamental parts that compose the system (see Figure 1-1):

- The **architecture** (or **algorithm**) used—This is the formal specification. In cryptography, the algorithm itself, in the case of MPLS VPNs, is the formal specification (as defined in RFC 2547bis, "BGP/MPLS IP VPNs." See www.ietf.org/internet-drafts/draft-ietf-13-vpn-rfc2547bis-03.text, which is a work in progress.)

- **Implementation** of that architecture or algorithm—This refers to how the architecture or algorithm is actually implemented in reality. Programming mistakes, such as buffer overflows, play a role here.

- **Operation** of the architecture of algorithm—This includes operator issues, such as choosing weak passwords on routers or workstations, or accidental disclosure of a shared key, such as if configurations are sent to untrusted third parties.

Figure 1-1   *Three Key Components of Security*

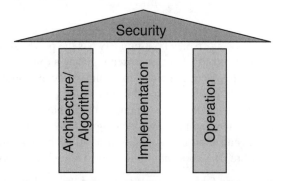

Whenever system security is discussed, it is paramount to separate these three components and to analyze the security of each single one of them. It also helps to understand this separation when defining security policies because the best algorithm is useless when operated in a weak way. In practice, one can find systems where a lot of effort was put into securing the architecture, but its operation was completely neglected. Password management in enterprises is an example of this: often, very good security systems are rendered useless because users choose weak passwords. The designers of such systems should keep in mind that the overall security depends on all three security components.

This book keeps these three parts of a system separate: Chapters 3 and 4 focus solely on the architecture as defined in the standard RFC 2547bis. In these chapters, there are no references to implementation or operation at all; the essential question answered in Chapters 3 and 4 is whether the standard is secure, or in other words, whether an MPLS VPN network as defined by the standard can be operated securely. Chapters 5 through 8 then describe the implementation and operational issues.

Principle of the Weakest Link

Earlier in this chapter, we made the observation that *a security engineer is unsuccessful if there is one single way to break into the system*. There is an important detail in this sentence: only one weakness is required to break the security of an entire system. The common analogy used to explain this is a chain: if one link breaks, the whole chain is broken.

In practical security systems, much effort is usually put into technical measurement, but quite often, the weakest link is the human factor. There are many well-known cases of this, such as users giving out their passwords freely to someone calling them on the phone, or configuration errors in otherwise very secure systems.

NOTE   In MPLS VPN security, the human factor is critical to the overall system security. An engineer might accidentally or deliberately misconfigure network elements, and this can lead to severe security breaches for the connected VPNs.

Because there must be a person who ultimately has the power to configure a router, there is always the possibility of that person misconfiguring a router. This problem cannot be completely averted. In practice, the way to minimize the exposure to human mistakes is to use automated tools as much as possible and to use a strict authorization system in conjunction with logging. Of course, automated tools have their own problems, but they provide consistency and prevent mistyping and transient mistakes, such as wrong parameters. The specific topic of operations in an MPLS network will be discussed in detail in Chapter 8, "Secure Operation and Maintenance of an MPLS Core."

Even though the human factor is, in practice, often the weakest link, other parts of the security system might also be flawed and need to be monitored carefully. The security policy should cover all parts of the system with their potential weaknesses, and it should be checked regularly. The only way to find and eliminate the weakest link in a network is with consistent monitoring and tight operational control.

Principle of the Least Privilege

Because human mistakes are an important security risk, the most secure way to design systems is to provide every operator only the authorization strictly required to perform the job. This is called the principle of the *least privilege*. The idea is that every privilege an operator or user has might lead to potential security breaches, and that therefore every privilege must be monitored and controlled. The less an operator is authorized to do, the less control and monitoring needs must be done and the smaller the overall risk of security problems.

In this area, MPLS networks do not behave any differently than other networks, and the normal controls for network operations apply equally. More information on how to secure a core network can be found in the book *Cisco ISP Essentials* (1-58705-041-2; published by Cisco Press).

The principle of the least privilege was originally devised in the context of human operators. However, the principle of the least privilege can equally be applied to general network security in that, on a network, everything should be restricted as much as possible. For example, it is not necessary for a user outside the core network (on the Internet or in a VPN) to send packets to core routers. Only very few protocols must reach the core routers from outside the core network—routing protocols are the obvious case (for example, BGP to and from the external peers). Therefore, the "privilege" to send traffic into the network should be limited from the outside to what is really required, such as routing. This type of traffic filtering is also referred to as *infrastructure access control lists (iACLs)*. Further discussion on this topic can be found in the book *Cisco ISP Essentials*, mentioned previously.

Other Important Security Concepts

Of course, security is a broad field, and it is impossible to capture all the details in a short introduction. However, some additional security concepts are worth mentioning briefly:

- **Confidentiality, integrity, availability**—These are the three basic properties of security (some text books add authenticity as a fourth). When defining security, one can be more precise by defining which of the security properties is required to which extent. For example in a military environment, the most important security property is probably confidentiality. In a bank, confidentiality is important, too, but even more important is the integrity of the data: it is imperative that no customer data such as account balances be accidentally or maliciously changed. For an online shopping site, however, availability of the web page is an important factor: every minute the web site is not available leads to direct loss of revenue. Overall, security can usually be defined using these three properties.

In the MPLS context, every VPN customer will have slightly different requirements for these parameters, but generally, customers will expect their data to be private (confidential), such that they are not accessible outside their VPN. They will expect the data not to change in transit, and they will expect the MPLS VPN service overall to be available to them—in other words, that it suffer very few or no outages.

- **Defense in depth**—Because one weak link is sufficient to endanger the security of an overall system, it is common practice to construct several "layers" of security around a solution, such that if one single component breaks, others still defend the assets. The best example of this in enterprise networks is the demilitarized zone (DMZ). In a DMZ, a company's servers are usually highly protected; however, even if this protection fails and a hacker gains access to a server, there is still a firewall to overcome to get into the network.

  It is good practice to add several layers of defense around everything that needs to be protected. This design principle is also important in MPLS networks.

- **Secure failure**—The primary mode of operation of any technology is usually well thought through and well secured. However, when the primary method fails, the backup method also needs to be secured appropriately. It is common practice today to use secure shell (SSH) for router configuration; however, a backup method of getting to a router is necessary in case the SSH server fails, for example. This is usually done through out-of-band access, mostly over the telephone network. It is important that this backup mode be as secure as the principal access mode.

There is ample literature available for more detail on security in general and in the networking context. Please refer to Appendix B for recommendations.

Overview of VPN Technologies

It is difficult to define precisely what constitutes a virtual private network (VPN) because the term means different things to different people. To some people, separation of their traffic on a network is sufficient to call it "private"; others expect encryption when they hear the word "private." The opposite seems clearer: a private network is strictly speaking completely separate from other networks. Of course, with this definition almost any network invented after the telegraph system in 1837 by Samuel Morse would be a virtual network. Today's "private" leased lines, for example, use a shared SONET or Synchronous Digital Hierarchy (SDH) infrastructure, and the physical lines or fibers carry many different "private" networks.

For any practical discussion in the context of MPLS, ATM, Frame Relay, and other VPN technologies, operators currently understand that services delivered over SONET or SDH are regarded as private because separation over these carrier technologies is so efficient that users cannot detect the sharing of core fibers.

VPNs thus exist in many different forms and have been classified in a variety of ways. All of these classifications exist because of different user requirements. VPN technologies can also be used in a nested way, that is, over an existing VPN such as a company intranet where it is possible to further define more detailed VPNs.

The criteria that distinguish VPN technologies from each other include the following:

- **Connection-oriented/connectionless technologies**—Many VPN technologies are connection oriented. That means that a VPN user who connects to the VPN service appears to have a connection to another VPN user. Examples for connection-oriented VPNs are IPsec, GRE, and IP-in-IP. Also point-to-multipoint technologies, such as multipoint GRE (mGRE), introduced in IOS Version 12.2T, are essentially connection oriented, even if the other endpoints might not be configured but discovered dynamically.

  MPLS is a connectionless VPN technology: a VPN user (customer equipment) does not have a direct relationship with any other VPN user; rather, it is connected to the MPLS service as a "cloud," which ensures that packets are forwarded correctly to the other VPN user site. Specifically, a VPN user does not have explicit knowledge of other VPN users. This is one of the key advantages of MPLS IP VPNs: they scale very well because less VPN information needs to be kept at the edge. Figure 1-2 shows the differences between connectionless and connection-oriented technologies.

Figure 1-2   *Connectionless Versus Connection-Oriented VPN Types*

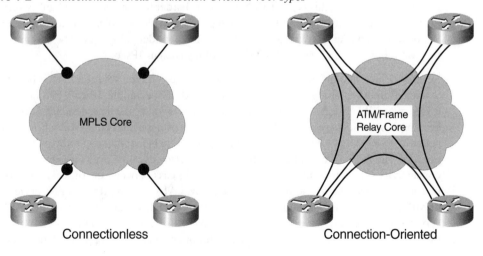

Connectionless   Connection-Oriented

- **Encrypted/non-encrypted**—Encrypted VPN types are typically used where confidentiality of data in transit is required, such as over a wireless network or the public Internet. The most widely used encrypting VPN technology today is IPsec, although other types based on transport layer security (TLS) or secure sockets layer (SSL) are on the increase. MPLS is by default nonencrypting. Encryption can be added (using PE-PE IPsec, for example).

- **Internet based/not Internet based**—Some VPN types can be used over the public Internet and thus allow easy interconnection of sites worldwide, assuming availability of Internet services in these locations. IPsec, GRE, IP-in-IP, TLS, and SSH are examples of VPN technologies that can be used over the Internet. The advantage of Internet-based VPN types is their mostly worldwide availability; the disadvantage is that often no quality-of-service guarantees are available for such services.

NOTE   Today, most MPLS VPN deployments use private infrastructure. The Internet is used within a core only in exceptional cases. Many deployments use Internet-based technologies such as IPsec to connect to a PE from the outside. So while the access to the MPLS VPN core is often Internet based, the core itself is usually built on private infrastructure.

VPN technologies can only be judged in the context they are being used in. There is no overall valid definition of "good" or "bad" VPN services. For a small public organization with few but far away offices, it might be perfectly acceptable to use a simple tunneling technique, such as GRE or IP-in-IP, to be able to interconnect sites over the public Internet. For larger companies, this type of VPN would be harder to manage for scalability reasons; they might prefer MPLS-based VPNs to keep their network simpler and easier to manage. For organizations dealing with secret information, confidentiality would be essential, and they would use some encrypting VPN technology such as IPsec.

Several VPN technologies can be used together in one common solution. This is being done where different technologies address different needs. For example, IPsec VPNs can be used on top of an MPLS VPN. This type of architecture is not necessarily redundant: IPsec might be chosen because there is a need for confidentiality on the data path. Many European countries, for example, by law require encryption of personal data over any public data network, and this is often addressed by using IPsec. However, the organization still requires connectivity between its sites for its IPsec traffic to pass between the offices. This could be addressed over the public Internet, but also over ATM, Frame Relay VPN services, or MPLS. Each of these options has its advantages and disadvantages, but MPLS VPN services have been used often in the past due to consistent service guarantees not available on the public Internet, as well as to often better prices than on other VPN technologies.

Fundamentals of MPLS VPNs

To understand MPLS VPN technology, it is important to know its basic concepts. This section explains the nomenclature used in MPLS VPN networks and how MPLS works in simple terms. One important differentiator of MPLS networks is that they employ a connectionless VPN technology. The concepts of MPLS and VPN technology are explained here.

Nomenclature of MPLS VPNs

RFC 2547bis, "BGP/MPLS IP VPNs," describes the nomenclature and definitions used in the MPLS VPN framework. More precisely, it defines IP VPNs, meaning that the VPN service accepts IP datagrams from customer sites and delivers them also as IP datagrams to other customer sites. The connection between a customer site and the core network, also referred to as an *attachment circuit*, may be a Layer 2 service such as ATM, but the VPN service handles only IP datagrams transmitted over this link.

Internally, an RFC 2547bis-compliant network uses the Border Gateway Protocol (BGP) to route VPN information across the core. This is invisible to the VPN customers, but it does have security implications for the operation of the network in that BGP is a vital part of the overall system and must be secured adequately by the service provider. On the CE-PE link, static routing can be used, as well as any dynamic routing protocol, such as BGP or RIP.

For the remainder of this book, the term "MPLS VPN" will be used for the type of VPN defined in RFC 2547bis unless explicitly stated otherwise.

This book uses the same nomenclature as the RFCs; they are listed here for your reference:

- **Service provider**—The organization providing an MPLS VPN service to a customer.
- **Customer**—An organization receiving an MPLS VPN service from the service provider. This organization can itself be a service provider, an enterprise or set of enterprises, an application service provider, or other organizational entities.
- **Core network**—The network, which is provided by the service provider and to which the customers connect.
- **Customer edge (CE) router** —Used to connect to an MPLS VPN. It is typically located at a customer site.
- **Provider edge (PE) router**—CEs connect to PEs on the MPLS core network. The PE is part of the MPLS core, and the service provider maintains it.
- **Provider (P) router** —Used inside the MPLS core, providing connectivity between the PEs. Normally, a P router does not have VPN information, but only information on how to reach the PEs.

Figure 1-3 shows an MPLS VPN network with connected VPNs. The core consists of PE and P routers. Customer routers (CEs) connect to the PEs. One PE can hold several CEs of different VPNs or the same VPN.

Figure 1-3 *MPLS VPN Structure*

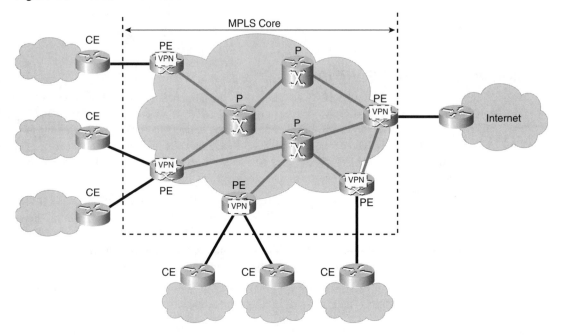

Three Planes of an MPLS VPN Network

Every network can be described by its three planes. This section describes the fundamentals of MPLS VPN networks by giving a brief description of the separate planes:

- **Control plane**—The way control information is exchanged through the network
- **Data plane**—How user traffic is forwarded through the network
- **Management plane**—How the elements of the network are managed

Especially when discussing security in a network, it is important to clearly analyze each plane on its own because security problems might arise in any of them.

How the Control Plane Works

In MPLS VPN networks, the *control plane* is defined by various routing instances. The CE announces the IPv4 or IPv6 routes from its site to the PE, and the PE announces to the CE the routes from other sites of the VPN. This can be done through static or dynamic routing. In principle, any routing protocol is suitable for this link (BGP or OSPF, for example).

NOTE   The content of this book is equally applicable for IPv4 and IPv6 networks. Unless there is a difference in the handling of IPv4 and IPv6, this book uses the term IP without referring to the version.

On the PE, routing information for each VPN is held in a *VPN routing/forwarding instance (VRF)*. Each VRF typically has some external interfaces to CEs associated with it, all belonging to the same VPN.

The ingress PE distributes the site's routes received from the CE and stored in the VRF to all other PEs that connect sites of this VPN. The routing protocol used for this is *Multi-Protocol Border Gateway Protocol (MP-BGP)*. MP-BGP needs another protocol to find the egress PEs. There are various ways of doing this, but they are beyond the scope of this book. (See Appendix B, "Reference List.")

To keep the control information of various VPNs separate, the PE must distinguish various VPNs. This is done by prepending a so-called *route distinguisher (RD)* to every VPN route received from the CE. This effectively creates a new addressing scheme: instead of using normal IP addresses, the MPLS core uses VPN-v4 or VPN-v6 addresses, which consist of the route distinguisher plus the IP address of the VPN. So between PEs, MP-BGP exchanges VPN-v4 or VPN-v6 routes.

On a PE, the VPN-specific routing exchange is controlled by *route targets* (RTs). RTs define which routes on the MPLS core are imported to and exported from which VRF.

NOTE   Misconfiguration of RTs can easily compromise the security of a VPN because they control which routes are imported into which VRF. In Chapter 2, "A Threat Model for MPLS VPNs," this security risk is explained in detail.

On the egress side, the egress PE uses the same mechanism as on the ingress side between PE and CE—that is, static or dynamic routing. The addresses exchanged here are normal IP addresses.

NOTE   The CE does not have to know that it is connected to a VPN service. From the CE's perspective, the PE is just a core router. It does not have visibility of any other VPN, nor of the MPLS core.

Figure 1-4 displays schematically which protocols are used in an MPLS VPN environment and where: The core itself runs MP-BGP for the VPN-specific information and runs an IGP plus typically LDP internally. The CEs are connected to the core through any standard routing protocol or through static routing.

Figure 1-4   *Control Plane in an MPLS VPN Network*

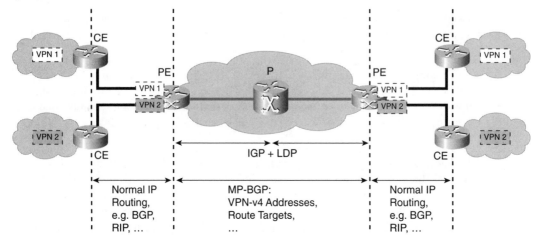

How the Data Plane Works

On the *data plane*, the CE forwards user traffic as normal IP traffic to the PE according to its routing table. Since the CE cannot "see" the core or other VPNs, the forwarding is the same as in any other network.

The PE forwards traffic from several VPNs, and because these VPNs may use the same address space, the forwarding on the MPLS core cannot use normal IP address space. Various methods are used to keep the traffic from different VPNs separate. This can be, for example, a *Label Switch Path (LSP)* or an IPsec tunnel. Common to all these methods is that the VPN traffic is carried in a type of tunnel. On LSPs, the most commonly used technique, the IP packet, is tunneled with a set of *labels*, as displayed in Figure 1-5. These labels distinguish the traffic of the various VPNs.

In most MPLS networks, the IP packet is attached to two labels:

- **Egress PE label**—Used by the core to direct the packet to the egress PE
- **VPN label**—Defines the VPN the packet belongs to

Both labels are removed before they are sent to the CE on egress, such that the egress CE receives a standard IP packet. The top label (PE label) is removed on the router before the egress PE, and before forwarding the packet to the egress PE. This technique is called "penultimate hop popping." This way the egress PE receives only the VPN label with the

underlying packet. The egress PE uses the VPN label to find the egress VPN, removes the
label, and sends the remaining IP packet to the CE.

Figure 1-5   *Labels Used in MPLS VPN Networks*

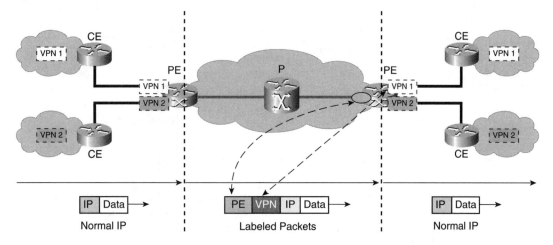

How the Management Plane Works

The *management plane* for the MPLS core is the same as in other IP networks. All devices
have in-band and out-of-band management channels, both of which are typically used.

The out-of-band channels are usually connected through a non-IP network, such as the
phone network, and controlled through terminal servers, where the routers of a service
provider's *Point of Presence (PoP)* are connected. These out-of-band channels are secured
through the terminal servers.

The in-band management channel connects the *network operations center (NOC)* of the
service provider to the devices that are to be managed over the IP network. Figure 1-6
shows in-band and out-of-band management channels. To secure this channel, several steps
are necessary:

- Each device needs to be secured by limiting access on the management channel to
  only the interfaces where this is required, and to only the source addresses that require
  access. In addition, strong authentication is required.

- The entire MPLS network should block the management channels that are used from
  the outside, such that outside users cannot send packets to the management ports. This
  practice is also referred to as infrastructure access control lists (iACL).

- The NOC must be protected against intrusions to avoid hackers to first take control of
  NOC systems, and then do device management from there.

All these points refer to operational best practices, which are described in detail in Chapter 5,
"Security Recommendations."

Figure 1-6 *Management Plane in MPLS VPN Networks*

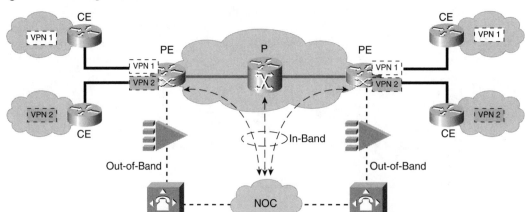

In some MPLS networks, the service provider also manages the CE routers, which are typically located at the customer premises. For out-of-band access to these CE routers, the same rules apply as for core network devices, which makes out-of-band access quite a secure channel.

In-band access to the CEs, however, has to be designed with more attention to security: In many networks, the service provider provisions two logical links between the PE and the CE, one for the VPN and one for management. Figure 1-7 shows the connection between the PE and the CE, where there is a separate logical link into the management VRF of the CE. The VPN link is part of the VPN, and VPN users are not able to intrude into other VPNs or the core. However, through the second logical link the CE has a direct connection into the management VPN and from there into the NOC. This needs to be secured against attacks from the CE or the site behind the CE. Chapter 8 discusses the options and gives recommendations on how to secure the management access.

Figure 1-7 *In-Band Management of CEs*

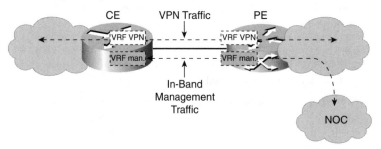

Another way to manage the CE is to use the single logical link between PE and CE also for management. In this scenario, a single loopback interface on the CE is imported into the management VRF, and the IP address of the management subnet is exported to the VRF of the customer, and from there to the CE.

From a functionality point of view, both setups are equivalent: the management stations can access the CE. However, if the CE-PE link is logically split into a VPN link and a management link, as shown in Figure 1-7, the management network can by default be better protected: only the CE has access to the management station, whereas in the model with a single link the entire VPN has access to it. This is due to the fact that in the first model the management routes are kept in a separate VRF on the CE. Access from the VPN to the management network can and should be restricted by ACLs. The best place to put those ACLs is the PE ingress interface.

NOTE   Remember that the CE is always untrusted because the service provider has no physical access control over it. A customer might, for example, swap the CE to circumvent any security measures configured on it.

More detail about managed CE solutions can be found in Chapter 8.

NOTE   For more details on the MPLS VPN architecture and its functionality, refer to RFC 2547bis.

Security Implications of Connectionless VPNs

MPLS-based VPN services have increased significantly over the past years. One of the reasons for this is that they can be provided more easily than traditional Layer 2 VPNs, such as ATM and Frame Relay. This ease of provisioning often leads to attractive pricing models for the customer.

One of the reasons why MPLS VPNs are easy to provision is that MPLS VPNs are not connection oriented. Whereas most traditional VPN types consist of a number of provisioned point-to-point connections, MPLS is connectionless, as illustrated in Figure 1-2.

The connectionless nature of MPLS VPNs has many implications for scalability of the overall MPLS network, but also for security: On an ATM network, for example, a VPN customer typically will be presented with a number of virtual connections from a given router to all other routers that need to be connected. However, the customer needs to configure the router to use these virtual connections. The disadvantage here is that many virtual connections have to be configured on both the customer side and the service provider side. The advantage is that the customer has full visibility of the VPN and controls the connections.

On an MPLS network, the same customer router will in most cases be presented with a single connection into the MPLS network, and it is the MPLS network itself that decides where to forward packets to. The customer loses the view of the connections through the core. The advantage of this approach is scalability: the provisioning complexity is reduced to a single connection for each customer router; but the customer does not have visibility of the core network anymore. A service provider could maliciously or inadvertently introduce into a customer's VPN a router that does not belong there. The customer might not detect this and have lost the integrity of the network. In Chapters 5 and 8 this threat will be discussed further and solutions will be discussed.

A Security Reference Model for MPLS VPNs

Whenever discussing security for a given system, it is important to define the security zones within this system. In a bank, for example, there are a number of security zones with defined "interfaces" between them: there is the outside of the bank, the open customer area inside the bank, the tills which are again separated from the customer area, and further security areas such as the safe room. In a security policy, the various security zones have to be described, security levels have to be assigned to them, and the "interfaces" have to be defined—that is, how to get from one zone to another.

The same procedure must be applied in the context of networks to define a security policy. The network must be divided into security zones, which must be clearly defined, and "interfaces" between the zones need to be described and defined. The Internet draft "Security Framework for Provider Provisioned VPNs" defines such a security reference model for MPLS VPNs. This RFC coins the generic term of *PPVPN network*. Since this book covers specifically BGP/MPLS VPN networks, the term *MPLS network* is used here.

Figure 1-8 illustrates the generic model used in the just mentioned security framework document, here applied to the MPLS VPN environment. An MPLS network consists of an MPLS core network and MPLS VPNs distributed over various VPN sites. An MPLS VPN is a service provided over an MPLS core network to a number of VPN users in various sites.

Figure 1-8   *Basic Security Reference Model for MPLS VPNs*

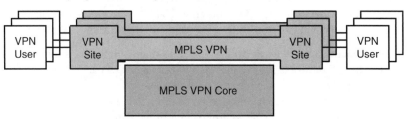

In this basic model, there are several restrictions: the VPNs cannot interconnect, and there is no extranet or Internet connectivity yet. Important for security considerations is that the zones are separated for any practical consideration: This separation means that it is not possible to send traffic from a VPN to another VPN, nor to the core. How this separation is achieved will be discussed in detail in Chapter 3. In principle, it is also not possible to send or receive packets from the core network to a VPN. However, Chapter 8 will show that operators of the service provider can change configurations and add new sites, implying that in practice a service provider operator or a hacker, who has obtained similar permissions, can intrude into VPNs provided on the network. Chapter 8 will also outline how this type of threat can be controlled.

In practice, MPLS networks are more complex than the basic concept previously shown: Many VPNs have interconnections to other VPNs, to extranets, or to the Internet. When two or more VPNs are merged on the MPLS core, they form logically one single VPN from the MPLS point of view. Further divisions of those VPNs by firewalls or packet filters are outside the scope of this work, although they are probably standard configurations in many cases. The MPLS backbone sees these two merged VPNs as a single VPN. Extranet connections can similarly be seen as a connection of one of more VPNs with an extranet site, which is another VPN viewed from the MPLS core (see Figure 1-9). The extranet might prevent direct connectivity between the different VPNs, but this is, again, outside the scope of the MPLS security model and this book.

Figure 1-9 *Security Reference Model with Extranet*

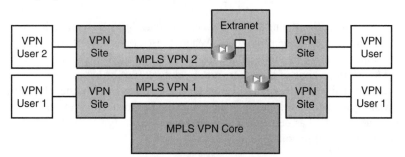

Similarly, if a VPN receives Internet access through the MPLS core network, this can be seen as a connection of this VPN to the Internet (see Figure 1-10). Typically, some type of firewall would be provided between the VPN and the Internet. This firewall can be provided by the service provider or by the VPN user. In either case, the MPLS core does not lose its status as a separate security zone.

Figure 1-10 *Security Reference Model with Internet Access*

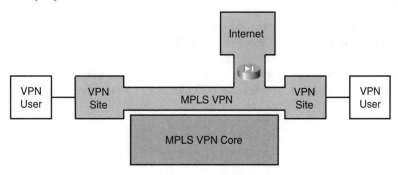

The MPLS core could also be provided by more than one provider, via advanced MPLS VPN architectures such as Inter-AS or Carrier's Carrier (see Figure 1-11). The fact that there is more than one provider involved in the provisioning is invisible to the VPN users from a technical point of view, except that they do not connect all the various VPN sites to the same providers, but to a set of different providers. The new aspect here is that the service providers involved in the provisioning of shared VPNs also have to secure their own MPLS core against intrusions from other MPLS cores. In all cases, the VPN users have to trust all the providers involved. This issue is discussed in more detail in Chapter 4, "Secure MPLS VPN Designs."

Figure 1-11 *Security Reference Model with Several MPLS Service Providers*

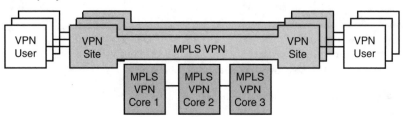

All these scenarios define security zones, or *zones of trust*, with their respective connections to other security zones. Where these zones are not connecting, intrusions are impossible: for example, it is impossible to intrude from a VPN into the MPLS core. Within a single zone of trust there are, by default, no further security measures. For example, a single VPN spans all sites normally, unless within the VPN further security divisions are added such as by using firewalls. For intrusion prevention, this means that once an intruder has penetrated a single zone of trust, typically the intruder has gained access to the entire zone.

The model of zones of trust is important for creating security policies and risk assessments. In the context of MPLS, this model also has to be applied to be able to analyze security and threats. The following chapters build on this zone model when analyzing security and proposing security measures.

Summary

This chapter introduced the fundamentals of MPLS VPN networks and the specific nomenclature used in these environments. You now understand the key security concepts for analyzing MPLS network scenarios—for example the fact that a secure solution consists of the basic components of architecture, implementation, and operation, and that all of those need to be secure in order for an overall solution to be secure. You have seen various types of VPNs, with an emphasis on the security implications of their specific characteristics. At the end of the chapter, you were introduced to a security model that you can reference in later chapters.

A very important concept for security considerations is the *zone of trust*, which was also introduced here. This concept makes analysis of security architectures easier by defining clear boundaries where security needs to be checked.

In this chapter, you learn about the following:

- How a threat model is constructed
- Which threats exist against a VPN, the core, an extranet, and the Internet
- Specific threats in an Inter-AS and CsC environments
- How threats within one zone and reconnaissance attacks are classified

CHAPTER 2

A Threat Model for MPLS VPNs

To be able to evaluate MPLS security, it is necessary to define a threat model for the various zones of trust. This chapter uses the zones of trust that were defined in Chapter 1 and outlines the threats against those zones. Later in this book, MPLS VPN security is analyzed based on this threat model, and mechanisms are discussed to defend against the threats.

A complete threat model (for example, one designed for use as a security policy) must identify threats from outside and inside a trusted zone. This is because, in practice, many threats come from the inside. For example, a thief might come from the outside of an office building, but more frequently in many enterprises, thefts occur by internal trusted staff members. Therefore, a complete threat model must consider both internal and external threats.

For the analysis of MPLS VPNs, however, only threats from the outside of a trusted zone are relevant, because internal threats are, in most cases, independent of the VPN architecture. A virus, for example, can propagate independently within a bank's VPN (within the trusted zone), whether the bank is using ATM or MPLS VPNs. It must, however, be examined whether such a virus could also intrude from another VPN or from the Internet.

In the example of the office building, this means that when analyzing the security of the building itself, internal thefts can be ignored. Translated to the networking world, this means that someone executing attacks on a LAN (for example, with tools such as ARP spoofing) can do so independently of whether the site attacked is connected via MPLS to the other VPN sites or via Frame Relay.

In the following sections, threats are viewed from each of the trusted zones and are explained.

Threats Against a VPN

This section discusses all threats from the point of view of a VPN customer or user. Any VPN user (for example, a bank that is using an MPLS VPN service) needs to analyze security based on the threats against its VPN. Threats that are potentially related to the MPLS VPN architecture are

- **Intrusions** from the outside (for example other VPNs, the core, or the Internet)
- **Denial of service (DoS)** from the outside (for example, other VPNs, the core, or the Internet)

Figure 2-1 depicts where threats might come from in a specific VPN. Threats might come primarily from other VPNs (1), the core itself (2), or the Internet (3). Threats internal to a VPN are not considered here. Those are typically independent of the VPN architecture; that is, the threats would be the same over, for example, Frame Relay.

Figure 2-1   *Threats Against a VPN*

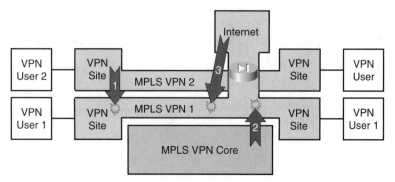

There is one exception to this rule: the PE is, by default, "visible" from the VPN user's network on Layer 3, and needs to be specially secured. This does not constitute a direct threat against a VPN, but against the core. Indirectly, however, a DoS attack against a PE might also affect availability of other connected VPNs. The PE is therefore a critical part in MPLS VPN security, and PE security is discussed in various sections of this book—in Chapter 3, "MPLS Security Analysis," in the section "Robustness against Attacks"; in Chapter 4, "Secure MPLS VPN Designs," in the section "Hybrid Provider Edge Recommendations"; and in Chapter 5, "Security Recommendations."

MPLS provides the possibility to connect VPN sites with any-to-any connectivity; therefore, traffic can flow from a given VPN site to any other site on that VPN. Sometimes, critics of MPLS point out that, inside a VPN, this may make secure traffic management such as firewalling and intrusion detection harder because there is not necessarily a central point where all traffic can be controlled. While this is true, MPLS gives the VPN user the choice of topology; and if more centralized services are required, MPLS allows the possibility to create hub-and-spoke topologies. This is a choice of the VPN user.

Intrusions into a VPN

Intrusions give an outsider control over parts of the VPN. This could be network elements, servers, PCs, or other networking equipment. To execute an intrusion, the attacker has to insert control traffic into the VPN; in the simplest case, a single IP packet to a destination in the VPN.

NOTE   Although most of today's intrusions use IPv4 packets, other data traffic can also be used to intrude into a network. This could be Layer 2 packets, IPv6 packets, or even the telephone system when dialing into a modem. Labeled packets also have to be considered, although the standard PE-CE interface does not allow labeled packets, which would be dropped. In the Inter-AS and Carrier's Carrier cases, labeled packets are an important consideration. See Chapter 3 for details on how labeled packets might impact security in those cases.

Figure 2-2 depicts the potential intrusion vectors into a VPN. Intrusions could potentially come from another VPN (1), the core itself (2), or from the Internet (3). What they have in common is that they must target a piece of the VPN infrastructure directly.

Figure 2-2   *Intrusion Vectors into a VPN*

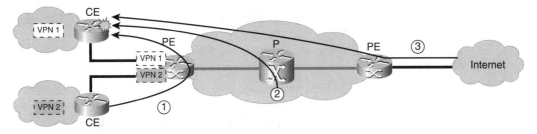

Therefore, to control intrusions into a trusted zone, it is sufficient to block all illegitimate data traffic from the zone. In traditional networks, this is being done using a firewall that controls traffic into a site and by separating the network from other outside networks, such as the telephone system.

In the MPLS VPN environment, the principles of separation against outside networks and control of inbound traffic into a VPN prevail as well. Chapter 3, "MPLS VPN Security Analysis," shows that VPNs are fully separated from each other such that intrusions from other VPNs or from the core cannot occur. When two normally separate zones, such as two VPNs, are connected at the IP layer (for example, in an extranet or for Internet access), additional firewalling is usually required. This firewalling, however, is independent of the MPLS network, as it would also be required over any other network architecture.

However, this assumes correct operation of the MPLS core network. If the MPLS service provider engineer misconfigures a PE router, an external site might become a member of a VPN, which would enable intrusions from this external site. This misconfiguration could be accidental or malicious. Note that the same threat exists in Layer 2 networks. This is discussed further in Chapter 3.

Some Inter-AS architectures can introduce an additional risk to the VPN user. Under certain conditions, a service provider (SP) that is providing part of the Inter-AS MPLS core can send unidirectional traffic into VPNs of other Inter-AS SPs. However, a VPN user must always trust the SPs involved in the provisioning of their VPN; any core provider can make VPNs insecure. Therefore, while Inter-AS security is a concern, the fundamental issue is that the SPs must be trusted, no matter what form of VPN (also non-MPLS VPNs). Inter-AS security is discussed in detail in Chapter 4.

The threat of the accidental PE misconfiguration in this context is probably somewhat less important than the malicious misconfiguration because there is not necessarily a malicious intent in this case. The possibility of the SP engineer to maliciously insert an external site into a given VPN, however, is a serious threat against the security of that VPN because that external site effectively becomes a member of the VPN and has the possibility to intrude into it. Chapter 8, "Secure Operation and Maintenance of an MPLS Core," explains how this threat can be controlled.

Denial of Service Against a VPN

Another threat against a VPN is denial of service (DoS) from the outside. Again, this threat could come from other VPNs, the core itself, or the Internet. However, there is a key difference between intrusions and DoS: intrusions allow full access to internal data, whereas DoS does not give such access, but prevents access for all users.

To intrude, a hacker needs to be able to send packets into the trusted zone of the VPN. Therefore, it is possible to protect a VPN effectively by securing its own network edge. This action involves assuring that the intrusion points are controllable; that is, that there are no hidden intrusion points. Chapter 3 discusses this question in detail.

The threat model for a DoS attack against a VPN is different, however: A given VPN site might receive a DoS attack against its own networking infrastructure (that is, targeting parts of the VPN that are under control of the VPN user); but, as opposed to an intrusion, a DoS attack can also affect a VPN user indirectly. For example, if a PE router is under a DoS attack, this might affect a given VPN connected to that PE, even though the attack is not directly against the VPN. The result might be slower performance for VPN sites connected to this VPN. This increases the exposure to DoS attacks.

In principle, any shared part of the network under DoS might affect a given VPN. Figure 2-3 shows that the attack points for a DoS attack against a VPN include any point of that VPN, but also any points in the shared infrastructure. This applies to core devices such as PE and P routers, core lines, and shared accesses (for example, accesses to the Internet or to extranet sites).

Although protecting a VPN against intrusions is relatively straightforward with controlling the ingress points into the VPN, protection against DoS is more complex due to the indirect effect of DoS attacks on the infrastructure. The solution to this threat lies in the correct architectural design of the MPLS network. How an MPLS VPN infrastructure can be designed to appropriately secure against DoS attacks is described in detail in Chapter 4.

Figure 2-3   *Attack Points for DoS Against a VPN*

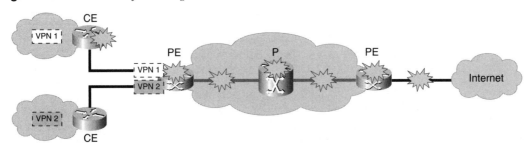

Threats Against an Extranet Site

There are various definitions for the term *extranet*. Generally speaking, an extranet allows different VPNs to interconnect and potentially share common resources. In MPLS VPNs, there are two main ways to implement extranets:

- **Integrated intranet and extranet**—Sites of different VPNs interconnect directly by controlling the route targets on the PE routers. In this case, the extranet consists of existing sites of the various VPNs, and from a security point of view, this type of extranet is just another way to interconnect VPN sites.

- **Central services**—In this model, there is a dedicated extranet site (for example, to host a server farm), which is to be accessed from all involved VPNs. The route targets in the PE routers define how the sites, including the extranet site, are connected.

From a security point of view, both extranet models are similar: As seen from the core, there are a number of VPN sites, and the route targets configured on the PE routers define how these sites are interconnected. If two sites are interconnected, they can exchange traffic freely. Whether the two interconnected sites belong to the same VPN, or whether one is a VPN site and the other an extranet site, is a question of interpretation—technically the configuration is the same.

This means that if some control of security is required between a VPN and an extranet site, that control has to be implemented using standard security technology such as firewalls. Such implementations are, however, independent of the fact that the infrastructure is based on MPLS.

Therefore, threats against an extranet site, from an MPLS point of view, are equivalent to threats against VPN sites, and the considerations discussed in the previous section also apply here.

Until now, all threats are of direct interest to a VPN customer because they directly threaten the integrity of the customer's VPN. In the remainder of this chapter, threats to the other zones of trust are discussed. Those threats might indirectly also be threats to the VPN, but where this is the case it has already been mentioned in the above sections.

Threats Against the Core

This section discusses security from the service provider's point of view, when securing its own core network. Security threats against VPNs are, of course, also indirectly of concern to the service provider, but here the focus is on the core as a zone of trust and threats against it.

There are different architectural options for building an MPLS core network. It can be a single autonomous system (AS) forming a monolithic core under one administrative control. There are also various options for connecting several autonomous systems in an Inter-AS architecture and in Carrier's Carrier (CsC) topologies. All the multi-AS architectures (Inter-AS and CsC) have in common that the core is itself divided into several different zones of trust. (Refer to Figure 1-11 for an illustration of this.) In all those cases, the threats are not only coming from VPNs or the Internet, but from a new threat vector— other parts of the core, in most cases under the control of another service provider.

NOTE   The fact that the MPLS core is potentially divided into several autonomous systems is mostly irrelevant to the VPN user: to the VPN user, the core appears in all cases as a single zone (apart from the fact that the user might be dealing with several providers). However, as shown in Chapter 4, the VPN user must trust all providers involved in the core. A detailed discussion of Inter-AS–specific issues can be found in Chapter 3.

The service provider's network operations center (NOC) can be seen as a logical part of the core, in the sense that it must be protected from attack as well as the core and probably forms a single zone of trust with the core. Therefore, the NOC is included as a separate section in the following threat model against the core.

This section discusses the threat models for these various types of core architectures, as seen from the core network.

Monolithic Core

The *monolithic core* refers to the standard MPLS VPN architecture as defined in RFC 2547, "BGP/MPLS VPNs." One single AS defines the core network, and all VPN sites connect to this single AS. The threats against a monolithic core are

- **Intrusions** from the outside, such as attached VPNs or the Internet.
- **DoS** from the outside, such as attached VPNs or the Internet.
- **Internal threats**—Operator errors or deliberate misconfigurations can cause security problems on the core or on a connected VPN. As opposed to internal threats to the VPNs, which are not considered here, internal threats to the core might have an impact on the VPNs as well. Therefore, they must be taken into consideration.

Intrusions

Intrusions can first be targeted at core equipment such as routers. The technical scope of this threat and the protection against it is comparable to normal Internet core networks. However, the potential business risk is higher in the MPLS VPN case because security of connected VPNs depends on the correct operation of the core, whereas sites connected to the Internet mostly do not rely on security of the service provider network.

NOTE	An MPLS core without any connection to the Internet naturally has lower exposure to attacks from the Internet. It is thus seen as more secure than an MPLS core with Internet connectivity. However, as explained in Chapter 1, it is wrong to assume you can achieve full separation from the Internet because VPN users may have their own Internet connectivity. Attacks may come from the Internet through the VPN in this case. This form of attack is much harder to carry out, but not impossible.

MPLS core routers are not accessible from connected VPNs or the Internet. The only exceptions are protocols that a PE uses to communicate to the "outside," because on the corresponding ports for each protocol the PE must accept packets. It is important to minimize the number of protocols used to the outside and to secure those protocols specifically. Chapter 5 gives examples on how this can be done.

Intrusions can also target the NOC and NOC equipment, such as AAA servers, TFTP and FTP servers, and management stations. The associated risk is high for both the core itself and for the connected VPNs. For example, a maliciously modified PE configuration can allow external sites to access a targeted VPN. Therefore, the threat of intrusions into the core or NOC carries a high business risk, typically higher than in normal IP service provider networks, but comparable to other VPN core networks such as ATM or Frame Relay.

Intrusions can be prevented with standard security measures such as securing access to devices, managing users securely through AAA, firewalling, etc. This is discussed in detail in Chapter 5, "Security Recommendations."

DoS Attacks

The threat of a DoS attack against the core is technically equivalent to the threat of a DoS attack in normal IP core networks. However, the business risk is potentially higher in MPLS VPN core networks, depending on the contracts with the VPN customers: usually, VPN contracts have significantly higher service level guarantees than Internet services. Any part of the MPLS core is potentially vulnerable against a DoS attack from a VPN or from the Internet, unless that part has been appropriately secured and designed. In a correctly configured MPLS core, it is impossible from the outside (that is, from VPNs or the Internet) to send traffic directly to a piece of core equipment. While this prevents intrusions completely (as discussed in the previous section), it is still theoretically possible to overload routers with transit traffic and thus cause a DoS attack.

The solution against a DoS attack threat is to design the core network appropriately: the routers and lines have to be correctly dimensioned; that is, even if an attack from a VPN loads an access line of that VPN completely, with minimum size packets, the connected PE router must be able to handle all the received traffic. The same principle applies to core lines. Where the aggregate traffic might exceed the provisioned capacities, appropriate quality of service (QoS) measures need to be taken to ensure that transit traffic meets the required service level agreements. This is discussed in detail in Chapter 5, "Security Recommendations."

Internal Threats

The last threat against MPLS core networks is insider attacks. This category contains all errors or deliberate misconfigurations made by internal service provider staff. The threat is relevant to the core and to VPNs because such misconfigurations might also affect the security of connected VPNs.

A relatively simple misconfiguration of a route target could have potentially serious security consequences. For example, if all the sites of the VPN of a bank use a certain route target for import and export of routes, and if this route target is accidentally added to another VRF, the connected sites of this VRF are effectively part of the other VPN.

Example 2-1 shows a correct configuration on a PE router. There are two VRFs configured, each with its own route target. CEs are connected to the VRFS on the PE through the serial interfaces, and the route targets in the VRFs define how the routes from a given VRF should be treated. Here, there are different route targets, and the routes will be kept in their respective VRFs.

Example 2-1 *Correct Configuration of Two VRFs with Correct Route Targets on a Singe PE Router*

```
ip vrf bank_A
  rd 1234:10
  route-target both 1234:33

ip vrf bank_B
  rd 1234:11
  route-target both 1234:34

interface serial 0/1
  ip vrf forwarding bank_A
interface serial 0/3
  ip vrf forwarding bank_B
```

Assume now that an operator accidentally typed the wrong route target. Example 2-2 shows the new configuration. Here, the routes from bank B will be exported with a route target that belongs to bank A, and vice versa.

Example 2-2   *Incorrect Configuration: Wrong Route Target in the Second VRF*

```
ip vrf bank_A
  rd 1234:10
  route-target both 1234:33

ip vrf bank_B
  rd 1234:11
  route-target both 1234:33   <--- ERROR: 33 instead of 34

interface serial 0/1
  ip vrf forwarding bank_A
interface serial 0/3
  ip vrf forwarding bank_B
```

The effect of this simple error is that all sites of bank B connected to this PE router will belong logically to bank A and have full access to the entire VPN of bank A. For routing to work in this scenario, the address spaces of the two now "merged" banks would have to be unique overall, and this is not necessarily the case in an accidental misconfiguration.

The danger in this type of situation is that bank A, which just suffered a potential intrusion from an outside site, might not even detect this easily. After all, the existing network of bank A is not affected by this move unless there is now some address space overlap with potential connectivity problems. Bank B, on the other hand, would probably discover quickly that its site is not connected correctly, because many operations like connecting to intranet sites (www.bank_B.com, for example) would fail while its site is logically connected to bank A.

So a simple misconfiguration on a PE router can connect one or several VPN sites to a wrong VPN, thus breaking VPN separation.

Therefore, if this misconfiguration was made accidentally, the security exposure of bank A is probably limited because staff in this particular site of bank B probably would not notice which VPN they are connected to. Viruses and worms, of course, or peer-to-peer applications would now spread freely between bank A and the wrongly connected site of bank B.

However, if an operator of the service provider deliberately made this type of malfunction, the potential exposure is relatively high. In this case, the operator probably has enough knowledge to avoid overlapping address space, and bank A might not discover the intrusion.

There are a number of such potential misconfigurations, all of which might have severe security implications for the connected VPNs, and some of which are hard to detect. It is important to understand that although in the previous threats the solution was based on design, here this does not work: the threat here is from the inside (from the people designing the solution). An analogy might be an operator configuring a firewall: the operator is controlling the security device and therefore automatically has the power also to subvert security by opening additional ports.

NOTE	**Recommendation**
	It is of paramount importance that service providers also secure their operations next to the architecture and the implementation, such that misconfigurations are prevented where possible, but at least detected.

In practice, many service providers use automated provisioning tools, which make such misconfigurations unlikely. So the more realistic threat is coming from deliberate misconfigurations of an operator. On the other hand, operational tools control running configurations and compare them against a correct configuration, such that even malicious changes would normally be detected.

More details on how to secure the operation of an MPLS core network can be found in Chapter 8, "Secure Operation and Maintenance of an MPLS Core."

Inter-AS: A Multi-AS Core

In the case of a monolithic core, there is only one service provider, and the threats come from the VPNs or the Internet. If a core consists of several autonomous systems and, with that, possibly several service providers, there is an additional threat to be taken into account: attacks from one part of the MPLS core to another part. Figure 2-4 shows a schematic Inter-AS architecture with two core autonomous systems.

Figure 2-4 *Schematic Inter-AS Architecture*

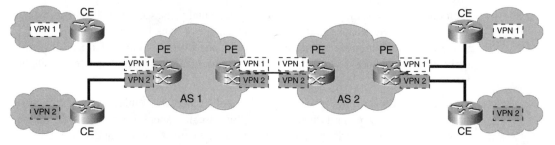

The Inter-AS architecture is described in RFC 2547bis. It allows an MPLS core to contain several autonomous systems, connected in different ways. If those autonomous systems are under the control of one single service provider, there is no difference between the threats against a monolithic core and an Inter-AS core.

However, in many implementations, the Inter-AS architecture is chosen to provide a transparent MPLS VPN service across several provider networks. In all those cases, there is the additional threat coming from the other AS.

As in previously discussed zones of trust, the threats are intrusions into an AS from another AS, and DoS attacks from one AS to another.

RFC 2547bis describes three basic ways to interconnect autonomous systems with the purpose of forming an overall MPLS core. These cases are referred to as case (or type) A, B, or C. The security exposure varies with each model, but the overall threats remain the same for all three models. The threats affect the connected VPNs and the other autonomous systems.

The details are explained in Chapter 4, but to summarize here:

- Model A is the most restrictive model and does not increase the exposure significantly.
- Models B and C allow for more interaction between autonomous systems and thus increase the risk of intrusions and DoS attacks from the other autonomous systems.

There is a difference in exposure for VPNs depending on whether or not they are shared over several autonomous systems. If a VPN is shared (that is, each service provider has sites of that VPN), the exposure is higher than if the VPN is present only on a single service provider network.

Depending on the model chosen (case A, B, or C), the threats in an Inter-AS architecture are

- For each shared VPN, each AS can introduce new sites with new addressing into the VPN, and these sites will be fully connected to the VPN. This can be used to intrude into a shared VPN or to attempt a DoS attack against it.
- In cases B and C, each AS can send traffic into any VPN of another AS, whether this VPN is shared or not, although it cannot always receive return traffic. This can be used for DoS attacks or simple intrusions.
- Routing between autonomous systems potentially allows for a DoS attack from one AS to a PE router of the other AS.

From a VPN perspective, the fact that the core is provided by several service providers in an Inter-AS architecture does not add new threats to the already existing ones. However, the VPN user must trust all involved service providers because either of the service providers could endanger the security of its VPN.

From a service provider perspective, the Inter-AS architecture adds additional threats, depending on the type of interconnection model chosen.

Carrier's Carrier: A Hierarchical Core

In the Carrier's Carrier architecture, which is also described in RFC 2547bis, several service providers provide an overall MPLS core. However, in this case, the autonomous systems follow a hierarchical architecture—not a peer architecture, as in the Inter-AS model. Figure 2-5 depicts the schematic architecture of a Carrier's Carrier solution. Only the Carrier, AS 2 in Figure 2-5's example, has the information of the customer VPNs. The

"Carrier's Carrier," here AS 1, treats everything coming from AS 2 as a VPN, and has essentially no visibility of the customer VPNs. From AS 1's point of view, there is only one VPN in this configuration, the VPN for AS 2.

Figure 2-5 *Schematic Carrier's Carrier Architecture*

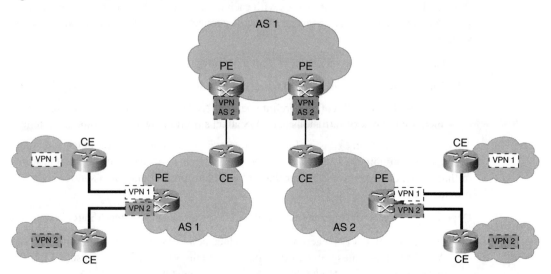

The data traffic on AS 1 consists of packets with the standard MPLS labels for AS 2. Only those two top labels have significance on AS 1; the rest of the packet is ignored on AS 1. This is equivalent to encapsulation of a VPN packet on a standard MPLS core, except that the VPN packet in this case is in turn an MPLS packet—the data packet as seen on AS 2. This one has in turn a VPN label and encapsulates a VPN packet. The VPN 1 data packet is in turn ignored on AS 2, which only works with the AS 2 VPN label. (See Figure 2-6.)

Figure 2-6 *A Packet on the Carrier's Carrier Network, AS 1*

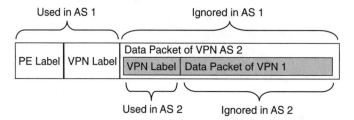

This has a significant advantage from the security aspect: AS 1, the Carrier's Carrier, only sees VPN information on the first level, that is, AS 2. This means that AS 1 only needs to know the next hop within its network for the AS 2, and only needs to look at the first labels, as if it was a normal RFC 2547 network. However, because AS 1 does not even look deeper into the packet than the first two labels, it also cannot be attacked based on information there. This reduces the security problem seen from AS 1's point of view to the standard RFC 2547 issues, discussed previously.

RFC 2547bis states specifically for this case that a PE router does not accept labeled packets from a CE "unless it is known that such packets will leave the backbone before the IP header or any labels lower in the stack will be inspected." This condition is true here: essentially, AS 1 tunnels packets from one part of AS 2 to another part of that same AS. Therefore, there is no threat against AS 1 in this model. But note that AS 1 has the power to forge packets such that a VPN of AS 2 is affected. (This is, however, a threat against the VPN, not against AS 1.) As in all previous cases, a VPN user always has to trust the service provider(s).

Of course, AS 2 can still forge packets, do source address spoofing, or intend a DoS attack against AS 1. But all such attempts would stay within its own domain, or in the case of DoS, would be the same issue as in standard RFC 2547 networks. In other words, a higher-level provider can affect the security of a lower-level provider, or his VPNs, but not the other way around.

Threats Against a Network Operations Center

Generally, a network operations center (NOC) is logically separated from the core network. There might be more than a single NOC, in which case each NOC site can be treated as a standalone entity.

A NOC needs connectivity to the network it needs to operate, and in most cases, there are also links to outside networks: the corporate intranet, the Internet, and possibly other networks. Figure 2-7 depicts how a NOC connects to its surrounding networks. Often a NOC also manages parts of a VPN, such as the CE routers. In this case, there are also connections between the NOC and the VPN, and these need to be secured.

Figure 2-7   *Schematic View of a NOC*

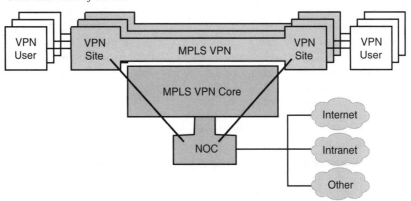

Threats from the Internet and other external networks include intrusions into the network management system and various other systems, such as FTP and TFTP servers, AAA servers, and so on. These threats are extremely serious, because they might endanger the secure operations of the entire network, but they are the same as in any other NOC environment and not discussed here in detail.

From the MPLS side, the same threats prevail in principle: intrusions into management systems with the potential to alter any type of network operations, introduce fake sites into VPNs, or to join VPNs. Also, DoS attacks against any part of the network or its operations center are possible. Overall, from a security point of view, the NOC is the most important part of a network because the entire network can be controlled from it.

NOTE   Especially in the case of managed CE solutions, the NOC must have "reachability" of all CE devices in the respective VPNs. This means in turn that the NOC is in principle reachable from all those VPNs. While most providers spend serious efforts in securing their NOCs, it is important also to consider accidental cross-connection of two managed VPNs through a management network. This must be prevented by appropriate design and ACLs where applicable. However, this threat is not MPLS specific; it exists in all VPN environments.

Threats Against the Internet

The Internet is usually positioned as the insecure part in any network deployment, thus threats are normally coming from the Internet. Although this view is completely correct, it is incomplete: in other parts of the Internet, there are other users that require security, and from their point of view, the threat also comes from "the Internet," which now includes their own network. For any given service provider network—MPLS or not—this means that there is a threat originating in this network toward the Internet.

Some service providers take the view that security is unidirectional and that they have to secure their part of the Internet, including their customers, against the rest of the Internet but not the other way round. There are at least two reasons why this attitude is inappropriate in the global Internet: First, the Internet is a global system and requires all participants to do their share in securing access to it. Second, more practically, an attack from a service provider's customer often affects the service provider network itself or other customers of that service provider. This can be observed where worms are spreading, with e-mail spam relays and many other security incidents.

NOTE   **Recommendation**

For all these reasons, it is necessary that operators of networks connecting to the Internet also secure the Internet from their customers—for example, by applying source address spoofing prevention as described in RFC 2827 (BCP 38), "Network Ingress Filtering: Defeating Denial of Service Attacks which Employ IP Source Address Spoofing."

In the specific context of MPLS VPNs, the threat originates from every VPN customer who has Internet connectivity through this MPLS VPN service. Customers who do not receive

Internet connectivity from the MPLS provider may still be the source of security incidents through other paths, such as through other Internet service providers (ISPs). But this is outside the scope of this book.

Threats from Within a Zone of Trust

The 2004 CSI/FBI Computer Crime and Security Survey shows that about the same number of security incidents have their origin on the inside as on the outside of an enterprise. More generically speaking, this refers to a zone of trust. Without any doubt, in many networks, insiders represent at least the same threat to a network as an outsider.

This principle applies in the same way to MPLS VPN deployments, for each zone of trust separately:

- **Zone of a given VPN**—This is essentially the enterprise intranet, and the CSI/FBI report referred directly to this zone of trust.

- **Core network**—In the core, an insider can easily modify configurations, endangering the security of the core or connected VPNs. Where this affects VPNs it is strictly speaking not a threat from within the zone. This is discussed earlier in this chapter.

- **Extranet**—For extranets and other external networks, threats such as accidental interconnection of VPNs can be originated in these zones.

A number of potential security issues originate in the same zone of trust and are thus not related to the fact that the underlying infrastructure is an MPLS network. Examples of such issues are

- An unsecured wireless access point in an enterprise that has an MPLS VPN service.

- A DoS attack from the Internet to a web server in a VPN network, where the VPN with Internet service is provided on the same MPLS core: if an MPLS core provides Internet connectivity to a given VPN, then this connectivity can also be used to attack the VPN from the outside. The same would be true in other VPN deployments such as Frame Relay or ATM.

- An intrusion from one MPLS VPN into another VPN, where the packet flow went through interconnection points which are specifically designed for this purpose, for example Extranets. Such deployments should normally be secured by a firewall, and the security depends on correct configuration of that firewall.

- Worm infections from a VPN site to an extranet site, where such connectivity was deployed consciously. Also, firewalls are typically deployed where VPNs connect to extranets, and security depends on correct operation of the firewall, plus standard security measures within the end systems.

In summary, within a single zone of trust, or wherever connectivity between zones of trust has been specifically designed, security issues relating to such connectivity are outside the scope of this book. In these cases, traditional security solutions such as firewalls need to be used to separate the zones as required.

Reconnaissance Attacks

To effectively launch certain types of attacks, a hacker usually needs some knowledge about the network topology or hardware used. The technique that gathers this type of information is called *reconnaissance*. Reconnaissance on its own is, in many environments, not a threat, but the intelligence found by employing it is often used later to attack a system or network. So, the threat of reconnaissance attacks is mostly an indirect one: after the network has been scanned, this information is used subsequently for attacks.

NOTE Often reconnaissance attacks go undetected for considerable time because they have usually no impact on the network. At best, this type of activity may be seen in some log files, but often it is not found.

It is good current practice to make networks and devices as "stealth" as possible, to make gathering information harder for potential attackers.

In the MPLS context, the core is already, to a large extent, hidden to the outside, as is shown in Chapter 3. So by default, only the PE-peering addresses are visible from the outside. These interfaces should be protected with ACLs so that the PE router does not accept packets targeted to the core or send any response. This hides the core and makes reconnaissance from outside the network very difficult.

NOTE VPN-specific infrastructure ACLs, which prevent the PEs from being targeted from the VPN, can be complicated depending on the addressing scheme used for all the CE-PE links in a VPN. Each PE, on the interface to each CE of a VPN, needs a deny statement for all PE addresses reachable from that VPN. See Chapter 5, "Security Recommendations."

There are two exceptions to this overall rule:

- **MPLS traceroute**—There is a feature to allow visibility of MPLS core routers in a traceroute, even though this is not possible by default in such a network. MPLS traceroute first became available in Cisco IOS Release 12.0(9)ST and 12.1(3)T, and is, by default, enabled. The command is **mpls ip propagate-ttl**.

  By default, on a PE, the Time-To-Live (TTL) value is copied from an IP packet header to the MPLS packet header. Each PE and P router decrements the MPLS TTL value. If a packet expires within the core, an ICMP TTL-expired message is sent back to the originator. An MPLS traceroute shows internal PE and P routers and reveals important information about the network topology to a potential attacker.

NOTE	**Recommendation**
	Disable **mpls ip propagate-ttl** from the outside of the MPLS core. The keyword "forwarded" can be used when the feature is required from within the MPLS core but when it should not be available from outside the MPLS core.

- **Unprotected Internet on core routers**—Many MPLS backbones provide Internet services and VPN services on the same core. By default, if the Internet runs on the global routing table, the core routers are visible to the Internet and can be seen, for example, with a traceroute. This enables relatively easy mapping of the core network from the outside. The recommendation is to block by default access from the Internet into the core. This topic is detailed in Chapter 5, "Security Recommendations."

Although reconnaissance is not a direct threat, it enables further attacks and should therefore be taken seriously. Also, depending on the way the reconnaissance is carried out, it might consume resources on the core routers, and in the worst case lead to a DoS attack against a core device. For all those reasons, an MPLS core should be operated as a "black box"—that is, without giving any information about itself to outsiders. The most effective way of doing this is by using infrastructure ACLs, described in detail in Chapter 5, "Security Recommendations," which block all access from the outside into the core.

Summary

To be able to analyze security in any environment, a threat model is required, against which security requirements are then evaluated. This chapter defined the threats against the various zones of trust in the MPLS VPN environment.

Threats against VPNs contain intrusions and DoS attacks from other VPNs, the Internet, or from the MPLS core. Each other zone has similar threats.

The core can be attacked from either VPNs or the Internet, and the Internet can be attacked from VPNs. If the MPLS core consists of multiple autonomous systems in an Inter-AS architecture, the various autonomous systems could attack each other, and in some cases affect the security of connected VPNs.

Special care must be taken in securing the NOC: in many designs it can be attacked from the VPNs, and it may accidentally cross-connect VPNs if the network is not designed carefully.

Based on this threat model, the overall security of the MPLS VPN environment can now be evaluated.

PART II

Advanced MPLS VPN Security Issues

In this chapter, you learn about the following:

- How MPLS provides security (VPN separation, robustness against attacks, core hiding, and spoofing protection)

- How the different Inter-AS and Carrier's Carrier models work, and how secure they are compared to each other

- Which security mechanisms the MPLS architecture does not provide

- How MPLS VPNs compare in security to ATM or Frame Relay VPNs.

CHAPTER 3

MPLS Security Analysis

VPN users have certain expectations and requirements for their VPN service. In a nutshell, they want their service to be both private and secure. In other words, they want their VPN to be as secure as with dedicated circuits while gaining the scalability benefits of a shared infrastructure. Both concepts, of privacy and security, are not black and white, and need to be defined for a real world implementation.

This chapter defines typical VPN security requirements, based on the threat model developed in the previous chapter, and discusses in detail how MPLS can fulfill them. The typical VPN security requirements are

- VPN separation (addressing and traffic)
- Robustness against attacks
- Hiding of the core infrastructure
- Protection against VPN spoofing

We also explain which security features MPLS VPNs do not provide, and compare the security capabilities of MPLS VPNs with Layer 2–based VPN services such as ATM and Frame Relay.

NOTE   This chapter analyses the *architecture* of MPLS/VPN networks, that is, how the standards define the architecture and protocols. In other words, for this chapter, we assume that the MPLS core is configured and operated correctly. Implementation issues are discussed in Chapter 4, "Secure MPLS VPN Designs," and Chapter 5, "Security Recommendations." Operational aspects are covered in Chapter 8, "Secure Operation and Maintenance of an MPLS Core."

VPN Separation

The most important security requirement for VPN users is typically that their traffic be kept separate from other VPN traffic and core traffic. This refers to both its traffic not being seen in other VPNs, and also other VPNs traffic or core traffic not intruding into their VPN. Referring to the threat model from the previous chapter, this section analyses a threat against a VPN, specifically intrusions into and from other VPNs.

Another requirement is that each VPN be able to use the complete IP address space without affecting or being affected by other VPNs or the core.

NOTE	The CE-PE links belong logically to the VPN, even though they are usually addressed with provider address space. The reason provider address space is used is that management from the NOC requires unique CE addresses.

The service provider has the requirement that the core remain separate from the VPNs in the sense that the address space in use does not conflict with any VPN and that VPN traffic remains separate on the core from the control plane traffic on the core.

In other words, a given VPN must be completely separate from other VPNs or the core in terms of traffic separation and address space separation. We will now analyze how the standard, RFC 2547bis, meets these requirements. In the first section, we see how it achieves address space separation, and in the following section how data and control traffic are kept architecturally separate—between VPNs, but also between a VPN and the core.

NOTE	Again, this chapter assumes that the network is securely implemented and operated, and the analysis concentrates completely on the standard.

Address Space Separation

To be able to distinguish between addresses from different VPNs, RFC 2547bis does not use standard IPv4 (or IPv6) addressing on the control plane for VPNs on the core. Instead, the standard introduces the concept of the *VPN-IPv4 or VPN-IPv6 address family*. A VPN-IPv4 address consists of an 8-byte *route distinguisher (RD)* followed by a 4-byte IPv4 address, as shown in Figure 3-1. Similarly, a VPN-IPv6 address consists of an 8-byte *route distinguisher (RD)* followed by a 16-byte IPv6 address.[1]

Figure 3-1   *Structure of VPN-IPv4 Addresses*

The purpose of the RD is to allow the entire IPv4 space to be used in different contexts (for VPNs, in our example). On a given router, a single RD can define a VPN routing/ forwarding instance (VRF), in which the entire IPv4 address space may be used independently.

NOTE   RFC 2547bis defines a semantic for RDs, but this serves only administrative purposes, to make it easier to select unique RDs. For security considerations, it is only important to understand that the RD makes the IPv4 routes of a VPN unique on the MPLS VPN core.

Due to the architecture of MPLS IP VPNs, only the PE routers have to know the VPN routes. Because PE routers use VPN-IPv4 addresses exclusively for VPNs, the address space is separated between VPNs. In addition, because they use IPv4 internally in the core, which is a different address family from the VPN-IPv4 address family, the core also has independent address space from the VPNs. This provides a clear separation between VPNs, and between VPNs and the core. Figure 3-2 illustrates how different address spaces are used on an MPLS IP VPN core.

Figure 3-2   *Address Planes in an MPLS VPN Network*

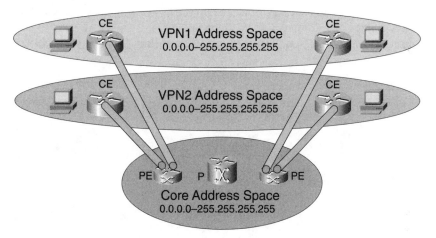

There is one special case in this model. The attachment circuit on a PE, which connects a VPN CE, is part of the VRF of that VPN and thus belongs to the VPN. However, the address of this PE interface is part of the VPN-IPv4 address space of the VPN and therefore not accessible from other interfaces on the same PE, from other core routers, or from other VPNs.

For practical purposes, this means that address space separation between VPNs and between a VPN and the core is still perfect because this PE interface to the CE belongs to the VPN and is treated as a VPN address. However, this also means that addresses exist in the VPN that belong to a PE. Consequently, a PE can by default be reached from a VPN, which might be used to attack that PE. This is a very important case and is discussed in detail in Chapter 5, "Security Recommendations."

All security mechanisms explained in this chapter work only when configured correctly and
           when the network is correctly implemented. Operational and implementation issues are
           discussed in later chapters. Here, we concentrate on the standards.

Traffic Separation

VPN traffic consists of VPN data plane and control plane traffic. For the sake of this
discussion, both will be examined together. The VPN user's requirement is that their traffic
(both types) does not mix with other VPNs' traffic or core traffic, that their packets are not
sent to another VPN, and that other VPNs cannot send traffic into their VPN.

On the service provider network, this definition needs to be refined because VPN traffic will
obviously have to be transported on the MPLS core. Here, we distinguish between control
plane and data plane traffic, where the control plane is traffic originating and terminating
within the core and the data plane contains the traffic from the various VPNs. This
VPN traffic is encapsulated, typically in an LSP, and sent from PE to PE. Due to
this encapsulation, the core never sees the VPN traffic. Figure 3-3 illustrates the various
traffic types on the MPLS VPN core.

Figure 3-3   *Traffic Separation*

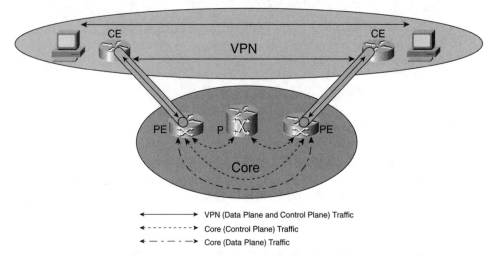

VPN traffic consists of traffic from and to end stations in a VPN and traffic between CEs
(for example, if IPsec is implemented between the CEs).

Each interface can only belong to one single VRF, depending on its configuration. So for
VPN customer "red," connected to the PE on a fast Ethernet interface, the interface
command **ip vrf forwarding** *VPN* determines the VRF. Example 3-1 shows the
configuration for this.

Example 3-1 *VRF Configuration of an Interface*

```
interface FastEthernet1/0
 ip vrf forwarding red
 ip address 1.1.1.1 255.255.255.0
```

Traffic separation on a PE router is implemented differently, depending on the type of interface on which the packet enters the router.

- **Non-VRF interface**—If the packet enters on an interface associated with the global routing table (no **ip vrf forwarding** command), the forwarding decision is made based on the global routing table, and the packet is treated like a normal IP packet. Only core traffic uses non-VRF interfaces, thus no further separation is required. (Inter-AS and Carrier's Carrier scenarios make an exception to this rule and are discussed later in this chapter.)

- **VRF interface**—If the packet enters on an interface linked to a VRF using the **ip vrf forwarding** *VPN* command, then a forwarding decision is made based on the *forwarding table* (or *forwarding information base, FIB*) of that VRF. The next hop from a PE perspective always points to another PE router, and the FIB entry contains the encapsulation method for the packet on the core. Traffic separation between various VPNs is then achieved by encapsulating the received packet with a VPN-specific header. There are various options for how to encapsulate and forward VPN packets on the core—through a *Label Switch Path (LSP)*,[2] an *IPsec* tunnel,[3] an *L2TPv3* tunnel,[4] or a simple *IPinIP or GRE* tunnel.[5] All of the methods keep various VPNs separate, either by using different tunnels for different VPNs or by tagging each packet with a VPN-specific header. Figure 3-4 shows how packets are encapsulated within the MPLS core.

Figure 3-4 *Encapsulation on the Core*

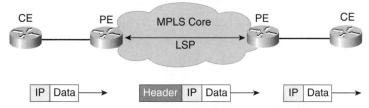

P routers have no active role in keeping traffic from VPNs separate: they just connect the PE routers together through LSPs or the other methods just described. It is one of the key advantages of the MPLS VPN architecture that P routers do not keep VPN-specific information. This aids the scalability of the core, but it also helps security because by not having visibility of VPNs the P routers also have no way to interfere with VPN separation. Therefore, P routers have no impact on the security of an MPLS core.

NOTE	In this chapter, as always, we assume correct operation and implementation. It is conceivable to construct a P router with the capability to also modify VPN traffic. However, this would constitute an operational mistake. (Current IOS and IOS-XR versions used for P routers do not permit modification of the tunnel content.) It is also possible for a service provider to use a packet generator to produce crafted packets and insert them into the core—anything can be faked that way. As mentioned before, the service provider must be trusted by the VPN users, or VPN-specific security such as IPsec is required.

In summary, VPN users can expect their VPN to be separate from other VPNs and the core because

- An interface on a PE (for example, the interface holding the user's attachment circuit) can only belong to a single VRF or the core.

- The attachment circuit (PE-CE link) to this interface belongs logically to the VPN of the user. No other VPN has access to it.

- On the PE the address information of the VPN is held as VPN-IPv4 addresses, making each VPN unique through unique route distinguishers. VPN-IPv4 addresses are only held on PE routers and route reflectors.

- VPN traffic is forwarded through the core through VPN-specific paths or tunnels, typically tagging each packet with a VPN-specific label.

- P routers have no knowledge of VPNs, thus they cannot interfere with VPN separation.

The service provider can expect its core to be separate from the VPNs because

- PE and P addresses are IPv4 addresses. VPNs use exclusively VPN-IPv4 addresses and cannot access PE and P routers. (Exception: The attachment circuit on the PE, which needs to be secured. See Chapter 4, "Secure MPLS VPN Designs.")

For more technical details on how VPN separation is technically implemented, please refer to RFC 2547bis.

Robustness Against Attacks

Over the last years, there have been an increasing number of attacks not only against application servers, but also directly against networking infrastructure. Service providers, therefore, have to be extremely careful about securing their core network well. The drastic effects of DoS attacks are mostly understood, but on MPLS VPN networks there is an additional, much more serious danger: if an attacker can control a PE device, the security of any VPN on the MPLS core can be compromised, whether connected to this PE or not. It is therefore of paramount importance for the service provider, but also for the VPN users, that the core, specifically the PEs, are properly secured and not attackable.

Where an MPLS Core Can Be Attacked

As the previous section shows, VPNs are separated from each other and from the core. This also limits potential attack points: Figure 3-5 illustrates the only interface point where a VPN can "see" the core and send packets to a core device: this is the PE router because the attachment circuit between CE and PE belongs to the VPN. Therefore, the only attack points seen from a VPN are all the PE interfaces that connect to CEs of that VPN. In the figure, VPN 1 can only see the PE interface it connects to and no other interface on that PE. Note that there is an attack point for each CE-PE connection, so that all of those PE interfaces must be protected from the entire VPN space. A VPN can*not* see any other interface on the PE, nor any core routers (for example, P routers or route reflectors).

Figure 3-5   *Visible Address Space from a VPN*

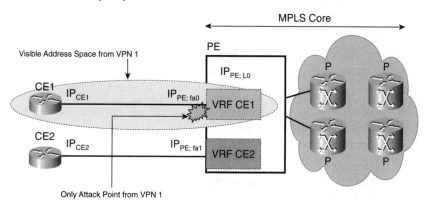

| | |
|NOTE| A CE router is *always* untrusted, even if the CE is managed by the service provider. The reason is that the CE is usually placed on customer premises and could, for example, be replaced by another router or even, in some cases, a workstation. A PE router, on the other hand, is *always* trusted, and *must* be trusted, because an intruder on a PE could jeopardize the security of *all* VPNs. This implies that a PE must always be in a physically secured environment. |

Each VPN can see and, by default, reach all of its PE peer addresses. These are the only direct attack points in an MPLS VPN environment, and this needs to be examined in more detail. How can a PE router be attacked from the outside?

| | |
|NOTE| P routers cannot be directly attacked from a VPN because they are not reachable from there. |

How an MPLS Core Can Be Attacked

In principle, a PE can be attacked with either transit traffic (not destined to the PE itself) or with targeted traffic to the PE. Traffic that is destined to a router is generally also called *receive traffic.*

Transit traffic is usually less of a problem because routers are designed to forward traffic fast. A router must, of course, be appropriately dimensioned to handle all potential transit traffic, which is a question of network design. This will be covered in detail in Chapter 4, "Secure MPLS VPN Designs," and Chapter 5, "Security Recommendations." However, certain forms of packets cannot be handled in hardware and can cause additional load on a router. Therefore, floods with such packets can lead to a DoS situation on the router.

Packets with *IP options* are one example. A packet with IP options has a variable IP header length and cannot, therefore, be looked up in current ASICs (microchips). This means that IP option packets must be switched in software, which lowers the performance of the router. Ways to protect against this are explained in Chapter 5.

Receive traffic, or traffic destined to the PE, is more of a concern because it affects the PE more directly. Two forms of attack are possible with receive traffic:

- **DoS**—In this case, an attacker tries to consume all resources on a PE router. This could be done, for example, by sending too many routing updates to the router, consuming all available memory.

- **Intrusion**—Here an attacker attempts to use a legal channel to configure the PE router. Examples are password guessing attacks against the telnet or SSH port, or SNMP writes to the router.

How the Core Can Be Protected

All of the potential attacks can be well controlled by appropriate configuration. In short, the recommendation is to block via an *access control list (ACL)* all access to all reachable PE interfaces. If routing is required, the routing port should be the only port on the PE not blocked by the interface ACL. Now an attacker can only attack the routing protocol directly, and that needs to be secured separately.

NOTE   Theoretically, if the PE is correctly configured, it should not be necessary to configure interface ACLs to protect it. However, in practice, two types of security problems arise: 1) operational issues, such as an erroneous AAA configuration or a weak password, and 2) implementation issues, where the operating system may have a security vulnerability. For better protection, it is therefore always recommended not to rely on a single layer of defense, but to configure additional security measures, such as interface ACLs in this example.

Following these recommendations, the PE will exclusively accept packets on the port for the routing protocol. This can also be secured, as explained in detail in Chapter 5. Any other packet destined to the PE will be dropped by the ACLs.

For overall security, of course all of the interfaces into the core need to be considered. Up to here we have covered the PE-CE interfaces. Another important point to control is the access to the Internet, and the question is whether an MPLS core or its VPNs can be attacked from the Internet.

If Internet access is provided in a VRF as if it were just another VPN, then all the above considerations apply equally to the Internet access: the Internet PE has to be dimensioned correctly, secured with ACLs, and the routing has to be secured separately.

If Internet is provided from the global routing table, then this access has to be secured in a different way. How Internet can be provisioned, what the security consequences are, and how to secure it is discussed in the Chapter 4.

NOTE   This chapter discusses only architectural security of MPLS, that is, whether an MPLS/VPN core *can* be secured. In real life the question arises whether the service provider actually implements and operates the core correctly. Overall security also depends on correct operation and implementation of the core. This is discussed in detail in Chapters 4 and 8.

Assuming proper implementation and operation, an MPLS VPN core provides a very high level of security: First of all, the interface into the core is limited to peering PE addresses only, and these can be secured well. This way, an MPLS/VPN core has considerably less exposure to attacks from the outside than a traditional IP backbone, where every interface on every core router might be a target for an attack. One of the key advantages of MPLS, then, is that it has small, well securable edges to the outside, making it easier to secure.

A traditional IP core, in comparison, is by default quite open, and each network element is reachable from the outside. This can in principal be limited by various means, such as ACLs or some core hiding techniques. But the advantage in an MPLS core is that the majority of the core is unreachable by architecture. Note that this depends how Internet routing is carried on the core: if it is carried in the global table, the risks of traditional IP cores apply as well. The key to security on an MPLS core is limited access to the global routing table from the outside. Chapter 4, "Secure MPLS VPN Designs," discusses the various options on Internet provisioning in detail.

Hiding the Core Infrastructure

Traditional Layer 2 VPNs such as Frame Relay or ATM have the characteristic that the VPN user cannot "see" the core infrastructure. In these cases, the reason is that the user connects a Layer 3 device to a Layer 2 network, such that the Layer 2 infrastructure is mostly hidden to the user. In general, most VPN users prefer to have details of the core hidden to them.

MPLS VPN networks hide most of their core infrastructure in the architecture. As shown previously in Figure 3-5, only the peering PE addresses are exposed to the VPN user; P routers are completely hidden. It is important to understand that the hiding of the core is not due to ACLs but to the intrinsic way of handling separate address spaces on an MPLS core: even if an address of a P router would be known to an outsider, this address does not belong to the address space of the VPN user, and therefore it not reachable.

The only exception to this is the peering address of the PE router. However, the address space of the CE-PE attachment circuits belongs to the VPN, not to the core. In fact, the same CE-PE address space could be used in several VPNs without address conflicts. Therefore, even though a PE address might be visible to the VPN, strictly speaking, no core information is passed to the outside because the address in question is VPN address space.

However, in reality, the reason to keep core infrastructure hidden is to avoid attacks against it. Therefore, considering which address space the PE peering address belongs to can be seen as mainly academic.

There is, however, a way to completely hide the PE routers from the VPN user: by using unnumbered address space and static routing between PE and CE. Here, an ACL could be applied to all PE peering interfaces of that VRF (where they exist), dropping any IP packet to the PEs' peering addresses (don't forget that *all* PE peering addresses toward *all* CEs of the VPN have to be secured this way).

In many cases, there are advantages to keeping the attachment circuit numbered—to monitor the health of the link, for example. Figure 3-6 shows a numbering scheme for such a case.

Figure 3-6 *PE-CE Addressing*

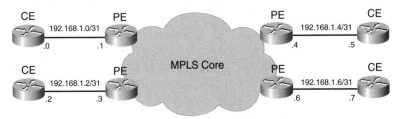

NOTE **Recommendation**

All attachment circuits of a given VPN should be addressed out of a contiguous supernet to simplify aggregation and protection of the PE via an ACL.

Example 3-2 shows how to implement this complete access control to the PE.

Example 3-2   *ACL to Protect PE Peering Interfaces*

```
access-list 101 remark 192.168.1.0/24 is the space used for PE-CE addressing
access-list 101 remark throughout this particular VPN, which is connected to
access-list 101 remark interface serial 0/1.
access-list 101 deny ip any 192.168.1.0 0.0.0.255
access-list 101 remark The next line permits transit traffic (important!)
access-list 101 permit ip any any
!
interface serial 0/1

ip access-group 101 in
```

In this example, the first line in the ACL covers all the PE-CE address space of that particular VPN. Note the following:

- In many real life implementations, this would require more lines to cover all the PE-CE address spaces (attachment circuits).

- Don't forget the last line: it permits all transit traffic.

- Other PE addresses, which do not belong to the VPN, do *not* have to be included, nor does any P addressing, because they are not reachable by architecture.

- This example assumes static routing (that is, no routing protocol) between CE and PE. If routing is required, the specific protocol must be permitted in the above ACL.

- The ACL as described here also blocks access to the interfaces of the CEs that are facing the PEs (see Figure 3-6). For example, 192.168.1.5 belongs to a CE, but this address is blocked by the ACL. Therefore, other CEs cannot ping that address. Also, a ping from this CE across the MPLS core would not work because return packets would be blocked, unless another source IP was chosen manually for the ping (using extended ping). This might not be desirable if, for example, a network management station pings these CE interfaces. To avoid that, you can either list all PE addresses of the VPN separately as host entries (/32) or ping loopback addresses on the CEs instead.

Implementing Example 3-2 for a given VPN, the core is entirely protected from that VPN.

Should routing be required, then the required ports need to be permitted from the CE and only the CE. This is described in more detail with examples in Chapter 5, "Security Recommendations." In this case, the peering PE address is not hidden, but as mentioned before, the address space belongs to the VPN.

Regarding core hiding, the main goal of service providers is to provide higher resistance against attacks. The previous section shows that even with the peering PE address exposed, sufficient security can be achieved.

VPN users asking for core hiding usually want to keep the network as simple as possible. The fact that a routing relationship with the PEs might be required is usually not seen as a strong impediment against using an MPLS service.

Protection Against Spoofing

When the Internet was in its early stages, the source address of a packet itself was considered sufficient to prove that the packet was really sent by this IP address. In early versions of UNIX, there is a whole command suite, the so-called "r-commands," such as **rlogin**, **rcp**, **rsh**, and so on, which rely on the IP address for authentication.

Today, IP address spoofing is an everyday occurrence in various types of attacks, and engineers have learned not to rely on the IP source address.

Since MPLS is a Layer 3 technology, users are concerned about spoofing on the MPLS network, both on the IP level and with the labels used by the MPLS protocols. Questions asked include "Can another VPN user spoof my IP address range to get into my VPN?" and "Can someone spoof VPN labels to intrude into my VPN?"

These questions can be easily answered:

- **IP address spoofing**—As discussed previously and shown in Figure 3-2, each VPN can use the entire theoretical IP address space, from 0.0.0.0 to 255.255.255.255. A certain VPN site or host may indeed spoof IP addresses, but the spoofing will remain local to that VPN. This is, in fact, a strength of MPLS VPNs: the VPN user may use the entire address space, including fake addresses, and the VPN behaves like a physical network with just that VPN user. This is possible because the PE routers keep all packets within the VRF context, such that even fake packets cannot "escape" that VPN context. Therefore, IP address spoofing in a VPN does not affect VPN separation.

- **Label spoofing**—Within the MPLS core, packets of different VPNs are distinguished by prepending a VPN label to the packet. A malicious VPN user may try to create specifically crafted packets with a fake VPN label and insert those into the MPLS core, trying to get those packets into another VPN. This is also impossible because PEs do not accept labeled packets from CEs. Therefore, such a faked packet would simply be dropped by the PE.

NOTE   The Inter-AS and Carriers' Carrier topologies are an exception to this rule because they do allow labeled packets to be sent to a PE router from the outside. These cases are discussed in the following sections in more detail.

But what if the packet with a spoofed VPN label is inserted within the core? Then this packet may really be routed to a random VPN, assuming the attacker knows (or can guess) some internal details of the MPLS core, such as VPN label numbers and egress PE label numbers.

The assumption made in this chapter is that the MPLS network is an integer (in other words, that the core is secure). This assumption includes the fact that the only interfaces into the network are the PE-CE interfaces. This may seem an unrealistic assumption at first, but in fact, any VPN technology is insecure if someone can insert packets in the core, because it would allow, for example, the insertion of random ATM cells with crafted virtual path and circuit information, and the same effect: getting packets into another VPN.

Therefore, the MPLS core is treated as a zone of trust where packets can only enter on well-known interfaces. See Chapter 1, "MPLS VPN Security: An Overview," for more details on zones of trust and this concept.

NOTE	In a standard MPLS VPN network consisting of a single AS, as defined in RFC 2547, a VPN user can assume a "virtually private" service with full separation, but the user has to trust the service provider to configure and operate the MPLS core correctly. Configuration mistakes or operational mistakes on the side of the service provider may break the security of the VPN. Also, data in transit are not encrypted and can be sniffed anywhere between the CEs. (This is discussed in more detail in Chapter 6, "How IPsec Complements MPLS.")

Assuming that packets can only enter the MPLS core through defined PE-CE interfaces, spoofing is not possible. RFC 2547, the first version of the standard for BGP/MPLS IP VPNs, describes only IP interfaces into the core, which allows this relatively simple security analysis.

RFC 2547bis, the second version of the standard, however, adds another form of interface—the Inter-AS and Carriers' Carrier architectures—which allow labeled packets entering the core. This changes the security exposure significantly and is therefore discussed in the following two sections in more detail.

Specific Inter-AS Considerations

The drawback of RFC 2547 is that it requires a single *autonomous system* (AS) to provide VPNs across it. RFC 2547bis allows VPNs to be provided across several ASs and thus several service providers. The standard describes three basic models for Inter-AS connectivity (models A, B, and C) that have different security properties.

Model A: VRF-to-VRF Connections at the AS Border Routers

This model is the simplest one, as it uses interfaces or subinterfaces between *autonomous system border routers (ASBRs)* to keep the VPNs separate. Figure 3-7 shows this principle: the two ASBRs each hold a VRF for each VPN that is shared between the autonomous systems. The ASBRs are then connected, and subinterfaces are used to link the VRFs directly.

Figure 3-7 *Inter-AS Model A*

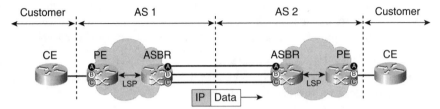

This model is equivalent in security to the standard RFC 2547 implementation because all external interfaces (seen from either AS) are IP interfaces.

In fact, an ASBR in this model behaves exactly like a normal PE router, and the configuration on an ASBR is also exactly the same as if it connected to a CE router in each VRF. Figure 3-8 shows how an ASBR in this model sees the other connections around it.

Figure 3-8 *Inter-AS Model A: How an ASBR Sees Its Peers*

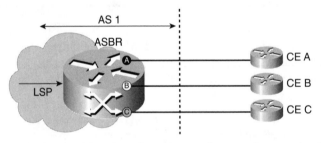

Therefore, all the considerations from the previous sections apply also in this model: there is strict separation between VRFs, label spoofing is impossible because no labeled packets are accepted by the ASBR from the other ASBR, and the other AS cannot "see" the core.

A further advantage of Inter-AS model A is that existing provisioning systems require little or no changes to support this model because the ASBR is essentially a normal PE, with attachment circuits to untrusted routers. To the provisioning system, such an Inter-AS connection looks like a number of normal CE connections.

For the same reasons, this model is also the easiest in other aspects, such as quality of service (QoS): everything that is possible on a subinterface can be supported automatically in this model. Because consistent QoS is important, especially when several service providers are involved in the provisioning of a VPN, it is important to have clear interfaces.

A service provider can deploy this model without further security implications over the standard MPLS VPN model, just as it would deploy more CE connections.

A VPN user in a single-AS RFC 2547 network has to trust the service provider for correct implementation and operation of the core. In Inter-AS model A, the user must trust *all* service providers that provide parts of the user's MPLS VPN in this way, but there is no further risk of interference with third parties. The only potential risk is that a service provider connects the VPNs from the other service provider wrongly, but this problem also exists in standard single-AS MPLS networks and has to be controlled operationally.

Inter-AS model A is the most secure interconnection model, but it has scalability issues on the ASBR: the ASBR must be configured with all shared VPNs (VPNs spanning more than one AS) and thus hold all VPN routes of shared VPNs. VPNs that exist only on one AS do not need to be kept on the ASBR. Furthermore, the interface between the ASBRs is not very flexible: a new subinterface must be configured on both sides for each new shared VPN.

The limiting scalability factor in Inter-AS model A is the number of interfaces or subinterfaces required, the number of VRFs required, and the memory required to hold all the routes from the various shared VPNs. Only Inter-AS model A has VRFs configured, so VRF memory is a deciding factor between the different Inter-AS types.

Two more MPLS interconnection models are defined in RFC 2547bis, with the goal of making the interconnection between ASs more scalable. Model B removes the need for separate subinterfaces, and model C even removes the need for configuring VRFs on the ASBRs. Both models are more scalable than model A, but this scalability has security consequences.

Model B: EBGP Redistribution of Labeled VPN-IPv4 Routes from AS to Neighboring AS

Model B removes the need for separate (sub-) interfaces per shared VPN on the ASBR. Here, only a single interface is required between the ASBRs. To be able to still distinguish the data packets from each VPN, packets must now be labeled on the data plane. This essentially creates a type of "tunnel" for each VPN on the single connection, defined by the label. These labels could be configured manually, but for ease of use, the control plane controls the labels in use. The *Multi-Protocol Exterior Border Gateway Protocol (MP-eBGP)* is used to pass VPN routes between ASBRs, and it assigns the labels to be used for each VPN prefix.

How Model B Works

Figure 3-9 illustrates model B: On the control plane, a single instance of MP-eBGP is used, exchanging all VPN-IPv4 routes, together with the required parameters (RD, label, and so on). On the data plane, all VPN packets are labeled to distinguish the VPN they belong to. In model B, the ASBR still needs to keep all VPN routes of the exchanged VPNs, as in model A, but here there is only a single interconnection.

Figure 3-9 *Inter-AS Model B*

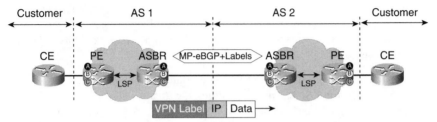

The standard for Multi-Protocol extensions for BGP (MP-BGP) is defined in RFC 2858. Although BGP only uses IPv4, MP-BGP uses the concept of an *address family* to enable BGP to carry VPN-IPv4 routes as a new address type. For this purpose, MP-BGP introduces two new attribute types, MP_REACH_NLRI and MP_UNREACH_NLRI, to announce and withdraw multiprotocol *Network Layer Reachability Information* (NLRI). The NLRI contains the VPN-IPv4 prefix (which in turn contains the RD) and the label. Example 3-3 shows how VPN label information can be seen on an ASBR.

Example 3-3 **show ip bgp vpnv4 vrf A labels**

```
PE#    sh ip bgp vpnv4 vrf A labels
   Network          Next Hop      In label/Out label
Route Distinguisher: 100:1 (A)
   10.10.10.10/32   192.168.10.10    10/12
```

This model makes the security between the service providers somewhat more complex. For the VPN user, however, nothing changes in comparison to model A: The VPN user must still trust both service providers, but third parties still can not interfere with this solution.

Security of Model B

To analyze the security between service providers, we examine the data plane and control plane separately.

On the control plane, there is a single MP-eBGP session between ASBRs, nothing else. Specifically, there is no *Tag Distribution Protocol (TDP)* or *Label Distribution Protocol (LDP)* running between ASBRs. This session can be and should be secured as any other BGP session: peer authentication with *message digest 5 (MD5)*, maximum route limits per peer and per VRF, dampening, and so on. In addition, prefix filters can be deployed to control which routes can be received from the other AS. Details on how to secure such BGP sessions are discussed in Chapter 5, "Security Recommendations."

With the Chapter 5 recommendations implemented on the two ASBRs, the MP-eBGP control plane does not increase the security exposure over model A and can be considered sufficiently secure for both service provider and VPN user.

On the data plane, labeled packets are exchanged. The label is derived from the MP-eBGP session; therefore, the ASBR announcing a VPN-IPv4 prefix controls and assigns the label for each prefix it announces. On the data plane, the incoming label is then checked to verify that this label on the data plane has really been assigned on the control plane. Therefore, it is impossible to introduce fake labels from one AS to another.

This control on the data plane means that packets with labels that were not assigned to the other ASBR will be dropped; however, it is *not* possible to check *which* of the correctly assigned labels is being used.

As an example, assume that an ASBR has announced two prefixes: one from VPN A with label 20, and another prefix from VPN B with label 21. On the data plane, packets with labels other than 20 or 21 can be dropped, but it is not possible to verify that a packet with label 21 really belongs to VRF B.

However, in reality, this does not add a new security exposure: each service provider involved in the provisioning of a VPN has the power to make each VPN insecure (which is not a specific MPLS problem). This does not change when VPNs are shared. As previously mentioned, the VPN user must trust all service providers involved in the provisioning of the VPN.

NOTE   Current versions of IOS (as of February, 2005) do not check the front label of an incoming packet on the data plane if the incoming interface terminates in the global routing table. The front label is only checked if the incoming interface terminates on a VRF (such as in the CsC case). Therefore, an additional security issue currently exists for Inter-AS case B: since the top label is currently unchecked, packets might enter an LSP to a PE router. At the penultimate router, the top label is popped and the resulting packet is presented to the egress PE, which would route it normally. This cannot happen accidentally and would be hard to execute deliberately. Also, such an attack could only come from the other service provider core, not from any of its connected customers.

There is one more potential issue to look at: Layer 2 security. All the considerations so far have been exclusively on Layer 3 and above. However, for a Layer 3 service such as MPLS VPNs to be secure, the lower layers must be secure as well. We have already discussed one Layer 1 issue: a wiretap on core lines or CE-PE lines reveals VPN data, unless encryption is used on top of MPLS.

A potential Layer 2 issue relates to using a shared switch to interconnect various MPLS networks in the Inter-AS model: if the connection between the ASBRs is provided (for example, on an Ethernet switch), Layer 2 security must be taken into consideration. This type of security threat is detailed in Chapter 4, "Secure MPLS/VPN Designs." (A quick summary here: VLANs can usually be assumed to be separate from other traffic on the switch, but within a VLAN there are security issues such as a third party inserting labeled traffic.

NOTE   Never connect ASBRs over a shared Layer 2 infrastructure such as an *Internet Exchange Point (IXP)*. Use a private connection, or at least a private VLAN.

In comparison with model A, model B is more scalable in that it requires only one connection between the ASBRs over which all VPNs are propagated. For this to work, MP-eBGP must be run between the ASBRs, and traffic is exchanged with labels. This can be secured adequately, but with more configuration the likelihood of error and a subsequent security breach increases.

Model B still requires each ASBR to hold the VPN routes for each shared VPN, and this is another scalability concern. To solve this issue, model C was invented.

Model C: Multihop eBGP Redistribution of Labeled VPN-IPv4 Routes Between Source and Destination ASs, with eBGP Redistribution of Labeled IPv4 Routes from AS to Neighboring AS

Model C was introduced in RFC 2547bis to remove the requirement to hold VPN-specific information on the ASBR. In this model, the VPN-specific information is propagated between the ingress PE on AS 1 and the egress PE on AS 2 directly. To improve scalability further, it allows the usage of *route reflectors (RRs)*.[6]

How Model C Works

Figure 3-10 depicts model C without RRs. The PEs of both autonomous systems have visibility of each other through a multihop MP-BGP connection, and they exchange the VPN-specific information (VPN-IPv4 NLRIs, labels, and so on) end to end, using the loopback addresses of the PEs without involving the ASBRs. This means that the ASBRs do not need to hold VPN-specific information.

Figure 3-10 *Inter-AS Model C, Without Route Reflectors*

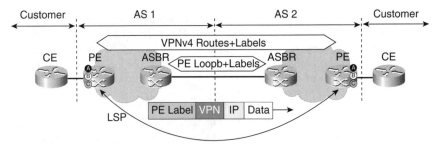

The ASBRs need only to exchange host routes (/32) to the PE routers involved in the VPN, with the labels needed to get there. In this way they facilitate the multihop BGP connection between the PE routers on both sides.

A Label Switch Path (LSP) is built from the ingress PE router in AS 1 to the egress PE in AS 2 (using loopback addresses). VPN traffic uses this LSP to reach the other AS. As far as the data plane is concerned, the ASBRs act as P routers, with no knowledge about the VPNs concerned. Also, between ASBRs the VPN traffic looks like traffic between P routers: each data packet is prepended with the VPN label and then with an egress-PE label.

Model C can be further scaled by using route reflectors in each AS. Figure 3-11 depicts this mode of operation. Because many networks require RRs internally, MPLS VPN model C also usually uses RRs.

Figure 3-11 *Inter-AS Model C, with Route Reflectors*

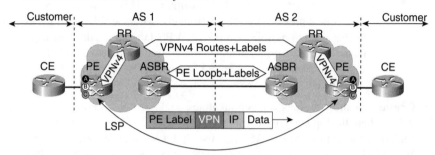

Here, the PEs in both autonomous systems maintain an MP-BGP peering only with the RRs in their own AS. The RRs in turn maintain an external MP-BGP peering. LSPs are established end to end from ingress PE to egress PE, as before.

Security of Model C

The security of this model is considerably more open than in models A and B.

On the control plane, model C has two interfaces between autonomous systems:

- The ASBRs exchange IPv4 routes with labels via eBGP. The purpose is to propagate the PE loopback addresses to the other AS so that LSPs can be established end to end. This route exchange and the whole BGP session can be controlled as in standard BGP. On this connection, no VPN information is passed on—only information relevant to the two ASs. Details on how to secure this connection are explained in Chapter 5, "Security Recommendations."

- The RRs exchange VPN-IPv4 routes with labels via multihop MP-eBGP. The prefixes exchanged can be controlled through route maps, equally the route targets. This makes it possible to ensure that only the required VPNs are exchanged, and within the VPNs, only specific prefixes.

On the data plane, the traffic exchanged between the ASBRs contains two labels:

- **VPN label**—Is set by the ingress PE to identify the VPN

- **PE label**—Specifies the LSP to the egress PE

Model C is considerably more open in terms of security than the previous models, for the following reasons:

- To be able to establish end-to-end LSPs, the service provider must be able to reach all PEs of the other AS, which hold connections of shared VPNs. This can be a considerable number of PEs, exposing important parts of the normally internal infrastructure of an AS to the other AS. This also means that considerations that are usually local to an AS in terms of addressing need to be coordinated with the other AS. It also means that traffic can be sent to a number of internal addresses from the outside, making possible attacks from the outside. The recommendation is to filter IP packets into the core as tightly as possible to prevent these issues. Labeled packets cannot be filtered currently.

• The ASBR does not hold any VPN information. This is a scalability advantage, but at the same time it prevents the ASBR from checking the VPN label for its validity. This means that it is impossible to verify the VPN label in the data path. (In model B, the ASBR holds this information and can therefore validate the VPN label.) The egress PE cannot verify the packet anymore because at this point the origin of the packet can no longer be determined.

Considering these reasons, a potential attack could be AS 1 sending labeled traffic into AS 2, where the top label represents the label to a valid egress PE in AS 2. AS 1 holds PE labels for all those PEs in AS 2, on which it has shared VPNs. However, because the VPN label cannot be checked by the ASBR, AS 1 could send packets with random VPN labels into AS 2 without AS 2 having a way to block this. Figure 3-12 illustrates this vulnerability. AS 1 has an LSP to the egress PE in AS 2. This PE has two VPNs configured: VPN A, which is shared with AS 1, and VPN B, which is not shared with AS 1. By sending the packet shown in Figure 3-12 with a VPN label for VPN B, the packet will be forwarded into VPN B. At the time of writing this book there was no solution to this issue.

Figure 3-12 *Case C Security Issue*

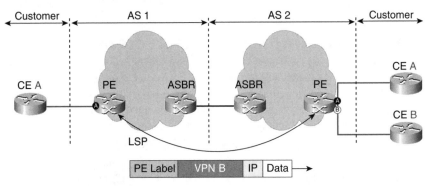

But how dangerous is this issue? First of all, AS 1 would need to know the VPN label for VPN B. The MPLS VPN network does not expose the label externally, so there are two ways of getting it: by espionage, or simply by trying the entire label space. A label has 20 bits, yielding $2^{20} = 1,048,576$ potential label values. Assuming a single packet attack with a 500-byte packet size, in the worst case an attacker would need to send 524 MB, which would take approximately 7 minutes on a 10 Mbps link, and 9 hours on a 128 k link. Note that in practice this number would be statistically smaller, and also, label numbering is not random, so intelligent guessing could reduce this number significantly.

Then, a malicious user in AS 1 could only send traffic into the VPN, but not receive a reply. However, there are a large number of examples in the history of security where a single unidirectional packet was enough to propagate a worm, for example. So while this limits the scope of an attack, it does not rule it out. In any case, the potential attacker would not receive feedback as to whether the attack was successful.

Therefore, it is not easy to carry out a sophisticated attack against a VPN from a given AS. But a single-packet unidirectional attack, as frequently used in the propagation of worms, is possible, even though statistically unlikely.

The consequence of this is that in model C the service providers must trust each other also in areas that are not shared. Therefore, model C is most commonly used today where a single operator uses several ASs on the backbone. In this case, implicit trust exists between the ASs because they have the same operational control.

As in model B, Layer 2 security between the ASBRs is extremely important. Therefore, here again is the recommendation from the previous section:

NOTE   **Recommendation**

Never connect ASBRs over a shared Layer 2 infrastructure such as an *Internet Exchange Point (IXP)*. Use a private connection, or at least a private VLAN.

Since the various Inter-AS connectivity options are confusing and their differences often subtle, the next section puts all options in context for easy comparison.

Comparison of Inter-AS Security Considerations

Table 3-1 compares the three Inter-AS connectivity options in simple terms.

Table 3-1   *Properties of Inter-AS Models*

	Model A	Model B	Model C
Required protocols between ASBRs	None (although intra-VRF routing is typically used)	MP-eBGP	eBGP
Complexity	Simple	More complex	Very complex
Scalability	Not very scalable	More scalable: one ASBR interconnection only	Very scalable: ASBRs don't carry VPN information
Visibility of other AS	None	ASBR only	All PEs, which carry shared VPNs and route reflectors
VPN user must trust	All service providers	All service providers	All service providers
Service provider must trust	Nobody	Nobody	The other service provider

So which Inter-AS option is the right one for you? Here are some decision guidelines, from a security perspective:

- If the number of shared VPNs and prefixes is small, consider model A. ("Small" is a relative term, depending on your ASBR capabilities.) It is simple, most provisioning systems easily support it, and it is the most secure option because of its simplicity: the more complex a solution, the more risk for errors and security issues. Model A has almost nothing to configure and no global protocols running (only possibly inside the VRFs). In security, nothing can beat simplicity! If the number of VPNs and prefixes is too large for model A, consider one of the other models.

- If you are peering with another operator, that is, the other AS is not under your direct control and you cannot fully trust it, use model B. If you cannot fully trust the other side, you need to control the interface. Model B has a clear-cut interface, which is relatively easy to control. Model C is not recommended here.

- If you are a single operator controlling all involved ASs, feel free to use model C. In this case, all your ASs behave a bit like a single AS, where ingress and egress PEs are in direct contact. The boundaries between ASs are less clear, but if there is one operator for all ASs, this is controllable.

NOTE	As a general security guideline, never use a new technology or protocol without a good reason. Adding complexity usually reduces security. So if in doubt, use the simpler model!

A number of risks exist in any environment and are independent of the Inter-AS model:

- Service provider 1 sends faked or crafted IP packets into any shared VPN on AS 2: this cannot be prevented. The VPN user must trust both service providers.

- Service provider 1 can bring a fake CE into any shared VPN, endangering the integrity of that VPN: this also cannot be prevented. Again, the service providers are trusted.

- A service provider can sniff traffic on any trunk, endangering the confidentiality of the VPN data. Here, too, the VPN user must trust the provider.

This appears to be quite an insecure model, but in fact the same risks exist in any VPN technology, although sometimes these trust issues are not clear. The service provider must always be trusted. The only solution if the service provider cannot be trusted is to provide additional security on top of MPLS, such as through IPsec. Chapter 6, "How IPsec Complements MPLS," describes this option.

Another model involving several providers is the Carrier's Carrier model. It allows a hierarchical structure, where a service provider resells a service from an MPLS provider. The next section covers this case.

Specific Carrier's Carrier Considerations

The *Carrier's Carrier (CsC)* architecture is described in RFC 2547bis, and can best be described as hierarchical MPLS VPNs: CsC provides an MPLS VPN service that other carriers use to resell their services.

How CsC Works

Figure 3-13 shows how the CsC architecture looks. The first-level service provider is commonly called the *backbone carrier*; the second-level provider is called the *customer carrier*.

Figure 3-13 *CsC*

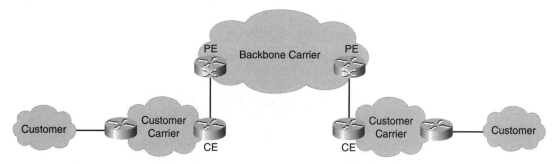

From a security point of view, the model is similar to standard RFC 2547 networks, with the exception that here on the interface between PE and CE, labeled packets instead of IP packets are exchanged. Although in the standard RFC 2547 network, all labeled packets can be discarded on ingress into the MPLS core, this model allows them.

There are two main cases for the application of CsC:

- The customer carrier is an Internet service provider (ISP).
- The customer carrier is an MPLS VPN provider.

If the customer carrier is an ISP, Internet traffic will be sent across the entire ISP network (spanning several VPN sites). For this to work, each router on the path must know all Internet routes. This includes the ISP's routers, but also the backbone carrier's PEs. For the backbone carrier, this does not scale: the PE would need to keep the entire Internet routing table for each VRF.

The solution is to use LSPs over the backbone carrier's network, essentially tunneling the Internet traffic over the core. This way, the PEs only need to know the address of the LSP endpoints, instead of the entire Internet routing table. In this solution the PE passes prefixes with a label to the CE, so the CE must be able to receive prefixes with labels and must be able to send labeled packets.

If the customer carrier is an MPLS VPN provider, the requirement is to connect VPN users transparently on several sites of the customer carrier's network. This can also be done with standard RFC 2547 MPLS, but it would require the backbone carrier also to configure on the core a VRF per customer of the customer carrier: essentially the VPN user would have to be configured on both the customer carrier network as well as the backbone carrier network. In addition, this does not scale well.

The solution is to exchange only *Interior Gateway Protocol (IGP)* loopback addresses with labels over the backbone, such that the CE will impose a new label for the traffic between sites. This way, the PEs from the customer carrier run MP-iBGP (interior BGP) sessions directly, and the backbone never sees the VPN user information. Figure 3-14 shows this behavior.

Figure 3-14 *CsC: Hierarchical VPN*

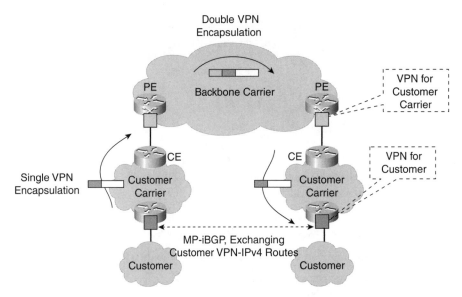

The original IP packet from the customer is encapsulated with a VPN label on the customer carrier's network. For this purpose, the customer's carrier has a VPN configured for each customer. This is exactly as in normal RFC 2547. The backbone carrier again configures a VPN for each customer's carrier on the customer's PE, the effect of which is that packets are again encapsulated on the backbone carrier's network.

There are several ways to configure the CsC solution for each case, but they are not discussed here because they do not differ from a security point of view: for security considerations, the important point is that the CE-PE interface now allows labeled packets. Therefore, CsC—like Inter-AS—is an exception to the general rules discussed in previous sections.

Security of CsC

To examine the security of the CsC solution, we address again both the control plane and the data plane. The interface between customers and the customer's carrier is a standard RFC 2547 interface and follows the considerations of the previous sections. The new part in the CsC architecture is the connection between the backbone PE and the customer carrier CE.

On the control plane, this interface has two basic options:

- To configure an Interior Gateway Protocol (IGP) with LDP or TDP. The IGP distributes the routes, while the LDP/TDP distributes labels for those routes.

- To configure BGP with label distribution, which combines the two tasks in one protocol.

All of these protocols can be appropriately secured, and this is described in detail in Chapter 5. The key concept is to ensure that the control connection is made with a known peer. This can be done using the MD5 authentication, which is available for all these protocols.

Label distribution on this interface is controlled in all cases by the backbone carrier. RFC 2547bis states for the CsC case: "The PE must not distribute the same label to two different CEs" (with some exceptions) for the control plane. For the data plane, it specifies that "when the PE receives a labeled packet from a CE, it must verify that the top label is one that was distributed to that CE."

This means the backbone carrier issues the label uniquely and then, on the data plane, controls all packets so that they use only the label(s) issued to them. This makes spoofing from the customer carrier impossible.

Attacks against the backbone carrier can be carried out with the protocols in use (IGP plus LDP/TDP or BGP), so they must be secured against DoS attacks and against propagation of false information. The backbone cannot be attacked through the exchanged packets, however, because the packets sent from the CE to the PE are not interpreted. Only label swapping takes place, which, again, is controlled by the backbone carrier. RFC 2547bis states for this case that packets cannot break the VPN separation if "it is known that such packets will leave the backbone before the IP header or any labels lower in the stack will be inspected." This is the case on the backbone level.

In CsC Layer 2, as in the Inter-AS architecture, security is paramount for any critical interface. Therefore, we repeat this warning:

NOTE   Never connect PEs and CEs over a shared Layer 2 infrastructure such as an Internet Exchange Point (IXP). Use a private connection, or at least a private VLAN.

The Carrier's Carrier architecture provides a secure way to operate multilevel VPNs, assuming correct implementation and operation. It is the backbone carrier that assigns and polices policy for the customer carrier, as the customer carrier does for its customers. On both levels the "customer" has no way to break the VPN separation of the level above. On both levels the lower level needs to trust the upper level to correctly implement and operate the network. For the end customer, this trust is transitive: the customer needs to trust the customer carrier, and implicitly also the backbone carrier.

Security Issues Not Addressed by the MPLS Architecture

In discussions about MPLS security, a number of questions typically arise that are outside the scope of the MPLS architecture. This means these issues have nothing to do with the standards and cannot, therefore, be controlled by the architecture. The following list describes these issues and explains why they are outside the scope of the architecture.

- **Protection against misconfiguration or operational mistakes**—The standards describe the architecture. This whole chapter examined MPLS VPNs based on this architecture. This architecture can also be misapplied, leading to security issues. Here's an example: As long as the PE is configured correctly according to the standard, the solution is secure. However, any operator could misconfigure a PE, breaking the security. This is not an architectural issue, but an operational issue. These problems are discussed in Chapter 8, "Secure Operation and Maintenance of an MPLS Core."

- **VPN data confidentiality, integrity, and origin authentication**—There is no guarantee to VPN users that packets do not get read or corrupted when in transit over the MPLS core. MPLS as such does not provide any of the above services. It is important to understand that a service provider has the technical possibility to sniff VPN data, and VPN users can either choose to trust the service provider(s) not to use their data inappropriately, or they can encrypt the traffic over the MPLS core, for example with IPsec, as described in Chapter 6, "How IPsec Complements MPLS."

- **Attacks from the Internet through an MPLS backbone**—If the MPLS backbone provides an Internet access to a VPN, attacks from the Internet into this VPN are outside the scope of MPLS. The task of the MPLS core is to forward packets from the Internet to the VPN and vice versa. This includes potential attacks. It is, however, within the scope of MPLS security to make sure that an attack against a given VPN does not affect other VPNs or the core itself. (This is discussed in Chapter 4.) Also outside the scope of the MPLS architecture is any kind of firewalling required for such cases.

- **Customer network security**—Every attack that originates in a customer VPN and terminates in that same VPN is outside the scope of MPLS security. The MPLS VPN architecture forwards packets between VPN sites; it is not concerned with the nature of these packets, which could also be attack packets. This also includes IP spoofing within a VPN.

NOTE   When discussing the security of MPLS VPN networks, take care to maintain a balanced view of the overall risks to a customer. For example, it is in relative terms close to irrelevant to argue about chances of an attacker sniffing a core line, if the customer network has unsecured wireless access points; it is also not important to worry about a service provider misconfiguring a PE, when attackers have uncontrolled physical access to hosts in an enterprise. Security is a question of balance: there is no point in putting extra secure locks on the door of your house if the windows are left open.

Comparison to ATM/FR Security

Many enterprises have been using VPN services based on ATM or Frame Relay (FR) in the past and are considering moving to MPLS VPNs. Unfortunately, the discussion about this topic has often been emotional and unbalanced.

New MPLS users are often concerned about the fact that an MPLS VPN service has a control plane on Layer 3. However, as shown in the previous sections, Layer 3 services can also be correctly secured and are fit to provide VPN services.

ATM/FR might be perceived as more secure because they are mostly not vulnerable to Layer 3 attacks (also ATM/FR switches typically have a Layer 3 control plane such as telnet). However, the security of Layer 2 in those technologies is typically assumed rather than actually proven. As we discuss in various parts of this book, Layer 2 has its own security issues that have to be considered. Many ATM/FR users are asking very hard questions about MPLS VPN security, while never having questioned whether a flood of signaling packets to an ATM switch might not affect that switch. It is good to discuss security of a technology, but it should be discussed in a balanced way.

This section discusses the features of both technologies and compares them.

VPN Separation

A VPN user requires his VPN to be separate from other VPNs and the core. In Layer 2 technologies, this is achieved implicitly by layering: the core exclusively uses Layer 2, so that the Layer 3 information of a VPN is separate. In MPLS VPNs, separation is achieved logically, by maintaining separate contexts on a provider router. Both ways are different, but both achieve the same result: each VPN can use the entire IP address space in their VPN, and it is impossible to send packets into other VPNs on the same core.

Misconfigurations are a problem in both technologies: an ATM circuit can be misconfigured, connecting a VPN router to a router from another company. Because many topologies are hub-and-spoke with default routing, this might lead to serious security breaches.

On the MPLS side, misconfigurations can equally break security. For example, a wrong route target on a PE router can bring a CE into a wrong VPN. You can argue about which misconfigurations are worse or more likely, but the fact is that if the core is misconfigured, VPN separation might be broken—in any VPN technology.

Robustness Against Attacks

VPN users demand a stable service, and most of all a service that cannot be attacked from the outside. For many VPN users, it would not be acceptable if a VPN service could be affected by a DoS attack from the outside. Even worse, an attacker gaining control of a network element could control any VPN. Therefore, any VPN technology must be resistant against attacks.

MPLS VPNs have been heavily scrutinized for the Layer 3 control plane and their frequent accessibility from the Internet. The issue was raised that given enough time, a good hacker would get access to a PE router over the Internet.

As shown previously in this chapter, an MPLS core has few and well-defined interface points to the outside. An MPLS core is not at all comparable to a traditional IP core, where every router was accessible (assuming the MPLS core has no global interfaces to the outside, only VRF interfaces). Rather, only single interfaces can be reached, and those can be very well secured. Therefore, it is very difficult to attack an MPLS network directly. An attack using transit traffic is the only possibility, and it might lead to a DoS condition. However, this can be controlled through appropriate dimensioning of the routers and architectural decisions, as is discussed in Chapter 4, in the section "Internet Access."

ATM or Frame Relay networks are also resistant against attack, assuming correct implementation. However, ATM switches and Frame Relay switches also have Layer 3 control planes (for example, telnet), and can be attacked if not appropriately secured. Frame Relay links depend on correct dimensioning of parameters such as Committed and Extended Information Rate (CIR/EIR). Misconfigurations of any of the above protocols or parameters can also result in a degradation or loss of service.

As long as both types of VPN technologies are configured correctly, they cannot be easily attacked.

Hiding the Core Infrastructure

In Layer 2 networks, the core is usually hidden because the VPN user works on Layer 3. Also, MPLS VPN cores are hidden to the VPN user, although using a different method: most addresses are hidden by architecture; the only visible part is the peering PE address. This address is, however, part of the VPN address space, so that in reality no core information is visible to the outside.

The fact that the PE router is reachable on this single interface is an exception to this rule. However, this usually is not a problem per se, but only in connection with attacks against the PE. As shown previously, this is very difficult if the PE is properly secured.

Impossibility of VPN Spoofing

As shown earlier in this chapter, it is impossible for an outsider to spoof another VPN, or the core, because a VPN user is always treated in his own context. Also, in ATM or Frame Relay, there are no known ways to spoof VPN signaling mechanisms such as the Virtual Path/Circuit Identifier (VPI/VCI) to spoof another VPN.

CE-CE Visibility

There is one area where ATM/Frame Relay point-to-point services do have an advantage over MPLS IP VPNs: Because the former are Layer 2 services, CEs can establish a direct Layer 3 adjacency and "see" the other CE. For example, the *Cisco Discovery Protocol (CDP)* can be used to find out basic properties of the peer router. This includes addressing of the Layer 3 link, so that a CE is able to verify to some extent the identity of the CE on the other end of the point-to-point link.

This is not possible in MPLS IP VPNs, and a given CE has no direct visibility of other CEs in his VPN. The reason for this is the connection model of MPLS IP VPNs: Although ATM and Frame Relay provide mostly point-to-point connections, where such a check is possible, MPLS IP VPNs provide connectivity from a CE to a "cloud." This avoids the overlay issue of having to establish a tunnel between all CEs (the so-called n^2 issue), but it has the disadvantage of losing the direct peering information.

This problem is not only theoretical. There is a real issue when a service provider accidentally or maliciously adds a CE to a wrong VPN by configuring wrong *route targets (RTs)*. The VPN to which this CE has been added has no easy means to find the bogus CE. It can only monitor traffic, control routing, and watch the used IP address space. This must be controlled by the service provider operationally. See Chapter 8, "Secure Operation and Maintenance of an MPLS Core," for more information on this important issue.

Other MPLS services, such as the *Pseudo Wire Emulation (PWE)*, also implement point-to-point services based on Layer 2, where direct CE-CE visibility is possible.

Comparison of VPN Security Technologies

Table 3-2 compares all the aspects of VPN security for the different VPN technologies.

Table 3-2   *Security Comparison Between MPLS and ATM/Frame Relay*

	MPLS	ATM/Frame Relay
VPN separation	Yes	Yes
Robustness against attacks	Yes	Yes
Hiding of the core infrastructure	Yes	Yes
Impossibility of VPN spoofing	Yes	Yes
CE-CE visibility	Not in MLPS IP VPNs Yes for MPLS pseudo wire emulation	Yes

Overall, at the time of writing this book, the industry had mostly accepted that both MPLS and ATM/Frame Relay can be operated securely. It was also common understanding that operational issues such as misconfigurations are an issue for any VPN technology.

Summary

In this chapter, we defined common requirements that VPN users have for a VPN service and examined MPLS IP VPNs against these requirements.

The result is that, based on the architecture described in RFC 2547bis, MPLS IP VPNs can be provided securely, meaning that:

- VPNs are separated (addressing and traffic).
- The core cannot be easily attacked.
- VPN spoofing is impossible.
- The core is invisible to the VPN user.

MPLS VPNs provide mostly equivalent security compared to traditional Layer 2 VPNs such as ATM and Frame Relay.

We have also examined Inter-AS and Carrier's Carrier architectures on their architectural security. While CsC networks are quite secure, care must be taken with Inter-AS scenarios when connecting different carriers: not all architectures provide the same level of security between providers.

There are also a number of issues that MPLS VPNs do not address. Among those are the internal security of a VPN, attacks from the Internet into a VPN, and VPN data confidentiality. These issues are independent of MPLS and have to be solved separately.

MPLS VPN networks are only secure when the network implementation is correct and when the network is operated correctly. How to control operations is discussed in Chapter 8, "Secure Operation and Maintenance of an MPLS Core." How to design and implement an MPLS core such that VPN services are secure is the subject of the next chapter.

Footnotes

[1] We will generally refer to IPv4 in this book; IPv6 is supported in the same way as IPv4, as a different address family.

[2] See RFC 2547bis.

[3] See draft-ietf-l3vpn-ipsec-2547 (work in progress).

[4] See draft-townsley-l2tpv3-mpls (work in progress).

[5] See draft-ietf-l3vpn-gre-ip-2547 (work in progress).

[6] For general considerations about route reflectors, consult *Cisco ISP Essentials*, ISBN 1-58705-041-2; *MPLS and VPN Architectures*, ISBN 1-58705-002-1.

In this chapter, you learn about the following:

- How to design an MPLS core for Internet access
- How to provision secure extranet access and firewalling
- How to design a DoS-resistant core
- How to secure Inter-AS and CsC solutions

CHAPTER 4

Secure MPLS VPN Designs

The previous chapters analyzed MPLS VPN security from an abstract point of view based on the architectural standards. However, the requirements of VPN users often go beyond simple architectures:

- The MPLS core should support Internet access.

- Several independent VPN users need to access a common extranet.

- A VPN user's network spans several countries and involves several service providers.

- An Internet service provider (ISP) wants to resell MPLS VPN services.

All of these more complex designs have a number of security implications, and sometimes a small design change affects security significantly. This chapter discusses their security properties and gives guidance on how to build advanced MPLS VPN designs securely.

Internet Access

Probably the most common VPN user requirement is that their service provider offer them Internet access in addition to VPN connectivity. However, being accessible from the Internet automatically is assumed to carry a certain risk for the VPN customer as well as for the MPLS VPN provider. This section discusses the various options for how to design an MPLS core for Internet access such that VPNs remain secure.

But is the Internet really so dangerous? Is a service provider not also at risk from connected VPNs? Can one VPN be a threat to another? As in all security questions it is difficult to draw a clear line, and of course a VPN user can also attack an MPLS core network.

The difference in security between a VPN user and the Internet consists mainly in the order of magnitude: A VPN user can attack the core, and a worm can come from a VPN also. But the size of the VPN user's network is usually several orders of magnitude smaller than the global Internet; therefore, the impact of an attack from the Internet is much higher.

Moreover, a service provider holds a contract with the VPN user but not with the Internet at large. This contract usually allows for counter measures to be taken: for example if DoS attacks are detected from a VPN connection, the connection can often be cut until the problem is resolved. Such drastic measures are often not possible with the Internet.

NOTE	**Recommendation**
	Service providers should seek legal advice on how to write customer contracts that allow the service provider to take technical counter measures against attacks, worms, and other threats from a VPN, including the temporal isolation of VPN sites. Legal aspects are outside the scope of this book.

Therefore, the risk from VPNs versus from the Internet is not intrinsically different in type, but it is significantly different in the order of magnitude and in terms of legal possibilities. Internet provisioning must be done with security in mind.

Technically, there are a number of options for how to provide Internet services on an MPLS core. While all those options achieve their goal in connecting a VPN user to the Internet, their security properties are completely different. We therefore strongly recommended considering all of the Internet options in detail before making a design choice.

NOTE	While security is a very important consideration in the design of an MPLS core, it is not the only one. Before making design decisions, other requirements, such as core scalability and quality of service (QoS), should be taken into consideration.

Technically, there are several ways to provide an Internet service on an MPLS core:

* Internet routes held in a VRF.
* Internet routes held in the global routing table. Here we distinguish two subcases:
  — The entire core holds the Internet routing (PE and P).
  — Only PEs hold the Internet routing, the so-called "Internet-free" MPLS core.

At first sight, all of those options appear to have similar properties; however, their security exposure varies significantly. The following section examines a core without Internet connectivity as a baseline to compare the other design options to. Then those options, as well as generic Internet design guidelines, are explained in detail.

MPLS Core Without Internet Connectivity

In this model, the MPLS core has no connection to the Internet. Only VPNs connect to the core, which means that all external connections end in a VPN routing/forwarding instance (VRF). This is the purest form of an MPLS VPN core, and all the considerations from the previous chapters apply directly:

- VPNs are completely separated, including addressing, data traffic, and routing.
- The core can be well secured against intrusions and DoS attacks from the outside.
- The core is invisible from the outside.
- VPN spoofing is impossible.

Note that all these items depend on correct configuration and operation of the core.

In this model, the entire core is inaccessible to the outside—that is, the connected VPNs, with the exception of the peering PE interfaces, which are part of the VPN. Figure 4-1 shows that those PE interfaces are the only interfaces to the outside, allowing for the core to be easily secured. Chapter 5, "Security Recommendations," describes this in detail.

Figure 4-1   *MPLS Core Without Internet (VPN Only)*

In this model, the core is by architecture unreachable, the security of internal parts of the network (the internal routing, LDP, SNMP, and so on) is guaranteed against attacks from the outside (see the following recommendation, however). The only way to threaten the security of the core is to attack from the inside: service provider engineers have the power to change security by mistake or deliberately. This threat is covered in Chapter 8, "Secure Operation and Maintenance of an MPLS Core."

The fact that no packets can get into the core may lead to the conclusion that the internal parts of the core do not need to be secured. Why protect Interior Border Gateway Protocol (iBGP) sessions with routing authentication with MD5 if it is impossible to send packets to the routers? This statement is true if and only if the network is 100 percent correctly implemented and operated. An engineer might connect a customer connection by mistake to a wrong interface, for example, terminating this connection in the global routing table.

In this case, the customer *does* have access to the core, and the usual security mechanisms (routing authentication, for example) are required. Therefore, it is strongly recommended to configure *all* possible security mechanisms, even if a single one is theoretically enough.

NOTE   **Recommendation**

Never rely on a single security mechanism! Security should be designed in layers of protection, such that if one layer fails there are more mechanisms to fall back on. This principle is called *defense in depth*.

It is in reality impossible to know whether an MPLS core has Internet connectivity because a VPN customer might have a private Internet connection, unknown to the service provider. Figure 4-2 shows how, in this case, traffic from the Internet might travel over the core within the VPN of that customer. In the figure, VPN A has a private Internet connection at its left site, and a user on another site can access it. The VPN includes the peering PE interfaces, and that now makes the PE reachable from the Internet.

Figure 4-2   *Hidden Internet in a VPN*

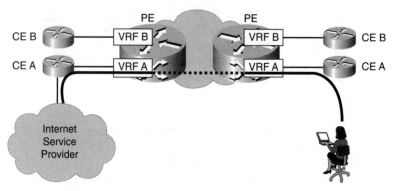

As a consequence, the Internet traffic is implicitly part of a VPN, here VPN A. Note that routing does not necessarily change significantly within the VPN because default routing can be used. Has the security exposure on the MPLS core changed because of this hidden Internet service? Are other VPN customers on the same MPLS core now at greater risk than before?

For the MPLS core, the situation does not change significantly: the Internet has effectively become part of a VPN, but the fundamental properties of the MPLS architecture listed at the beginning of this chapter still hold true. There is a possibility of DoS attacks from the

Internet across the core, but those would likely be limited by the access capacity of the VPN customer. In this example, if the user gets attacked from the Internet across the MPLS core, the maximum bandwidth on the core would be limited by the access line on the left VPN site. (In the section "Designing DoS-resistant Networks," later in this chapter, we examine the effect of DoS attacks against PE routers because theoretically an attack against a single PE may affect all VPNs connected to that PE.)

For other VPN users, the security also does not change significantly because of this hidden Internet connectivity: the separation between VPNs remains fully intact, and the only risk is flooding attacks. However, those attacks are limited by the access capacity, which in correct network capacity planning cannot do harm to core or other customers. And again, the service provider actually holds a contract with each VPN, which should allow for disconnection of sites if the site "misbehaves."

The important fact for security in this example is that all external routes are kept in a VRF. If there are hidden Internet connections, the security exposure is similar to the case where all the Internet routes are held in a VRF. This is also discussed in the section "Designing DoS-Resistant Networks."

In the following sections, we discuss various ways to provide Internet services on an MPLS VPN core: first some generic recommendations that apply to all models, and then each model in detail.

Generic Internet Design Recommendations

If the service provider chooses to provide an Internet service over its MPLS core, it has to follow general design guidelines. These are not specific to MPLS core networks but are listed here for completeness.

When providing Internet connectivity, the following factors have to be taken into account:

- The maximum ingress capacity from the Internet, limited by the line between Internet PE and CE or further upstream. Note that both the packet-per-second (pps) rate and the bit-per-second (bps) rate are important in this calculation: the capacity of routers and servers is determined by a pps rate, whereas the capacity of a core line is determined by bps.

- The switching capacity of the Internet PE and CE routers and of P routers in the core (measured in pps).

- The capacity of core lines (measured in bps).

- The capacity of PE routers where VPN customers are connected (measured in pps).

The MPLS core must be designed such that all components of the core can process a potential DoS attack from the Internet. Figure 4-3 illustrates the components to be taken into account.

Figure 4-3 *Designing the Core to Sustain DoS Attacks*

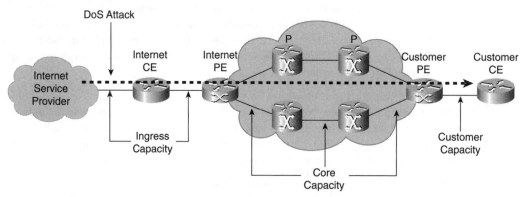

The network design has to accommodate the worst-case scenario: This is a DoS attack from the Internet where all connections from the Internet are completely loaded and all this traffic goes to a single destination (the customer CE)[1]. To design a network for this worst-case scenario, you must take into account the following considerations:

- The ingress capacity must be sufficient to serve the customers who have contracted an Internet service.

- Internet PE and CE routers must be able to forward the full theoretical maximum ingress bandwidth (in pps) from the Internet. In addition to pure packet forwarding, they must be able to apply security features on ingress. As a minimum, ACLs at line rate are required.[2] These routers are paramount security tools and must be fully operational under all circumstances, including under a DoS attack. (Note: While the core routers should be fully operational, the customer under attack will be affected by the attack. The goal is to keep the core operational and to limit the impact on other customers.)

Note   The stability of the core routers in a network, including the routers to upstream providers, is the single most important factor for core security. Counter-measures against DoS attacks frequently involve features such as ACLs and committed access rate (CAR) on ingress routers. These features can only be applied if those routers are 100 percent stable, even under the full theoretical load.

Modern routers, such as the Cisco 12000, can forward packets at full line rate, while applying features. This type of router is usually not affected by data plane DoS attacks.

- The core capacity must be designed such that even if a worst-case attack (full ingress capacity) is going to a single destination, VPN traffic can still be served according to the service level agreements (SLAs) with the VPN. In other words, even under extreme stress from the Internet, VPN users should not be affected. There are two ways of achieving this:

— By providing sufficient capacity in the core

— By using QoS mechanisms to prioritize VPN traffic over Internet traffic

- P routers must be able to switch traffic at line rate.

- Egress PE routers should be designed such that they cannot be affected by DoS attacks from the Internet. This requirement is hard to fulfill in practice: Internet capacity is usually larger than what small PEs can handle. The section "Designing DoS-Resistant Networks" discusses this PE design issue and explains ways to handle it.

NOTE	Any core network, including MPLS VPN networks, must be designed such that even DoS attacks are carried correctly to their destination, while the core remains completely stable. Only on a stable core can a service provider then counteract DoS attacks with specific techniques, which are outside the scope of this book.

The dimensioning of the customer capacity (the PE-CE link into a VPN), which requires Internet over this link, is not of concern to the service provider. It is the choice of the VPN customer, according to the customer's Internet needs. In practice, this link is usually overloaded under a DoS attack. This problem occurs on all types of networks and is not specific to MPLS VPNs.

NOTE	You cannot protect a customer's Internet connection (the PE-CE link, the CE itself, or anything behind that) from a DoS attack by core design. For this special DoS mitigation, techniques are required (for example, the Cisco Guard), which are not discussed in this book. The design goal of this chapter is to ensure that the core remains operational, that VPN traffic is not affected by the attack, and—if possible—that other customers' Internet traffic is not affected.

The Internet CE (as shown in Figure 4-3) is a normal router, such as a router connecting to an Internet Exchange Point (IXP). In theory, the Internet PE could directly peer with ISPs. However, Figure 4-4 shows why it is an advantage if the Internet CE is also controlled by the provider of the MPLS core: this way, the address space between PE and CE does not have to be announced externally. This means that even if this address space is public, it can be blocked on the Internet CE to make the PE completely inaccessible from the outside. Also, *infrastructure ACLs* can be applied here, which protect all address space that is visible to the outside: the Internet PE's external address and all PEs facing Internet customers (not shown in Figure 4-4). Infrastructure ACLs are explained in Chapter 5. Naturally, an Internet CE is an additional expense that has to be considered when designing the Internet access.

NOTE	The name *Internet CE* is misleading: this router is, of course, not a "customer edge" router in the traditional sense of MPLS VPNs. However, for consistency reasons, we maintain this naming scheme.

Figure 4-4   *Protection of the Internet PE*

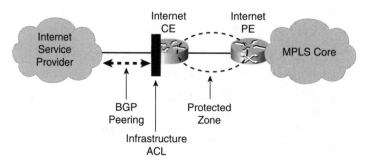

If the Internet PE does not carry any other VPNs, the recommendation to shield the Internet PE with another CE router can be disregarded. In that case, it does not make a difference if an attack goes against the Internet CE or the Internet PE. But if the Internet PE holds other VPNs as well, a DoS attack against the PE might affect those VPNs, too. In this case, the Internet CE adds significantly to the security of the VPNs connected to the Internet PE because it protects the Internet PE against direct attacks. The subject of PE routers that carry both Internet and VPNs is discussed in detail in the section "Designing DoS-Resistant Networks."

NOTE   **Recommendation**

When connecting to other service providers or an IXP, provision an Internet CE router, such that the Internet PE can be completely shielded from the Internet. Alternatively, do not provision any VPNs on the Internet PE.

Previously, we mentioned that the dimensioning of routers in the MPLS core (PE and P) should be done such that they can handle all traffic from all Internet connections concurrently, for example under a DoS attack. This is, of course, unrealistic in practice: a small, customer-facing PE router would often not be able to sustain a flood from the Internet. Therefore, if this issue cannot be solved by design, it needs to be addressed on the operational level: The service provider must be able to detect and counteract packet floods from the Internet quickly, so that the SLAs with the customer can be met.

In other words, most of today's Internet networks assume a certain traffic distribution, which can be severely distorted under a DoS attack. There are two ways to make sure that the overall service, specifically the VPN part, remains operational even under a severe DoS attack:

- **Design method**—Each backbone router (PE and P) and each line must be designed such that a DoS attack does not affect VPN traffic or the backbone itself. This is difficult to achieve because capacities are not normally sufficient to cope with a DoS attack, especially on the customer edge router and line. However, in the section "Designing DoS-Resistant Networks" we explain how in order to achieve this goal a core can be built such that VPN traffic remains separate from Internet traffic. One way to do this is to strictly separate Internet and VPN PEs such that Internet floods never touch a VPN PE.

- **Reaction method**—If the network design is such that a DoS attack from the Internet might affect a portion of the network carrying VPN traffic, the alternative is to have a fast DoS detection and mitigation scheme to avert the DoS attack. In other words, if you know parts of your network will melt in a DoS attack, you should be very fast in detecting and blocking the DoS attack. If this reaction happens within the timelines guaranteed in the SLAs, this is a commercially viable solution.

To define a DoS strategy for your network, consider several levels of priority when it comes to an attack:

- **Core**—The core itself must never be affected by a DoS attack, first because a single affected core router is likely to affect a number of customers, and second because the service provider must be able to apply counter-measures on the core devices. This works only if core devices are fully operational. So the core is top priority.

- **VPN traffic**—This traffic usually has higher SLAs than Internet traffic; therefore, the next priority is to make sure VPN traffic is not affected by a DoS attack.

These first two goals *must* be achieved by a service provider. With correct design and operations, this is possible.

- **Internet traffic to other destinations than the attacked one**—If the core and VPNs are still working, the provider should try to make sure that Internet traffic to nonattacked customers is working. However, this goal might *not* be achievable anymore; for example, if the entire uplink into the service provider network is overloaded, it will affect all Internet customers. This can only be solved by upstream providers and is thus not under full control of the service provider any longer.

- **Internet traffic to the site under attack is the lowest priority**—In a first approach, the customer is actually paying to receive traffic from the Internet, which ironically includes DoS attacks. However, often the customer is relying on the provider to mitigate DoS attacks. So the provider should offer help, even though this service might incur an extra charge.

NOTE   DoS attacks are only one form of distorting traffic patterns and thus potentially overloading parts of the network. If a significant number of users decide to access a service at the same time, the same technical phenomenon might be observed: overload of some network resources. This latter form is called *flash crowds*. Although there is no malicious intent in this case, the net effect can be the same as a DoS attack.

This section's recommendations are not only applicable to an MPLS backbone, but to a large extent to any Internet backbone. In the following sections, we go through the various MPLS-specific options for providing Internet services:

- Internet in a VRF
- Internet in the global routing table (with various suboptions)

Internet in a VRF

If the Internet is required on an MPLS VPN core, the most secure way is to provision it in a VRF. In this model, as in the previous example, Internet traffic stays within a VPN on the MPLS core, but here it is designed by the service provider.

Figure 4-5 illustrates the Internet in a VRF model. Upstream connections to other ISPs are connected to a PE router directly into a VRF. The MPLS core carries the Internet routes as if the Internet were just another VPN on the core network, and customers who need Internet connectivity connect into that VPN.

Figure 4-5   *Internet Provisioned in a VRF*

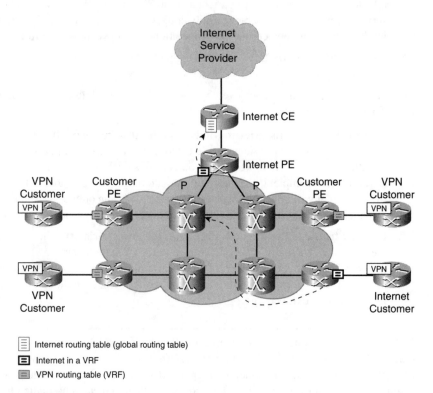

☰ Internet routing table (global routing table)
⊟ Internet in a VRF
▦ VPN routing table (VRF)

NOTE   A prefix held in a VRF requires about three times as much memory as a prefix held in the global table. If the full Internet routing table is required, the additional memory required is an important factor to consider.

The Internet router shown in Figure 4-5 is seen by the core as a CE. Since Internet is just another VPN on the core, all the statements at the beginning of this chapter hold true here.

The difference to a normal VPN is contractual: this CE is not a customer, but part of the overall service.

NOTE   In April 2004, Cisco announced an IOS vulnerability in TCP, where an attacker could reset an established TCP session in much shorter time than previously thought. This also affected BGP and LDP because both run on TCP. For MPLS core networks, however, which had either no Internet connectivity or Internet in a VRF, this vulnerability could not be exploited from outside the MPLS core because the core devices are by architecture not reachable from the outside. This is a good demonstration that because of its architectural separation MPLS core networks can be better secured than traditional "transparent" IP core networks.

All the security features discussed in previous chapters also hold true for the case of Internet in a VRF. Here's a summary of them:

- Separation between VPNs is maintained because Internet is handled just the same as a VPN.
- The core can be secured against attacks from the outside, specifically from the Internet; because just like other VPNs, the Internet has no access to the core.
- The core is invisible to the outside. This also applies if the Internet is provided in a VRF because it constitutes another VPN.
- Spoofing is impossible between VPNs and the Internet in a VPN, following the reasons discussed in Chapter 3, "MPLS Security Analysis."

These architectural features of MPLS VPN networks do not require specific configurations. As discussed in the previous section, packet floods are one remaining potential issue from the Internet: there is a possibility that large DoS attacks may have an impact on the PEs or on core lines. This might indirectly also affect VPN customers. The solution is to either overprovision the core or to use QoS to give VPN traffic a higher precedence. (Please refer to the previous section for details.)

If the Internet is provided in a VRF, the overall network benefits from the intrinsic security properties of the MPLS architecture. The downside of this approach is scalability, as previously discussed. Therefore, many service providers choose to carry Internet in the global routing table.

Internet in the Global Routing Table

Due to memory limitations and the previously mentioned issue of VRF prefixes needing more memory than prefixes in the global table, many providers prefer to keep Internet routing in the global table. There are two ways to implement this:

- Configure the MPLS core like a traditional IP core, with each router holding the full routing table.
- Use the option called *Internet-free core.*

Hop-by-Hop Internet Routing in the Core

Traditionally, the Internet follows the hop-by-hop routing paradigm, where every router makes a forwarding decision based on its local routing information. This paradigm requires every router to know a route to every destination on the Internet that needs to be reached. Smaller ISPs and their customers usually use default routing to avoid having to keep the full routing table. The large ISPs in the core of the Internet run their core "default-free," which means their core routers hold the full routing table and therefore do not require a default route.

MPLS offers an alternative to the hop-by-hop routing behavior: As described in the previous section, only the PE routers need to know routes external to the MPLS core. P routers only know routes within their own autonomous system (AS). The forwarding on the core is done using label switch paths (LSPs), ATM virtual circuits (VCs), or another encapsulation method such as GRE, L2TPv3, or IPsec.

However, the two paradigms can be combined on a single core network: the PEs carry VPN-related information in VRFs, and the Internet routing table in the global routing table. Figure 4-6 illustrates this setup.

Figure 4-6 *MPLS with Hop-by-Hop Internet Routing in the Core*

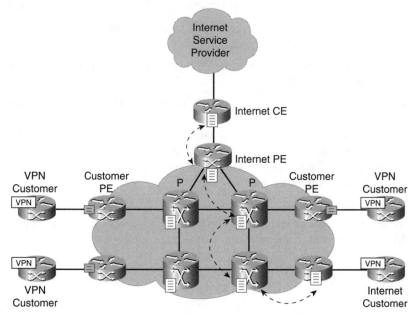

In most cases where such a design is used, all PE and P routers hold the entire Internet routing table. PEs that connect only VPN customers would not require the Internet routing table; however, for consistency reasons, service providers often have the same routing policy for all PE routers. Note that in a default MPLS core, all next hops on a PE router will resolve to an egress label, such that an LSP would be used. Special configurations are required to actually get hop-by-hop routing on an MPLS core.

In this model, one of the important security aspects of MPLS security does not apply: here, all routers are accessible from the Internet by default. From a security point of view, two aspects have to be analyzed for each router in the network:

- **Reachability from the Internet to a router**—Packets originating from the Internet can be addressed to a router. This exposes the router to directed attacks and should therefore be avoided or at least limited in scale if possible.

- **Reachability from a router to the Internet**—The router can reach destinations on the Internet. This may seem less relevant for security, but it is important: it allows connections to be established—for example, an SSH control connection. If the router does not know how to reach Internet addresses, return traffic will not reach potential attackers on the Internet, making two-way connections impossible.

To reach a router from the Internet, one of the addresses of this router must be routed on the Internet. To reach the Internet from a router, the router needs to keep the Internet routing table. In MPLS VPN networks without Internet, the core is never accessible from the outside. By importing the Internet routing table into the core, and by announcing at least some of the core address area to the Internet, the separation between the core and the Internet is fundamentally broken.

This in itself is not specific to this architecture: traditional Internet networks without MPLS have likewise always had this property; nevertheless they where operated securely. If the architecture of the core network does not provide separation, additional security measures must be taken.

NOTE   **Recommendation**

Even if your design does provide architectural separation, always secure each device as if it were freely accessible from the outside: use the defense in depth principle to secure on all levels. If one security mechanism fails, there should always be fallback security.

In traditional IP networks, each network element is secured independently. The assumption here is that the device might be hit by attacks any time; therefore, all possible device security measures have to be taken.

In addition, since about 2003, several providers have started to implement infrastructure ACLs. The idea is to block all traffic into the core on ingress (see Figure 4-7).

Figure 4-7   *Infrastructure ACLs*

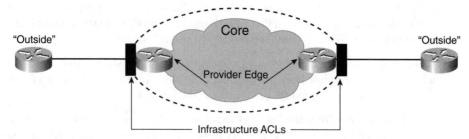

Infrastructure ACLs are applied on all edges into the core for all packets destined to core devices:

```
deny ip any core-address-space
permit ip any any
```

Because the core address space usually cannot be expressed in a single prefix, several deny statements are usually needed. There will also be exceptions in practice, such as for routing protocols to the PE router. The last line permits transit traffic across the core. Infrastructure ACLs are discussed in more detail in Chapter 5.

With infrastructure ACLs on the ingress ports into the core, reachability of the core can be controlled. There are other ways for achieving the same goal (for example, by not announcing the internal address space to the Internet or by using private address space on the core). All of those mechanisms have the common goal of securing the core against attacks from the outside by limiting reachability to the core. When Internet on an MPLS core is provisioned in the global routing table, such measures are required.

NOTE   **Recommendation**

Deploy infrastructure ACLs on all ingress ports into your network. See Chapter 5.

In summary, Internet in the global routing table makes all core devices accessible and, therefore, attackable from the outside by default. So a strong layer of defense around the entire core, limiting reachability of the core, is required. As in every model, every router must be individually secured.

NOTE   The integrity and separation of VPNs is not endangered by providing Internet in this way. The only threat is an attack against the backbone. This might, however, result in a reachability problem for some VPNs, and thus endanger their availability.

There is also a compromise between the two models (Internet in a VRF and Internet in the global routing table): the Internet-free core.

Internet-Free MPLS Core

The Internet-free core is a hybrid between Internet in a VRF and Internet in the global routing table. Although the Internet routes are carried in the global table on the PE routers, the P routers do *not* carry Internet routes. Instead, LSPs (or other tunnels) are used to forward Internet traffic. Figure 4-8 illustrates this setup.

Figure 4-8   *Internet-Free Core*

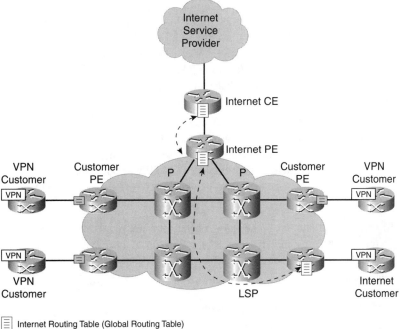

The PE routers hold the Internet routing table in their global routing table. Also, in the previous case, P routers held Internet routing information distributed by iBGP; here, the P routers only run an Interior Gateway Protocol (IGP), in which only reachability of PEs is advertised. The PEs maintain iBGP peering with all other PEs directly or through route reflectors. But because here the reachability of the egress PE is achieved through the IGP and because the Label Distribution Protocol (LDP) is used to establish LSPs between the PEs, these LSPs are also used for Internet traffic. Therefore, the P routers do not require Internet routing information in this model.

Schematically, this setup is the same as when forwarding between VRFs. But here, instead of the VRF table, the global routing table is used.

In this model, the PEs maintain Internet routes and are thus by default fully reachable from the Internet. Therefore, the PE routers need to be secured as in a traditional core network: every router independently, plus infrastructure protection, as described in the previous section.

It may appear at first glance that P routers are not reachable from the outside, but this is *not* the case. P routers do not hold the Internet routing table; therefore, they cannot send packets into the Internet. However, the opposite direction is open: the Internet PE router holds all Internet routes in its global routing table, but it also needs the IGP routes there for the interior routing within the core. Therefore, if a packet reaches the PE with a destination of one of the P routers, the PE router does have a route to the P router and will forward the packet.

The consequence is that, by default, traffic from the Internet can reach any PE or P router in this setup, but only PE routers have the route back to the Internet. Therefore, a PE router can receive and send traffic to the Internet, allowing full connections to be established. A P router may be accessible from the Internet *unidirectionally*, but it cannot send traffic into the Internet. This allows at least a DoS attack against the P router.

NOTE   VPNs can*not* be attacked directly from the Internet, and the separation of VPNs and the core remains intact. The threat here is a DoS attack against the backbone only, which might however have a follow-on effect on the availability of some VPNs.

To secure such a network, the same mechanisms are required as in the previous section: device security plus infrastructure ACLs. With those mechanisms, an Internet-free core can be secured like any other IP backbone.

Overview of Internet Provisioning

The Internet is perceived to be the source of attacks against network infrastructure. While attacks might come also from connected customers, those are usually easier to handle than attacks from the Internet. Therefore, you must be careful how you provision Internet services on an MPLS VPN core network.

NOTE   None of the Internet architectures described here put the separation between VPNs and between VPNs and the core or Internet in question: separation is always maintained. The difference between these options lies in the ways the backbone can be attacked. For the connected VPNs, the main threat is temporary loss or degradation of service under a DoS attack against the backbone.

Table 4-1 summarizes the default reachability for various options for providing Internet on an MPLS VPN backbone and compares it to an MPLS VPN backbone without Internet service.

Table 4-1   *Default Reachability for Various Options for Providing Internet Services*

	MPLS Without Internet	Internet in VRF	Internet in Global Table	Internet-Free Core
PE reachable	No	Yes	Yes	Yes
P reachable	No	No	Yes, bidirectional	Yes, unidirectional
VPNs reachable	No	No	No	No

Table 4-1 shows the default behavior of various MPLS VPN architectures. This does not necessarily imply a security issue! Reachable devices just require additional security measures. The traditional Internet was built with the paradigm that every router is reachable, yet it can be secured.

Specifically, MPLS VPNs are not reachable from the outside, independently of which of the before-mentioned Internet options is chosen.

The various options discussed here, however, impact two areas:

- **Security of the service provider network**—Devices that are unreachable cannot be hacked. If, for example, a PE router is reachable, it is exposed to attempts to intrude into the device and potentially alter the configuration. This may have a secondary effect on VPNs if security mechanisms on the PE are disabled, for example. This may also lead to a breach of separation between VPNs, depending on the PE configuration. This has to be secured with traditional security measures.

- **Exposure to DoS attacks**—A reachable device can also receive a DoS attack, which might affect availability of the backbone and, with that, potentially connected VPNs. If a router is not reachable, it can only be attacked with transit traffic, and that is significantly more difficult.

In addition, in an MPLS VPN environment all external connections, to the Internet as well as to customers, must be secured. Chapter 5 explains the necessary security measures in detail.

NOTE   **Recommendation**

When implementing any of the options just discussed, reachability of core devices should always be minimized to the absolutely necessary. So if, by default, a PE is reachable, additional measures such as infrastructure ACLs should be implemented on the edge to limit that reachability.

This way, either of the Internet provisioning models can be made secure; the difference lies in the number of security mechanisms that protect the core. Architectural security is in every case stronger because it cannot be misconfigured.

As you can see from Table 4-1, Internet in a VRF provides the highest security level of all Internet options. However, there are a number of other design considerations to be taken into account, such as memory consumption. Routes in VRF require significantly more memory than in the global table. Therefore, decisions on design options cannot be taken solely based on security considerations.

For all options, additional security mechanisms are available to further secure the backbone. Looking at the MPLS market, the various types of Internet architectures described here have all been successfully implemented.

In addition to VPN and Internet connections into an MPLS core, it is possible to provide extranets—shared areas that several VPNs can access.

Extranet Access

MPLS provides the flexibility to link VPN sites in a number of ways. When several VPNs get access to a shared part of network infrastructure, this is called an *extranet*. Figure 4-9 shows one type of extranet: a shared services extranet.

Figure 4-9 *Shared Services Extranet*

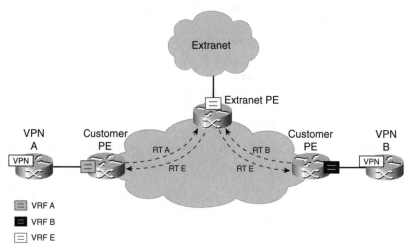

Technically, extranets are constructed by using *route-targets* to determine which routes get included into which VRF. In this example, the VPN routes from VPN A and VPN B are imported into the VRF of the extranet. This is achieved through the **route-target import** statement within the VRF configuration. This way, the extranet receives the routes of the two VPNs. In the other direction, the extranet VPN routes are imported into VPNs A and B with the same command.

The VPNs export their own routes, or a subset thereof, such that the extranet VRF can import them. The command **route-target export** in the VRF controls this behavior. The extranet VRF exclusively exports its own routes to both VPNs. This way, both VPNs know the route to the extranet.

NOTE   If the extranet VRF would accidentally export also routes from VPNs, connectivity between VPNs would result through the extranet. Therefore, it is important to operationally control the route-targets: misconfigurations may result in a break of separation of VPNs. (This applies to all route-target configurations.)

Normally, VPNs are free to use the entire theoretical IP address space within the VPN. In the extranet scenario, however, routes are exchanged with entities outside the VPN, in this case the extranet VPN. Therefore, the exchanged routes between the VPNs involved (A, B, extranet) must be unique. If the routes are not unique, a *network address translation (NAT)* function must be used to make all routes within this group unique.

What are the security consequences of linking two VPNs to an extranet? The primary goal of such a configuration is to permit various VPNs to access a shared network while maintaining the separation between the VPNs. Figure 4-10 shows which data flows are "legal" in a scenario like this and which ones would result in a security breach.

Figure 4-10 *Desired Traffic Flows in an Extranet Scenario*

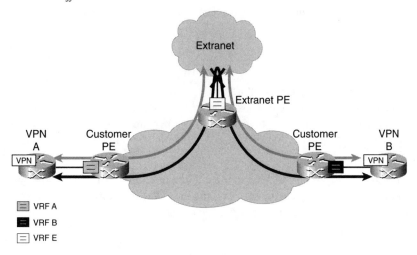

The traffic exchange between VPN A and the extranet and VPN B and the extranet is controlled by the route-target configurations on the respective PE routers, as previously explained. To prevent traffic from VPN A flowing to VPN B through the extranet, the first necessary step is not to export the routes from one VPN to the other, but only export the extranet routes. This way, both VPNs do not learn about the routes of the other VPN and therefore cannot send traffic to the other VPN through the extranet.

Assume, however, that a user in VPN A knows that VPN B, a competitor, is connected to the extranet and wants to send traffic into the other VPN. Would that user be able to connect to servers in VPN B by some means? Figure 4-11 shows in more detail the PE routers in this case, with the corresponding VRFs and route-target statements.

Figure 4-11 *VRFs and Route-Target Statements*

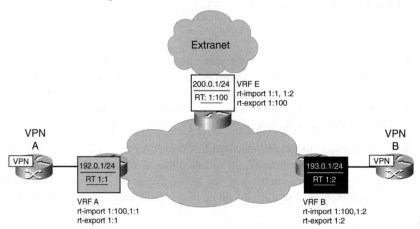

The VRF of the extranet imports the routes to both VPNs, such that the final VRF table would be as follows:

```
200.0.1/24; RT: 1:100  (the extranet route)
192.0.1/24; RT: 1:1    (the route for VPN A)
193.0.1/24; RT: 1:2    (the route for VPN B)
```

If VPN A knows the addressing of VPN B, it could send a local default route to the extranet, thus sending traffic to locally unknown destinations (as addresses of B would be) to the extranet VRF. There the route to VPN B is known, and traffic would flow to VPN B. However, since VPN B does not know a valid route to VPN A, return traffic would not get back to VPN A.

Therefore, it is possible to send traffic unidirectionally into another VPN that is connected in this way to a shared extranet, assuming the "attacker" knows the addressing of the target in the other VPN. Is this a realistic threat?

Yes, this threat does need to be taken seriously: Firstly because there are a number of attack forms that only require a single packet to be sent. The "ping of death" from the early 1990s is a historic example. Note that the way back might be different: for example, a one-packet exploit could open a connection to a host in the Internet. This way, a single command might be transmitted unidirectionally, opening a connection to the Internet for further exploits.

Secondly, many worms have spread this way. The "code red" worm is a more recent example of how a single packet might exploit a local vulnerability. Worms usually spread their infecting packets to random destinations, so if there is some form of default routing to the extranet, some of the packets with random destinations would be sent to the extranet.

This issue can be solved with firewalling, which is explained in more detail in the next section, "MPLS VPNs and Firewalling."

In the previous example, we have discussed an extranet scenario with two VPNs. However, look at Figure 4-11 again and imagine a hub-and-spoke setup within a single VPN: then VPNs A and B would be the spokes and the extranet the hub. Leaving the route-target import/export statements as they are, this would result in an architecture where spoke sites are allowed to exchange traffic with the hub but not with each other.

What are we trying to show with this? The route-target import/export functions control the flow of routing on an MPLS VPN backbone. If routing allows packets to flow either unidirectionally or bidirectionally, we have connected two networks (in the example, the two VPNs with the extranet).

NOTE   The configuration with appropriate route-target statements is from a security point of view just like connecting the networks with a cable: full connectivity between sites by default. What is important here, as shown in this section, is that unidirectional routing does not necessarily result in only unidirectional traffic because of static or default routing.

Therefore, when connecting sites through route-target configurations, you have to always assume full connectivity, even if route-targets only allow traffic to flow in one direction by default.

As a corollary from this exercise, note the importance of this single feature, the route-target statements, for security: A single line in the configuration of a PE router decides whether two VPN sites get connected or not. In large VPN environments, VRFs may have a long list of route-target statements. A single error in one of them may endanger the security of one or several sites.

It is, therefore, of utmost importance to control the route-target statements in an MPLS VPN backbone against misconfiguration—deliberate or accidental.

NOTE   **Recommendation**

Manual configuration of route-target statements is discouraged because operator mistakes are not only possible but likely long-term. The safest option is to let the provisioning software systems configure the route-target statements.

More about operational control of misconfigurations can be found in Chapter 8.

From these considerations, we deduce the following recommendation: when connecting sites of different security zones through route-target statements, always separate these zones through firewalling. How to do this is discussed in the next section.

MPLS VPNs and Firewalling

As previously described, it might not be sufficient to control VPN separation with the route targets. In an extranet scenario, for example, routes from various VPNs are brought together in a single context; therefore, additional security measures need to be taken. Firewalls offer a solution to this problem.

To find out where firewalls are needed, consider the following steps:

1   **Establish a map of the full network**—This may include several VPN sites, maybe some extranet zones, and probably the Internet. The key concept here is reachability: who can reach what (also considering routing changes, static routing, and so on).

2   **Divide this full network into *zones of trust***—The Internet and the MPLS core are always separate zones, each extranet is a zone, and each VPN is a separate zone. Depending on the security policy of a VPN, a single VPN might have several zones of trust (see Chapter 1) internally, divided by VPN sites. (Internal splits within a VPN site are outside the scope here.)

In principle, firewalls are required on all zone boundaries.

The concept of zones of trust was introduced in Chapter 1. We apply this concept to the previous example to show how it can be applied in practice.

Figure 4-12 depicts the various zones of trust in the current example, with both Internet and extranet connectivity.

Following this procedure strictly, firewalls would also be required between the MPLS core and the VPNs, a setup which is not normally seen in implementations. The reason for this is that the MPLS core has a special role in the provisioning: the MPLS core, or better yet, the service provider providing the core, is usually trusted by the VPN customers. And, in fact, the VPN customer has no choice here except to trust the service provider.

Figure 4-12 *Zones of Trust*

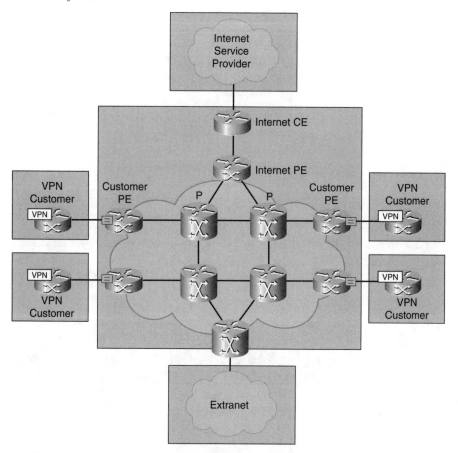

The reason is that every service provider has the power to make any VPN it provides insecure—for example, by adding additional VPN sites, by sniffing traffic on the trunk lines, or by inserting fake traffic into a VPN. This issue is common to all VPN service models: for example, in ATM VPN services, the service provider has the power to send fake traffic into a VPN.

Therefore, the MPLS core has a special status in that it is most implicitly trusted by the VPN customers. If the service provider cannot be trusted, firewalls would add little value: The service provider could still sniff connections and interrupt or "steal" them.

NOTE The only solution if the service provider is not trusted is to provision additional security on top of the MPLS VPN service, such as with CE-CE IPsec. In practice, this has so far rarely been done.

Thus, since the MPLS core is implicitly trusted, the zones of trust change for the VPN customers. Figure 4-13 shows the effective zones of trust as seen from a VPN user.

Figure 4-13 *Zones of Trust, Seen from a VPN User*

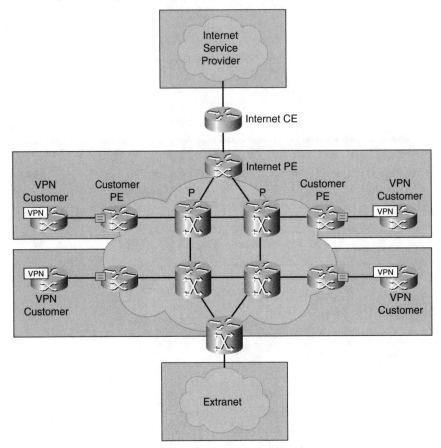

Therefore, firewalling is typically required between a VPN and the Internet, and between a VPN and an extranet.

NOTE   From a service provider point of view, the VPN customers are typically *not* trusted. Therefore, a service provider's view of zones of trust corresponds to Figure 4-12. To shield the core from VPN users, a service provider does not use firewalls but other measures: infrastructure ACLs, strict router security, as well as security of any routing protocol used. See Chapter 5 for more details.

The firewalling between VPNs and the Internet or extranets can be achieved in several ways. A firewall can be placed at the VPN site connecting to one of the "outside" zones. This would typically be under the control of the VPN customer. Alternatively, a central firewall can be used to shield VPNs against outside zones. Figure 4-14 depicts this scenario, which also solves the problem of nonunique address space. In this case, the extranet/ Internet PE holds a VRF for each VPN that requires access to the extranet/Internet. Only the routes from this VRF are imported from the MPLS side, plus a possibly static route to the outside. From the VRF on the shared PE, there is a connection to a *virtual firewall* and from there to the extranet.

Figure 4-14 *Firewalling Between VPNs and Internet/Extranets*

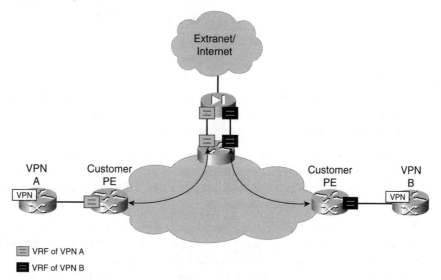

A virtual firewall maintains separate customer contexts, similar to a PE router. Between those contexts there is no connectivity, such that all customer contexts are completely independent. The firewalling function is performed between each customer context and the Internet context.

The added advantage here is that the firewall can also perform a NAT function, so that each VPN can keep using the entire theoretical IP address space. Therefore, each connected VPN perceives the virtual firewall as as a normal firewall.

The lines between the PE and the firewall can be implemented either physically or logically, that is, either with separate cables or as VLANs on a single ethernet connection, for example. Typically, a single physical connection is used, and virtual interfaces are configured for each virtual firewall.

When different VPNs are connected in an extranet, or within one VPN site with different security levels, firewalls should be positioned between the zones. Figure 4-15 shows an example of how this can be achieved.

Figure 4-15 *Firewalling Within a VPN or an Extranet*

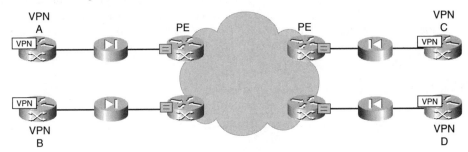

In this scenario, the firewalls are within the VPN they protect, and even the link between the firewall and the PE router belongs to that VPN. Therefore, no virtualization is required here, and normal enterprise firewalls can be used here.

It cannot be stressed enough that in all of these scenarios where routes are exchanged through route-target configuration, firewalls are essential: without them the sides are just interconnected on the IP level, without any protection. This applies clearly to sites within a single VPN but also to extranet scenarios.

A firewall protects primarily against intrusions: it prevents an outsider from accessing internal devices. However, there is another important threat: DoS attacks. Firewalls only provide limited protection against DoS attacks because there are other ways to degrade the service. For example, if the access line between the PE and the firewall in Figure 4-15 is overloaded, the firewall does not help. Even worse, if the PE router itself is overloaded, it might also affect the connected VPNs.

DoS attacks cannot be averted with features on boxes: the problem has to be solved by appropriate network design. The following section outlines the potential issues and design solutions for DoS attacks.

Designing DoS-Resistant Networks

A DoS attack prevents a legitimate user from accessing a resource, such as a web server. It is achieved through overusage of a shared resource, such as the following:

- Overloading a line in a network
- Exceeding the packet-forwarding capacity of a router
- Exceeding the packet-processing capacity of a server

In general, DoS attacks are directed toward exhausting one of the following shared resources:

- Bandwidth (for example, on a line)
- CPU (on a network element)
- Memory (on a network element)

Therefore, a DoS-resistant network must be designed such that none of the shared resources can be overloaded by a malicious user or a group of malicious users. In this section, we firstly discuss general DoS considerations, then various options to design a DoS-resistant network. The main consideration here is how a dedicated PE for VPN traffic helps increase DoS resistance. Various design options are discussed.

Overview of DoS

When large groups of legitimate users all decide to access a certain resource at the same time, and this resource has not been designed to handle that load, the effect may be similar to a DoS attack. However, the correct expression for this behavior is a *flash crowd*. Technically, the effect is exactly the same as a DoS attack. Flash crowds could be observed, for example, on September 11, 2001, when after the collapse of the World Trade Center in New York many people tried to access news servers.

NOTE   There is no 100 percent DoS resistance. Every solution has a maximum capacity. A network withstands a DoS attack if the attacker has less attack capacity than the network offers. A future DoS attack, however, might exceed the network capacity.

Most design principles for DoS resistance apply to any form of network and are not MPLS specific. These are in short:

- **Correct device positioning**—Each device in a network must be able to process the maximum inbound load. On the edge of the network, routers must also be able to handle equired features at full line speed—for example, ACLs, uRPF, NetFlow, and CAR.

- **Correct bandwidth planning**—The lines in the network must be able to handle bursts of traffic. This can be solved in two ways: *overprovisioning*, where lines are designed such that they cannot be overloaded even under worst-case circumstances; and *Quality-of-Service* (QoS), where the bandwidth of a line might not be sufficient, but traffic is divided into classes and the important class is always serviced.

- **Service overprovisioning**—Web services must be designed to worst-case assumptions. The content architecture with web caches, load balancers, and so on provides this overprovisioning.

- **Anti-DoS solutions**—Every network should dispose of a DoS solution that allows detecting, analyzing, and mitigating DoS attacks. The Cisco Guard[3], for example, provides a mitigation device. Operational procedures to handle DoS attacks are required as well.

For MPLS networks, all these points also apply. There are, however, some MPLS-specific considerations: the PE routers require special attention when designing a DoS-resistant MPLS core.

Designing a DoS-Resistant Provider Edge

Figure 4-16 describes the potential problem: A PE router typically holds connections to several VPNs. If a DoS attack is directed at one of those VPNs, and if it has a higher packet-per-second (pps) rate than the PE router can handle, other connected VPNs might also suffer performance degradation up to complete loss of connectivity.

Figure 4-16 *A PE Router Shared Between Several VPNs under a DoS Attack*

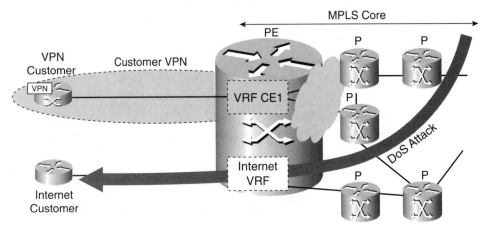

NOTE	DoS attacks are usually perceived as coming from the Internet; however, they can come also from connected VPNs. The difference is that the bandwidth from the Internet is usually much higher than from a VPN site and that a VPN site can be shut down if it attacks the core. Consider also worms that might originate from a VPN and have a similar effect to a DoS attack.

Most current PE routers in the industry use shared resources for different VRFs, which means that this problem affects most MPLS VPN networks. Many marketing slides suggest that a given router is not susceptible to this problem. The reader is encouraged to verify such claims in a lab setting. The Cisco CRS-1[4] offers a new operating system (IOS-XR) that does provide true memory and CPU protection for different VRFs. On such a router, only the VPN under direct attack would be affected, but not other VPNs on the same PE.

Because the vast majority of routers deployed today as PE routers does not offer any memory and CPU protection, the problem of the shared PE can only be solved by using a different design. Since DoS attacks from the Internet have likely a greater impact than attacks from a connected VPN, we propose to keep those two security levels strictly separate on the network. Figure 4-17 shows the principal idea: we split PE routers into PE routers that only hold VPN connections and PE routers that hold Internet connections. This way, if an attack is coming from the Internet, the VPN PE will not be affected.

Figure 4-17 *Separating Internet PEs from VPN PEs*

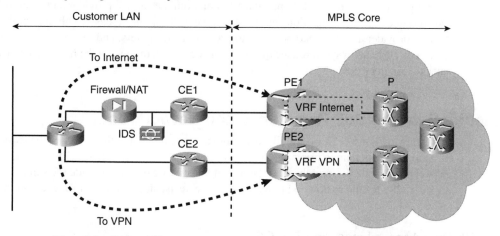

There may be customers who only have a VPN connection, which will be connected to the VPN PE; a customer who only has an Internet service will be connected to the Internet PE. Figure 4-17 shows a customer who requires both a VPN and an Internet connection: This set-up maintains the separation between the CE routers and separates routing internally between VPN and Internet traffic.

In such a setup, the Internet connection (upper part of the figure) can be treated as any other Internet service, for example with a leased line to an ISP. A firewall would typically be deployed, plus usual other-edge security features such as intrusion detection. If an attack hits this customer, in the worst case only the Internet part will become unavailable: the VPN part will remain unaffected. This offers very strong DoS resistance. The fact that the Internet part is still exposed is not any different to other network technologies. Customers with leased lines to ISPs may also be affected by DoS attacks; so this is not an MPLS-specific issue.

Routing must be set up on the MPLS core such that traffic from the Internet never passes through the VPN PE. In fact, to prevent a direct attack, the VPN PE must not be accessible from the Internet at all! (Reachability from VPNs should also be limited to a minimum, probably only routing.) If the VPN PEs are not hidden by architecture, infrastructure ACLs are a must to prevent packets from reaching VPN PEs.

The idea behind this separation is similar to the zone segmentation on firewalls: the assumption is that within one security zone attacks are less frequent and that the more secure zone needs protection from the less secure zone. As mentioned above, though, DoS attacks may equally come from VPN sites, so this assumption is not very strict.

NOTE If redundancy is required, this setup would have to be duplicated according to normal network design rules. Redundancy is not shown in the examples but can be provided with all options.

Although full separation of Internet and VPN on both the service provider and customer side provides optimal protection against DoS attacks, this is an expensive solution: both the service provider and the customer need to provision two routers, and two access lines are required. There are ways to reduce the costs for such a separation, but the resistance to DoS attacks also goes down.

Tradeoffs Between DoS Resistance and Network Cost

Referring to Figure 4-17, essentially any duplicated component of this setup can be reduced to a single component to bring down the overall cost of the solution—the PEs, the line between PEs and CEs, and the CEs. Note that all of those options provide the same functionality for the customers; however, the DoS resistance is different for each option.

Single PE, Two Access Lines, and Two CEs

The first alternative is described in Figure 4-18: the service provider may terminate both services on a single PE, whereas the enterprise separates the two services.

Figure 4-18 *Using a Single PE Router*

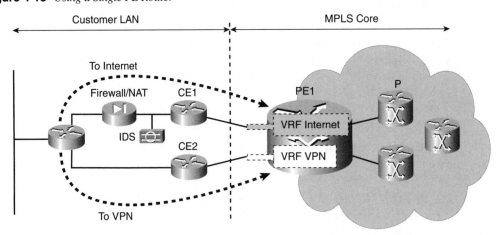

Since a potential DoS attack from the Internet would go over the shared PE, the VPNs connected to this PE might be affected as well. (Note that this might also be a different VPN customer.) Theoretically, this offers higher DoS resistance for the customer's VPN part because the customer's own VPN network is separated. In this case, a DoS attack against the Internet part of the customer would only affect the VPN part if it is strong enough to affect the PE router. Every other part of the setup is still separated.

The service provider will be able to offer this service at lower cost because only a single PE is required. On the customer side, there is still significant cost—the two access lines and the two CE routers.

NOTE   The customer cannot distinguish by technical means whether the two access lines are terminated on a single PE or two PEs.

Since one of the highest cost factors is the access line, customers have looked for solutions that allow providing both services, Internet and VPN, over a single access line.

Using a Single Access Line with Frame Relay Switching

There are various ways to share an access line. The common criteria for all of those are

- The access line technology must allow for separation between the two services; this could be done by using two Frame Relay circuits, VLANs on an Ethernet connection, or any tunneling technology such as GRE, IPsec, or L2TP. Frame encapsulation on top of Packet over SONET (POS) lines is a popular solution.

- The routers on both sides must be able to configure subinterfaces to terminate those circuits.

- The routers on both sides must be able to keep traffic separate. This could be done using Layer 2 forwarding (for example, Frame Relay switching).

In the first solution for shared access lines, shown in Figure 4-19, the access line is segmented with Frame Relay logical links. Packets of the two services, Internet and VPN, travel in different Frame Relay circuits.

On the PE side, the two circuits are terminated in the respective VRFs, providing full separation. On the CE side, the VPN circuit is terminated as a normal interface and thus is subject to normal routing. The routing table on this CE, therefore, holds only VPN routes. The Internet circuit is switched with Frame Relay switching, on Layer 2, without touching the routing table. It is terminated on Layer 3 on a second CE router, which acts as the Internet CE. From there, the traffic enters the Internet edge zone with firewall and other security services.

Figure 4-19 *Using a Shared Access Line: Frame Relay Switching*

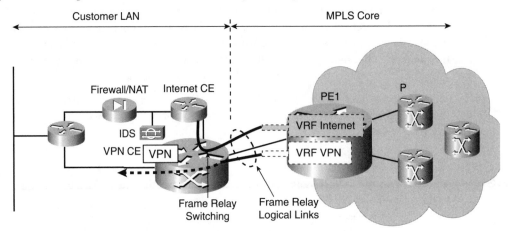

The separation between Internet and VRF is equally good as in the previous examples: the two traffic streams are perfectly separated and cannot mix anywhere. But the lower cost of this model comes at a price. Now all three elements—PE, CE, and access line— are shared, and the VPN part potentially might be affected by a DoS attack on the Internet part.

However, this risk is probably manageable: the overload on the line can be prevented by configuring correct Frame Relay parameters. The bandwidth of the Internet circuit must be configured such that there is always sufficient bandwidth on the VPN circuit. This also helps in securing the CE against overload: both CEs have a maximum forwarding capacity. The circuit bandwidths must be configured such that even if both are fully loaded from the PE side with minimum-size packets, both CEs can still fulfill their tasks. This should be tried in a lab environment.

Thus if the bandwidths are configured correctly, the only bottleneck in this scenario is on the PE router. If the bottleneck is just the access circuit, packets will be dropped on that circuit, but other services will not be affected. This is the desired state. The only problem might be if the attack is so strong that it exceeds the forwarding capacity of the PE, in which case the VPN might also be affected by the DoS attack.

Using a Single Access Line with VRF Lite

Instead of doing Frame Relay switching on the CE, an alternative would be to provision VRFs on the CE. This concept is illustrated in Figure 4-20. The line is segmented as before in some form (in the example, Frame Relay), but now the Internet circuit is terminated in a separate VRF on the CE. From there, another connection leads to the Internet CE, or alternatively, directly to the firewall because the Internet CE is not really required in this setup.

The concept of using VRFs on a router without any MPLS-based forwarding is called *VRF Lite* (or *Multi-VRF Support*). The VRF is exactly the same as a VRF on a PE router, except that here no MPLS switching is done. An interface can only be in the global table or in a single VRF, and the VRFs are strictly separated from each other and from the global table, just as on a PE. With these properties, VRF Lite offers a concept of virtualized routers.

In Figure 4-20, the Internet VRF and the global table are strictly separated. Packets from one side can never get to the other side, except if this is explicitly configured. The separation this solution offers is therefore very good, exactly as in the other examples. As in the previous example, this solution is more exposed to a DoS attack because several components are shared; but here as well correct design can overcome this problem: if the Frame Relay links toward the CE are dimensioned such that the CE will always be able to handle both ingress lines full with minimum packet size, both the access line and the CE cannot be affected by a DoS attack. Correct design is therefore of paramount importance.

Figure 4-20 *Using a Shared Access Line: VRF Lite*

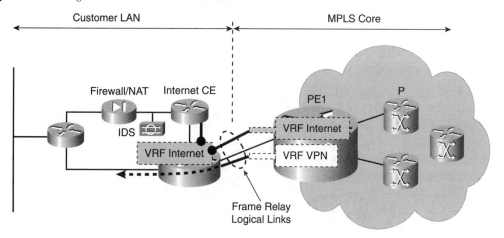

Why Policy-Based Routing Is Not Preferred

An alternative way to separate the two contexts on the CE has been proposed in the past: by configuring *policy-based routing* (PBR), where the packets entering on the Internet context would be policy routed. This means that all packets coming in on the Internet link would be forwarded to the defined egress interface without a forwarding table lookup. This also provides the required separation, in principle. However, PBR has an important property: if the egress interface is down, PBR is essentially disabled, and packets are again forwarded according to the forwarding table. This, of course, would break the separation.

NOTE   **Recommendation**

Never use PBR as a security tool, for example to separate different security levels because under some circumstances PBR falls back to the forwarding table. Although in later IOS releases there is a switch to disable this behavior, separation through VRFs is always more strict.

Among the various options to separate routing on the CE, the VRF Lite mechanism is the best one: both PBR and Frame Relay switching produce a higher CPU load, whereas VRF Lite is a CEF-based feature without performance impact. The separation on VRF Lite is the same as in MPLS: very strict.

NOTE   **Recommendation**

The best way to separate routing contexts on any router (specifically CEs) is using the VRF Lite concept.

Figure 4-21 gives an example of how a complete VPN can be implemented on an MPLS VPN core, applying the principles just discussed.

Figure 4-21 *Providing a Full VPN with Separation*

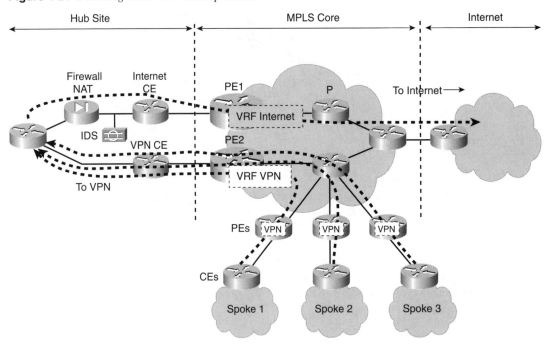

The principal VPN topology for Internet access is hub-and-spoke: all spoke sites send their Internet traffic through the hub site. VPN internal traffic can go directly between the spokes. This may seem like a restriction, but most VPN customers prefer this anyway so that all Internet traffic of the VPN goes through a central point of security control (firewalls, and so on). The hub site connects to the Internet service of the MPLS provider.

In this configuration, packets from the Internet can only be sent to the Internet part of the VPN customer: the VPN part is unreachable from the Internet (which must be enforced by the core design). This way an attacker from the Internet can only attack the Internet PE, CE, and the Internet servers on the VPN—not any of the VPN parts. Therefore, in the worst case, the Internet connection of this VPN might suffer degradation or loss of service, but the VPN part will be unaffected.

There are many ways to combine these principles: there can be two redundant hub sites laid out in the same way; there could be Internet connectivity to selected spoke sites; there could be Internet provided to all VPN sites. The consequences for each scenario have been described previously.

NOTE   All the discussed options provide perfect separation (apart from the PBR solution). The discussion here is exclusively to DoS resistance.

Comparing the Options

The remaining key question for an MPLS core design is how much difference it makes to VPN availability whether the core uses shared versus separate PEs for Internet and VPN. This question cannot be answered generally. Both solutions have their applicability and justification.

Because a shared-PE scenario is cheaper to provide, there is probably a large number of customers who would prefer such a service, simply because they do not feel the need for very high DoS resistance. This is a perfectly valid argument.

A VPN customer who has high exposure on the Internet, such as an online book shop or a bookmaker, might take a different view, however. Customers like these are under the permanent threat of DoS attacks, and if they have mission-critical applications on their VPN, they might not want to endanger the VPN with attacks from the Internet.

From the service provider perspective, a third point of view might be taken: if the security operation of the core network is very fast and efficient and if anti-DoS measures are deployed on the core, the service provider might have an extremely short response time to a DoS attack. In this case, one option is to deploy the cheaper variant with shared PEs and monitor the network very closely: if a DoS attack is noticed, the service provider can then divert the attack to a packet scrubber like the Cisco Guard, thereby "cleaning" the traffic and thus mitigating the DoS attack. The question now is, "Can a DoS attack be mitigated fast enough to not break the SLA with the customer?" If this is the case, the cheaper variant can be deployed even for customers with high security requirements.

Finally, high availability requires a number of different technologies in parallel: quality-of-Service, fast rerouting and convergence, device and line redundancy, management, and finally security. Therefore, a complete architecture must take many more considerations into account to achieve a highly available solution.

Following these recommendations, a standard RFC 2547 network can be secured and VPNs be made highly available, even with Internet provided on the same core. The next challenge for the service provider is how to interconnect securely to another service provider network, using one of the Inter-AS methods described in RFC 2547bis.

DoS Resistant Routers

All the previously discussed problems with DoS attacks potentially affecting a PE router have a common root cause: Most PE platforms in the industry have operating systems with shared memory and CPU. Therefore, there is no 100 percent resource separation between the VPNs as far as DoS resistance is concerned: A single VPN can potentially consume too much shared memory or CPU, which potentially affects other VPNs on that PE. This can be partially secured, as explained in Chapter 5, "Security Recommendations," but the root problem persists.

NOTE   There is no danger of intrusions: The VPNs remain separate. The risk is exclusively related to availability of resources; for example, if a PE is under a DoS attack, other VPNs on that same platform might also lose their VPN connection.

The Cisco CRS-1 is a notable exception: The architecture of the new operating system IOS-XR allows full memory and CPU separation between virtual routers. Therefore, even if a process in a given VPN is not fully secured, the operating system limits the central resources that this process can consume. This means that there is no additional risk of DoS for a given VPN on a Cisco CRS-1, and it is not necessary to split the PEs.

The resource separation is a feature of the new operating system IOS-XR, and will therefore also be available on other platforms that might run IOS-XR in the future.

Inter-AS Recommendations and Traversing Multiple Provider Trust Model Issues

Standard RFC 2547 MPLS VPN networks have a simple interface to the outside of the network: IP. Any VPN that connects to the MPLS core can only send IP datagrams into the core. Internally, MPLS core networks work mostly with LSPs, using labeled packets for forwarding. Because the inside uses different packet types from the outside and because the inside format of labeled packets is not accepted on ingress, there is no way to attack an MPLS core from the outside. However, because an RFC 2547 network uses iBGP to distribute VPN routing, this mechanism cannot be used across *autonomous system (AS)* boundaries.

RFC 2547bis introduced the concept of Inter-AS to connect various autonomous systems together with ASBRs and to provide VPNs over all ASs involved. Figure 4-22 shows the basic concept of Inter-AS topologies, here with two autonomous systems. There is no limit on the number of ASs involved in such a setup.

Figure 4-22 *A Generic Inter-AS Scenario*

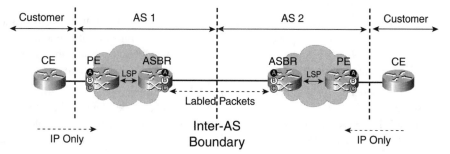

The key difference between this scenario and the traditional RFC 2547 networks is that, on the Inter-AS boundary shown in Figure 4-22, labeled packets may be exchanged. This changes the security exposure of an MPLS core significantly: because labeled packets are now accepted, those need to be checked to avoid attacks against the inside of the MPLS core.

Because the threat comes from exchanging labeled packets and because VPN customers can send only IP packets and not labeled packets, the threat we have to examine for this section is attacks from a connected service provider network, not attacks from a VPN customer. All the attacks described in this section assume that one of the providers in an Inter-AS scenario accidentally or deliberately makes certain configuration mistakes.

NOTE   If an Inter-AS scenario is used to connect autonomous systems that are under the operational control of a single service provider, this section can be ignored. The same applies if the autonomous systems are maintained by providers that trust each other fully.

Before discussing the various scenarios, it should be clear what we are trying to achieve by securing the Inter-AS boundaries. The goals of securing the Inter-AS boundaries are as follows:

- Each SP must be able to send packets across the Inter-AS boundary into all Inter-AS VPNs (VPNs that are shared between the autonomous systems).

- No SP must be able to send packets across the Inter-AS boundary into private VPNs (VPNs that are not shared between the autonomous systems).

- The various autonomous systems must be secure against each other: attacking one core from another must not be possible. To achieve this, it is highly desirable to limit visibility and reachability across AS boundaries.

The goals of Inter-AS scenarios are not the following:

- To provide any form of access control on the Inter-AS boundary: a given Inter-AS VPN is shared completely, without restrictions between the ASs. Specifically, there is no firewalling, packet filtering, or any other content inspection between the ASs for a given Inter-AS VPN.

- To separate Inter-AS VPNs: a service provider always has full access to all Inter-AS VPNs (and none to private VPNs). It can insert any type of traffic into any of the Inter-AS VPNs; specifically, it can "misconnect" two VPNs and send traffic from Inter-AS A into Inter-AS B. (However, it also has this capability in a standard RFC 2547 network.)

As a consequence of these considerations, VPN customers must always trust all of the service providers involved in provisioning their VPN. Depending on the interconnection model chosen, service providers must trust each other or not. (Refer to Chapter 2, "A Threat Model for MPLS VPNs.") In the rest of this section, we discuss the security properties of the three interconnection models for Inter-AS.

NOTE   For this section, a thorough understanding of Chapter 10 of RFC 2547bis is required. The architectures described there will be repeated in this book only briefly as a reference. Please refer to the RFC for detailed descriptions.

Case A: VRF-to-VRF Connection on ASBRs

In case A of the Inter-AS architecture, the two autonomous systems are connected separately per Inter-AS VPN. The ASBR in this model is equivalent to a PE router with VRFs for all Inter-AS VPNs and interfaces or subinterfaces to the other AS. Figure 4-23 depicts this scenario.

Figure 4-23 *Inter-AS Case A*

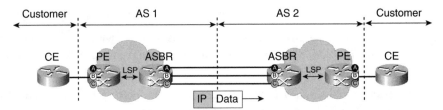

The only interconnections are VRF based. To keep the traffic separate, each Inter-AS VPN requires a separate logical connection between the autonomous systems, and this can be achieved by using separate cables or subinterfaces, such as VLANs on an Ethernet connection.

This model is equivalent in security to a standard RFC 2547 network because, here also, all external interfaces into the core are "IP-only" interfaces. The interfaces connect directly into the VRFs of the corresponding VPNs. Specifically, there is no connection between the global routing tables of the ASBRs.

The only potential security issues in model A are

- **Accidental misconnection at the ASBR**—When provisioning a VPN connection, service provider 1 will tell service provider 2 that VPN A is configured on a given interface or subinterface. Either service provider may make a mistake in connecting this interface into the wrong VRF, thereby connecting two VPNs that should not be connected. This risk, however, exists in all VPN environments, such as in ATM or Frame Relay, for example. It must be controlled operationally by making appropriate checks after a connection has been established.

- **Routing issues**—The VRFs on both ASBRs will exchange routing for a given Inter-AS VPN. The usual routing security mechanisms (for example, MD5 security) must be deployed here. Most importantly, the number of prefixes must be limited on each ASBR within a VRF to avoid the ASBR running out of memory because a single VPN announces too many routes. This could happen, for example, if the whole Internet routing table accidentally gets propagated into the VPN. See Chapter 5, "Security Recommendations," for more details. Note that these precautions also need to be taken on each PE. Again, the ASBR in this model is equivalent to a PE.

For the service provider, the security exposure is exactly the same as in a single-AS MPLS network: its network cannot be attacked from the other service provider if it is appropriately secured. See Chapter 3, "MPLS Security Analysis," for a detailed discussion of the security in this environment.

For the VPN customer, the security risk is also equivalent to that of a single-AS MPLS network, except that in the Inter-AS model the customer has to trust all the service providers involved in the provisioning of the VPN: any of the providers could make the VPN insecure—when misconfiguring routers, for example.

This model has a number of other advantages as well: because each VPN is connected individually, QoS control for a given VPN is easy. Also, because the ASBR is equivalent to a PE in this model, existing provisioning systems can be used for the provisioning of the Inter-AS connection. Essentially, an ASBR in this model thinks it is connecting to a CE for each VRF; the fact that there is another MPLS core "on the other side" is not visible.

However, model A is not very scalable: each Inter-AS VPN must be configured with a VFR and an interface or subinterface on the ASBR. This requires memory for all the VPN routes, plus potentially a large range of subinterfaces. To give an example, the limit on a Cisco 12000 router with POS frame encapsulation is in the range of 200 VPNs. Models B and C were, therefore, designed to improve the scalability of the Inter-AS architecture. However, the improved scalability comes at the cost of higher security exposure.

Case B: eBGP Redistribution of Labeled VPN-IPv4 Routes

As in case A, here there is only one connection between the ASs: The ASBRs are connected back to back, but this time in the global routing table, not in a VRF. The VPN-IPv4 prefixes of the Inter-AS VPNs are held in the BGP table, not in VRFs. There are also no separate interfaces per VPN in this model. Figure 4-24 depicts this architecture.

Figure 4-24 *Inter-AS Case B*

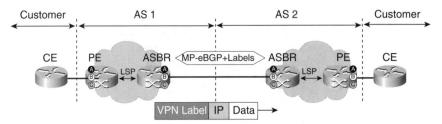

Because there is only one connection between the ASBRs, data plane traffic for different VPNs must be kept separate. This is done by labeling packets before sending them to the other ASBR.

NOTE	The fact that an external interface to an AS accepts labeled packets instead of just IP packets changes the security exposure completely because labeled packets are also used internally in the cores: the strict separation between "outside" and "inside" is broken!

To define which label to use for which VPN prefix, the ASBRs exchange on the control plane VPN-IPv4 routing information with labels, through eBGP. (MP-BGP, the multiprotocol extensions to BGP, are required to be able to exchange routes of the VPN-IPv4 family.)

In the following subsections, we examine the security of the control plane and data plane separately.

Control Plane

The control plane can be secured well with standard routing security measures:

- **Peer authentication with MD5**—This feature ensures that the routing updates are coming from the correct peer.

  ```
  neighbor 192.0.2.1 password si%e_3kee$i5
  ```

- **Route flap damping (RR-RR and ASBR-ASBR)**—To prevent quick announce and withdraw messages of a prefix from increasing the CPU load, new updates are ignored after a few flaps for a certain time.

  ```
  bgp dampening
  ```

- **Generalized TTL Security Mechanism (GTSM)**—This checks the TTL of an incoming BGP update; if the TTL is lower than an expected value (normally 254), then the packet has been originated "further away" than expected and is likely bogus. GTSM is described in RFC 3682.

  ```
  neighbor 192.0.2.1 ttl-security hops 1
  ```

- **Prefix filtering**—No IP prefixes should be exchanged in this model (only VPN-IPv4); therefore, all IP prefixes should be blocked.

  ```
  ip prefix-list abc deny 0.0.0.0/0 le 32
  ```

- **Route-target filtering**—Each VPN-IPv4 route comes with a set of RTs, defining to which VPN the prefix belongs. Wrongly propagated RTs might lead to intrusions into private VPNs of the other AS.

  ```
  ip extcommunity-list 101 permit RT:100:3+
  ```

  By default, a PE only accepts a VPN-IPv4 prefix if it is imported into a local VRF. Because model B does not have VRFs on the PE, by default no route would be accepted. To switch off this behavior, use the command

  ```
  no bgp default route-target filter
  ```

- **No IP routing**—By default, BGP carries the IP address family. This should be switched off.

  ```
  no bgp default ipv4-unicast
  ```

- **Measures against prefix flooding**—To avoid memory exhaustion on an ASBR or RR, a maximum number of prefixes for each BGP peer should be configured.

  ```
  neighbor 192.0.2.2 maximum-prefix 100 80
  ```

  (Case B does not have VRFs on the ASBR; therefore, the prefix limits per VRF are not applicable here.)

- **Standard router security**—Use standard router security features to protect the router against intrusions and DoS attacks. *Receive ACLs (rACLs) or Control Plane Policing (CoPP)* are important examples.

Please refer to Chapter 5 for detailed configuration examples.

NOTE   **Recommendation**

Configure all these security mechanisms as tightly as possible. A hacker only needs one weakness to succeed!

Following the assumptions at the beginning of this section, prefix filtering within one VPN is not required because the VPNs are shared between ASs in full. At the time of writing this book, it is not possible in IOS to filter on VPNv4 addresses. This is addressed in enhancement request CSCec32038.

VPN-IPv4 addresses contain route distinguishers (RDs). Those RDs must be chosen such that they are unique across all ASs. The convention is to use the AS number as part of the RD, which provides uniqueness. However, this is not enforced on the routers.

What can happen if the RDs are not unique across the autonomous systems? Figure 4-25 shows the flow of routing in such a case.

Figure 4-25 *Consequence of RD Overlap*

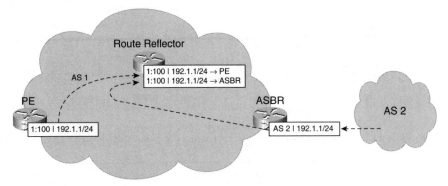

In the example shown in Figure 4-25, the left PE learns from a connected VPN the prefix 192.1.1/24. It is configured with an RD of 1:100 for the corresponding VRF, and therefore announces this VPN-IPv4 prefix to the route reflector (RR). The ASBR is learning a prefix from AS 2, which has the RD wrongly set to 1. This prefix happens to be the same as on AS 1. The RR will receive, therefore, two identical VPN-IPv4 routes with different next hops.

An important implementation detail: whereas PE routers can support multiple prefixes, RRs currently cannot. (This is addressed in enhancement requests CSCdu51714 and CSCdu51721.) Therefore, the RR will choose the better prefix by some metric (see "BGP Best Path Selection Process") and announce only that. The effect is that one of the paths for the VPN-IPv4 prefixes will be lost on the RR, such that one VPN might experience connectivity issues to the prefix in question. The separation of VPNs is not affected by this.

Which of the two VPN-IPv4 prefix paths will be chosen depends on the BGP decision process, which can be controlled on the corresponding router—here, the RR. The following list shows the BGP decision process. One of those criteria can be chosen to differentiate external from internal VPN-IPv4 prefixes and to give the internal one preference. For example, AS path length can be an option.

BGP Best Path Selection Process

1. If the next hop is inaccessible, do not consider it.

2. Consider larger BGP administrative weights first.

3. Consider the route with higher local preference.

4. Prefer the route from which the local router originated.

5. Prefer the shorter autonomous system path.

6. Prefer the lowest origin code (IGP < EGP < INCOMPLETE).

7. Prefer the path with the lowest Multi Exit Discriminator (MED) metric.

8. Prefer external paths over internal paths.

9. If IGP synchronization is disabled and only internal paths remain, prefer the path through the closest neighbor.

10. Prefer the route with the lowest IP address value for the BGP router ID.

Therefore, while the ASBR can be configured to keep multiple AS paths for a single VPN-IPv4 prefix in the BGP table, a decision must be taken on the RR according to this list. To avoid a potential RD overlap, we recommend using, for example, AS path length to prefer the internal path on the RR.

NOTE   **Recommendation**

Uniqueness of RDs across all autonomous systems is essential and must be enforced through operational means. The easiest way is for all service providers involved to follow the conventions to use the AS number as part of the RD.

Overall, the control plane can be well secured in case B. There are commands to provide security against most parameters that could be faked. One issue is that it is currently impossible to filter on VPN-IPv4 prefixes or RDs on the ASBR border. This allows the introduction of bogus prefixes within one VPN. This is probably not a serious issue in real implementations, but it must be considered.

Data Plane

To secure the data plane, two types of traffic need to be considered: IP traffic and labeled traffic. The traffic on the Inter-AS interface contains the following:

- BGP traffic (TCP with destination port 179 can be originated from either side) for the control plane. Usually the BGP session is established with the directly connected interface IP addresses, not with loopbacks.

- Labeled traffic (non-IP) for the data plane.

Following basic security rules, anything that should not happen should be blocked. Therefore, we strongly recommend filtering on this interface as tightly as possible. Because data traffic is exchanged with labels, most IP traffic can be blocked.

NOTE   **Recommendation**

On the ASBR-ASBR interface, filter all inbound IP traffic (and possibly outbound traffic, as well, to check your own policy) with the exception of BGP. Keep in mind that a BGP session may be originated from both sides, so the ACL needs to take both directions into consideration. Be conservative with exceptions to this rule!

Apart from BGP, all IP traffic is now blocked. BGP is secured with the mechanisms described in the preceding section, "Control Plane." If all these mechanisms are implemented well, IP traffic cannot create a security hole.

Therefore, the last type of traffic to consider is labeled traffic. All VPN traffic is exchanged with labels. From a security point of view, the question is whether the label or the packet underneath can be changed to create a security hole.

Labels are exchanged by the BGP peering between the ASBRs. This way, each ASBR learns from the other which label to use for which VPN-IPv4 prefix.

Therefore, the first check when looking at a labeled packet would be whether the label observed on the data plane has been assigned previously on the control plane. Figure 4-26 shows this principle.

Figure 4-26 *Assignment and Use of Labels in Model B*

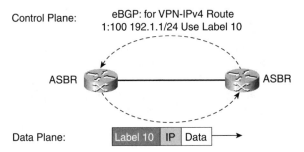

While, therefore, the ASBR theoretically has the capability to check incoming labels, this is not supported everywhere at the time of writing this book.

Currently, an incoming label can be checked when the interface terminates in a VRF; but it cannot be checked when the interface terminates in the global routing table. Therefore, this security check currently cannot be done in model B (nor in model C). Once this feature is available, it is strongly recommended to switch it on.

In addition, if the front label is faked to match a VPN label on the other ASBR, the packet would be forwarded to this VPN, effectively providing unidirectional traffic into a nonshared VPN. Also, if the top label matches a PE label on the ASBR, the packet would be forwarded to that PE, the top label would be popped before the egress PE, and the remaining packet would be interpreted there. This would effectively also allow intrusions into nonshared VPNs, as well as into the IGP of the other AS if an IP packet is underneath the top label. Note that all of those potential attacks can only be carried out from within the service provider's core, not from connected customers.

To overcome the issue of not being able to check the incoming label, we recommend you check a specific design option where the incoming ASBR does not have any label except VPN labels of Inter-AS VPNs. This can be achieved by putting another router in front of the existing ASBR, which only knows labels to Inter-AS VPNs. Figure 4-27 shows this design. The new router is labeled "ASBR (external)" in this figure. It maintains an eBGP session to the internal ASBR, representing essentially another Inter-AS case B interconnection.

Figure 4-27 *Adding a Router for Label Checking*

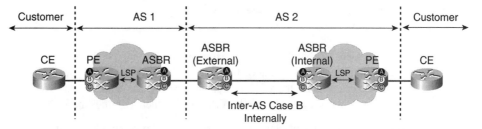

The external ASBR holds only labels of Inter-AS VPNs in its label forwarding information base (LFIB). If a packet is received with another label that is unknown, it is dropped. The trick is that the external ASBR does not have LSPs into the core of AS 2.

Between the internal and external ASBR, another instance of model B can be used. This way, the external ASBR does not hold labels in its LFIB that correspond to LSPs to egress PEs. However, this currently requires a separate AS number to be used on the external ASBR. This can, however, be a private AS number if that doesn't clash with the other provider.

In summary, model B can be secured adequately on the control plane. On the data plane there is as of today a lacking feature in that the incoming label cannot be checked. This creates a security hole that allows traffic to be sent from the service provider into other VPNs or the core of the other service provider. To work around this, another ASBR can be added to front-end the existing ASBR. With this setup, model B can be secured adequately.

In model B, the ASBR still needs to keep the full routing information of all Inter-AS VPNs in the BGP table. This can be a scalability limitation. Model C removes this requirement as well, and makes the ASBR even more scalable.

Case C: Multi-Hop eBGP Distribution of Labeled VPN-IPv4 Routes with eBGP Redistribution of IP4 Routes

Most MPLS core networks use route reflectors (RRs) internally to scale their network. The idea in model C is to exchange the VPN-IPv4 routes directly between the RRs so that the ASBRs do not need to hold any VPN information. The ASBRs exchange routing information about the PEs and the labels needed to get to them. This way, an end-to-end LSP can be established across the autonomous systems. Figure 4-28 depicts this setup.

Figure 4-28 *Inter-AS Case C*

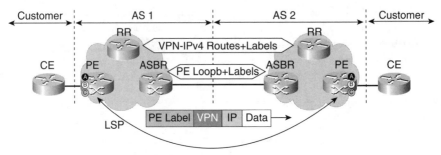

On the control plane, VPN information is exclusively exchanged between RRs. The ASBRs exchange routing and label information between the ASs involved via eBGP. On the data plane there are labeled packets for the VPN traffic, but these packets hold at least two labels: a PE label, which leads to the egress PE, and a VPN label, which identifies the VPN on that PE.

Also in model C, the control plane can be secured well with standard routing security measures. However, they now need to be applied twice: RR to RR and ASBR to ASBR. The full list is

- **Peer authentication with MD5 (RR-RR and ASBR-ASBR)**—This feature ensures that the routing updates are coming from the correct peer.

  ```
  neighbor 192.0.2.1 password si%e_3kee$i5
  ```

- **Route flap damping (RR-RR and ASBR-ASBR)**—To prevent quick announce and withdraw messages of a prefix from increasing the CPU load, new updates are ignored after a few flaps for a certain time.

  ```
  bgp dampening
  ```

- **Generalized TTL Security Mechanism (GTSM) (RR-RR and ASBR-ASBR)**— This checks the TTL of an incoming BGP update; if the TTL is lower than an expected value (normally 254), then the packet has been originated "further away" than expected and is likely bogus. GTSM is described in RFC 3682.

  ```
  neighbor 192.0.2.1 ttl-security hops 1
  ```

The ASBRs are usually only one hop away, which makes the configuration of GTSM easy. For the RR-RR peering, this is more complex because potential backup paths need to be considered as well. The maximum TTL value to be configured is the value of the longest possible path between the RRs.

- **Prefix filtering (RR-RR)**—No IP prefixes are exchanged between RRs (only VPN-IPv4); therefore, all IP prefixes should be blocked.

  ```
  ip prefix-list abc deny 0.0.0.0/0 le 32
  ```

  As mentioned in the section for model B, VPN-IPv4 routes cannot currently be filtered; but this is not a security threat because attacks would remain within the same VPN.

- **Prefix filtering (ASBR-ASBR)**—Only IP prefixes are exchanged here, and they define reachability of the PEs. We recommend configuring prefix filters that allow only the required PE IP addresses. (Remember, this is control plane filtering, not data plane.)

  ```
  ip prefix-list abc deny 0.0.0.0/0 le 32
  ```

- **Route-target filtering (RR-RR)**—Each VPN-IPv4 route comes with a set of RTs, defining to which VPN the prefix belongs. Wrongly propagated RTs might lead to intrusions into private VPNs of the other AS.

  ```
  ip extcommunity-list 101 permit RT:100:3+
  ```

- **No IP routing (RR-RR)**—By default, BGP carries the IP address family. This should be switched off.

  ```
  no bgp default ipv4-unicast
  ```

- **No VPN-IPv4 routing (ASBR-ASBR)**—This is not required, and therefore the VPN-IPv4 address family should not be configured.

- **Measures against prefix flooding (RR-RR and ASBR-ASBR)**—To avoid memory exhaustion on an ASBR or RR, a maximum number of prefixes for each BGP peer should be configured.

  ```
  neighbor 192.0.2.2 maximum-prefix 100 80
  ```

  Case C does not have VRFs on the ASBR; therefore, the prefix limits per VRF are not applicable here.

- **Standard router security**—Use standard router security features to protect the routers against intrusions and DoS attacks. Receive ACLs (rACLs) or Control Plane Policing (CoPP) are important examples.

Please refer to Chapter 5 for detailed configuration examples.

NOTE

Recommendation

Configure all these security mechanisms as tightly as possible. A hacker only needs one weakness to succeed!

The problem with overlapping RDs also exists in model C. Please refer to the description of model B earlier in this chapter.

NOTE

Recommendation

Uniqueness of RDs across all autonomous systems is essential and must be enforced through operational means. The easiest way is for all service providers involved to follow the conventions to use the AS number as part of the RD. Also, refer to the problem of overlapping RDs in the section "Case B."

In summary, the control plane in model C can be secured well, but this is a complex process, with many important details. However, the main concern at the moment for case C is data plane security.

Also in model C, two types of packets are exchanged between the ASBRs: IP packets and labeled packets. IP packets are used for eBGP between the ASBRs. All other traffic, including the eBGP peering between the RRs is over labeled packets. Therefore, it is recommended, as in case B, to filter all IP traffic with the exception of the required eBGP peering between the ASBRs. This prevents a large number of potential attacks where packets could be sent to routers in the other AS. This secures IP traffic well.

Labeled packets, however, are much harder to control. In case C, there are at least two labels for each packet: the PE label, which defines the LSP to the egress PE, and the VPN label, which defines the VPN on the PE the packet belongs to.

The top label could in theory be checked, but as described previously for model B, this check is currently not implemented for interfaces in the global routing table. This means that a service provider may send packets to any egress PE to which the peering ASBR holds an LSP. It includes at least all PEs which hold Inter-AS VPNs.

In addition, there is a fundamental architectural security issue in model C for which there is currently no solution: because the ASBR routers in this architecture do not hold any VPN information, the VPN label cannot be controlled at the ASBR. This means that it is possible for another service provider to insert packets with anything below the top PE label. Therefore, the security risk of this architectural model is very high: not only can a service provider send packets into any VPN for which it holds a valid PE label, it could also fake a packet such that there is an IP packet directly underneath the top label. This packet would be forwarded to the egress PE with the top label, and before reaching that PE, penultimate hop-popping would remove the top label. If there is an IP packet underneath, this IP packet would be routed in the other service provider's IGP and could thus reach any router in its network.

How easy are attacks of this form?

All of those attacks allow only unidirectional traffic: the return path to the attacker would never be open. However, there have been a number of security issues in the past based on single packets, such as the "ping of death" in 1990 and the "code red" worm in 2001. Thus this issue has to be considered.

Attacks where labeled packets are crafted can only be carried out from a point in the network where labels are accepted: this is normally only the service provider core because all customer connections accept only IP packets. The following section describes the Carrier's Carrier (CsC) case, which allows also labeled packets to enter from a customer, but the CsC architecture does not allow label spoofing: in CsC, the top labels on the data plane are checked. Therefore, the threat of label spoofing can only originate within a service provider network.

Spoofing of the top label can in principle only occur on the ASBR itself because labels have only a local significance to a single router and are swapped at every hop. Every router has a label binding for an incoming label to an outgoing label. To create a binding for a fake outgoing label, one would therefore have to statically configure a binding on the ASBR. This way, an LSP could be constructed hop by hop through the MPLS core. This LSP could be terminated on a packet generator as a source, in which case any type of packet could be generated. There are programs for PCs to generate random packets—also labeled ones.

Even though it is possible to spoof the top label in models B and C, it is not known which label values would lead to which destination. For a targeted attack, an attacker would therefore have to have access the routers in the other AS to check which labels to spoof.

A blind attack is easier, where the entire label space is tried out. A label has 20 bits, which yields one million distinct values. Therefore, by sending one million packets it is possible to test all values. With a minimum packet size of 60 bytes, this means that 60 MB need to be sent. Over a 10 Mbps connection, this would take less than a minute. Over a 128 kbps, it would take a bit more than an hour. Note that label allocation is not random, so in practice the attack would be easier than this. So if only a single packet is needed for an attack, it is quite feasible simply to try all possible label values.

To summarize the various Inter-AS options:

- Model A is as secure as standard (single-AS) MPLS as defined in RFC 2547. There are only IP interfaces into the core, providing a strong separation of the outside to the inside of the core. It is suitable for multiprovider MPLS networks, even if the providers do not trust each other.

- Model B can be secured well on the control plane, but on the data plane there is a problem currently in that the top label is not checked. This weakness could be exploited to send crafted packets from inside one MPLS core into the other one. It is not possible to establish bidirectional communications, but it is possible to send faked packets into the core of the other provider or VPNs connected there. There is a workaround: a separate ASBR can be provisioned that blocks faked packets. With this workaround, model B can be deployed today in Inter-AS scenarios.

- Model C can also be secured well on the control plane, but the data plane has architectural weaknesses: because the ASBRs do not have any VPN information, they cannot check the second label. This enables unidirectional packets to be sent into private VPNs of the other AS, and into the other core directly. This architectural weakness cannot be solved by configuration. As in case B, the top label cannot be checked, and the consequences are the same as in case B as well. Model C can therefore only be deployed where service providers trust each other fully.

Recommendation

To implement interprovider VPNs, the most secure option today is model A. We recommend using this model as long as the scalability requirements permit. Model B can be used in an interprovider setup only with some specific security measures put in place. Model C is not suitable for general interprovider VPNs.

As previously mentioned, if several autonomous systems are under one administrative control, all models—even model C—can be deployed today.

Another option for providing a multiprovider scenario is the so-called "hierarchical MPLS," where a carrier buys an MPLS VPN from another carrier and, in turn, offers VPNs to its customers: this is the Carriers' Carrier architecture.

Carriers' Carrier

Consider VPN customers of an MPLS carrier who would like to offer VPNs themselves to their customers. To separate the customers' traffic, they could use a label, as in a normal MPLS network. However, the interface to their carrier would normally be IP. If the carrier would allow them to use labels for their VPN, they could put another label underneath and pass their VPN customers' traffic end to end. This architecture is called Carriers' Carrier (CsC).

Figure 4-29 shows the CsC architecture. It is a hierarchical structure where the hierarchy is also reflected in the data plane: VPN labels are stacked (though the full label stack is not shown here). The main difference between this and a standard RFC 2547 network is that the CsC-CE routers need to support MPLS.

Figure 4-29 *CsC Architecture*

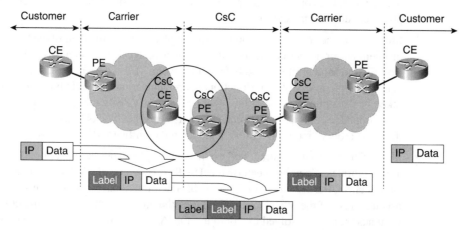

NOTE   For ease of reference, in this section we use the term "Carrier" for the top-level MPLS provider and "Internet service provider" or "ISP" for the second-level provider or customer of the carrier.

In this model, the interface between the CsC-PE and the CsC-CE allows labeled packets. In the Inter-AS section, we mention that this fact puts separation of "inside" and "outside" of the MPLS core in question. However, the CsC architecture has a fundamental difference that allows it to run securely: the connections from the ISP are terminated on the carrier's core CsC-PE in a VRF, not in the global table.

On the control plane, eBGP is used between the CsC-PE and CsC-CE to exchange routing and to assign labels to the ISP. This session needs to be secured with all the mechanisms described in the previous section: peer authentication, GTSM, maximum prefix limitation (here also for a VRF), prefix filters, and so on.

NOTE   **Recommendation**

Secure the BGP session between the CsC-PE and CsC-CE as tightly as possible, configuring all possible security features. Of particular importance are route flap damping and the configuration of maximum prefix levels per VRF and BGP peer.

The CsC-PE assigns a VPN label to the CsC-CE that is then used like a VPN label on a standard RFC 2547 backbone. This way, the carrier keeps traffic from different ISPs separate.

On the data plane, there are two types of traffic:

- BGP over IP between the CsC-PE and CsC-CE
- Labeled packets for the data traffic

Therefore, IP traffic can and should be restricted to only BGP traffic, and the routing protocol should be secured as previously described. This secures the IP data plane.

For labeled packets, the CsC-PE checks that the top labels received on the data plane were actually assigned to that CsC-CE on the control plane. This way, the top label cannot be spoofed.

Anything underneath the top label can be spoofed by the ISP; however, the carrier's network does not look underneath the top label: it only needs the top label to forward the packet to the egress CsC-PE and into the right VRF there.

RFC 2547bis states for data plane security that a backbone router does not accept labeled packets over a particular data link unless it is known that such packets will leave the backbone before the IP header or any labels lower in the stack will be inspected.

This is the case in the CsC architecture.

Therefore, if anything underneath the top label is faked, it can only affect the VPN of the ISP itself. So the security of the CsC architecture is equivalent to the security of a standard RFC 2547 network, even though labeled packets are exchanged at the edge.

Because the security of CsC is very good, this solution can also be considered to extend MPLS to the customer site. Often, this requirement is stated as a "PE at the customer site."

It is not recommended to position a PE at a customer site. The reason is that if the PE gets compromised, all VPNs of that MPLS core can be intruded. A PE router must be under complete physical control of the service provider to avoid problems such as password recovery through the console port. See Chapter 3, "MPLS Security Analysis," for more details on this issue.

However, the requirement in such cases is not, strictly speaking, to have a PE at the customer site, but to extend MPLS to the customer site. The CsC solution offers this in a secure fashion: MPLS can be extended to the customer site without jeopardizing the security of the PE, which remains in a secure environment at the carrier.

NOTE	**Recommendation** Never put a PE router on customer premises. Physical access to the PE routers must be fully controlled to avoid unauthorized password recovery. Where MPLS to the customer site is required, use the CsC architecture, which provides a secure solution while keeping the PE in a secure service provider location.

In summary, CsC is an architecture that can be deployed securely, even to nontrusted parties (customers and other providers, for example). It is ideal for cases where MPLS is required to the customer's premises.

NOTE	In both Inter-AS and CsC architectures, there is a threat that is often ignored. While considering all details at Layer 3, remember that the lower layers are also important. In fact, a wrong design, for example, on the switching interconnection between two service providers might endanger the security of all VPNs.

Layer 2 Security Considerations

Security is often overlooked at the lower layers, yet lack of security at these layers might jeopardize the security of all traffic passing on the higher layers unless some form of end-to-end security is used (for example, encryption or authentication). Consider an enterprise Ethernet switch, to which several PCs are connected, as well as routers. There are a number of attack forms that permit users of PCs on that switch to redirect traffic to themselves, with so-called *man-in-the-middle* attacks.

Here's one attack example: The malicious user sends a flood of *Address Resolution Protocol (ARP)* messages to the broadcast domain. The switch keeps track of Layer 2 (MAC) addresses and notes which port they are on. With each ARP packet, the user randomly changes the MAC address, thereby slowly filling the memory of the switch with fake entries. Once the address table of the switch is full, the switch will start broadcasting all packets from all ports to every port in the *virtual LAN (VLAN)*. This way, the attacker sees all data traffic going over the switch.

Some hacking tools available on the Internet allow someone to carry out this attack and then steal any session that is established over the switch. This is one of the reasons why telnet is not recommended. *Secure Shell (SSH)* prevents this problem by providing end-to-end security through authentication and encryption.

There are a number of attack forms of this type. (Refer to specific security literature for details on these attack forms.) There are also forms and tools for preventing all of these attacks: for the attack just described, for example, there is the **port security** command, which limits the number of MAC addresses on a port to a predefined level.

Despite all the attack forms, Layer 2 can be provisioned securely. Security is an important consideration that is often overlooked when designing Layer 2 infrastructure.

NOTE   **Recommendation**

On all external links into your MPLS network, check how the links are provided. Point-to-point technologies are usually secure, and dedicated links are best. Where external connections are provided over shared media such as Ethernet, special care must be taken to secure the connection at Layer 2.

Figure 4-30 shows an example of an interconnection between two autonomous systems, provided over an Ethernet switch at an Internet Exchange Point (IXP).

Figure 4-30 *Layer 2 Security at an IXP*

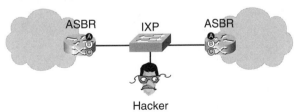

If the hacker is connected to the same VLAN as the ASBRs, security of all Inter-AS VPNs is jeopardized. The hacker could, for example, insert on Layer 2 spoofed labeled packets, which appear to come from one ASBR and go to the other. This way, the hacker could insert traffic into any Inter-AS VPN. Essentially, all attack forms on Layer 2 would be applicable in this design, so that the attacker could be the man-in-the-middle for any traffic stream. Confidentiality would also be lost for all data on this path.

NOTE   This book cannot list all Layer 2 security issues and solutions; it only can raise attention to the problems. All known Layer 2 security issues have solutions, so implementing security at Layer 2 is not an unsolvable task and must be done. Chapter 7 discusses Layer 2 security in more detail.

Layer 2 security must be considered on every shared connection. For example, if two CEs of different VPNs connect to a single PE over an Ethernet switch, it would be theoretically possible to put all CEs into a single VLAN and provide separation through some form of tunnel, such as generic routing encapsulation (GRE). If the two CEs are in the same VLAN and if the switch is not well secured, separation between those VPNs might be broken at Layer 2. RFC 2547bis explicitly states for this case:

"In the case where a number of CE routers attach to a PE router via a LAN interface, to ensure proper security, one of the following conditions must hold:

1   All the CE routers on the LAN belong to the same VPN.

2   A trusted and secured LAN switch divides the LAN into multiple VLANs, with each VLAN containing only systems of a single VPN; in this case, the switch will attach the appropriate VLAN tag to any packet before forwarding it to the PE router."

NOTE   **Recommendation**

Avoid providing connections of different VPNs on the same VLAN. If this is required, either secure the tunnels or provide end-to-end security over the VPN. Both can be achieved with Ipsec, for example. As a rule, always try to keep VPNs separate on Layer 2 also.

The Inter-AS scenario is a special case: Many service providers are peering with each other on IXPs and might consider using this connection for Inter-AS also. This is not secure! As previously described, a third party could introduce crafted packets into VPNs at the IXP.

NOTE   **Recommendation**

Always make Inter-AS peerings over a dedicated line, or at least over a dedicated VLAN.

Multicast VPN Security

At the time of writing this book, the architecture for multicast VPNs (MVPNs) has not been completely defined yet by the L3VPN working group of the IETF. However, already at this stage, some observations about MVPN security can be made:

- The MVPN architecture is being specified with the goal that a VPN has the same security properties independently of whether it is using multicast over the VPN or not. Therefore, it should make no difference to a VPN user from a security point of view whether this service includes multicast or not.

- The service-provider network must be equally resistant to attacks from VPNs or the Internet, independently of whether multicast is offered on this MPLS core or not.

When examining the security properties of MVPN, additional protocols must be taken into considerations — specifically Protocol Independent Multicast (PIM). PIM must be secured on the PE such that the PE cannot be attacked with PIM protocol messages.

In addition, it is recommended to keep resource intensive processes off PE routers. The rendezvous point (RP) is such a service; it can receive significant load, therefore, it is preferable to not have an RP on a PE.

For more information on how to secure multicast, please refer to *Developing IP Multicast Networks*, Volume I, by Beau Williamson (ISBN 1578700779).

Summary

While the RFC 2547 architecture is very secure, real deployments are usually quite complex. Increasing complexity, however, for example in the various Inter-AS scenarios, is usually a challenge for security. Not all security problems can be solved with features on a single router: the overall design of a network must be secure, on all layers.

This chapter discussed various network design options and discussed their implications for security. For example, Internet connectivity can be provided in various ways, with different security levels. DoS attacks are an increasing concern as well, and an MPLS VPN design must take this into consideration. When connecting several service providers' networks to provide VPN capabilities across them, new challenges arise: not all available architectures are suitable for a secure deployment today.

The practical examples in this chapter show that it is important to consider security at the time of designing the network because some design decisions can make an entire network insecure. However, when properly designed and secured, an MPLS VPN network can provide a secure service.

Footnotes

[1] This is the worst-case scenario considering attack forms known at the time of writing this book. It is conceivable that other attack forms might appear in the future with a different behavior. In this case, the design guidelines would have to be updated.

[2] Modern routers such as the Cisco CRS, 12000, or 7600 series can process many security features such as ACLs, NetFlow, committed access rate (CAR), and others at the same time at full line speed. This is required to counteract DoS attacks.

[3] The Cisco Guard XT is a product to clean packet floods from DoS attacks. The strength of it is that it lets valid user traffic get to the destination, whereas attack traffic is being dropped. For more information, please see www.cisco.com/go/guard.

[4] For more information on the Cisco Carrier Routing System (CRS), see www.cisco.com/go/crs.

In this chapter, you learn about the following:

- Security recommendations for network elements
- General router security measures
- Security recommendations for the core network
- IGP routing security recommendations
- Operational considerations for MPLS over IP

CHAPTER 5

Security Recommendations

In this chapter, we recommend security measures for every router and progress to customer edge, core infrastructure, and provider edge security mechanisms. The reader will find a full provider edge configuration example in Appendix A with a clarification of key security explanations.

In any network, security considerations devolve into essentially two areas of focus, this first area being compromises that can be either accidental or deliberate. Accidental compromises can occur as a result of misconfigurations or by anticipated changes in the network. Alternatively, compromises can be deliberate, such as attacks by some miscreant entity determined to cause havoc. In either case, the risk vectors are either external, such as issues driven by events external to the network in question, or internal, such as problems that are sourced from within the network itself.

The methods used to accomplish the compromises are the second area of focus. Most security-related problems fall into the categories of Denial of Service (DoS) or intrusion in any network. Security considerations devolve into essentially two sets of two types of issues. Compromises are either of the following:

- **Accidental**—Problems that occur due to misconfigurations or anticipated changes in the network
- **Deliberate**—Attacks by some entity bent on causing havoc

The risk factors of these compromises are either external (issues driven by events external to the network in question) or internal (problems sourced from within the network itself). Additionally, most security-related problems fall into two categories:

- **Denial of Service (DoS)**—These events may be intentional or accidental.
- **Reconnaisance**—These issues by definition are intentional.

It is essential to harden the network components and the entire system to minimize the likelihood of any of these scenarios. However, as with all resource-consuming features, you must strike a balance between maximizing security and offering the performance and usability the service is intended to provide. Clearly, a completely disconnected host or router has total security; however, its ability to forward data or provide services is substantially compromised.

The state of the network from an availability and security viewpoint may also differ with respect to the perspective of the interested party. That is, the concerns of the service provider and the customer intersect, but they do not completely overlap. Indeed, the perspective of the current status of the network may not be identical for the two parties.

General Router Security

This section focuses on elements required to secure a single router. Examples of network element security include generic router security measures that can be applied on a router. We build on these network element guidelines to provide best practice security recommendations for key MPLS network elements such as CE, PE, and P routers as an introduction to our core security recommendations, which follow this section.

In this section, we illustrate router security best practices that are valid on all routers in the network and include generic best practices such as using AAA, strong passwords, turning off unused services, and so on. We further introduce capabilities such as rACL, CoPP, and autosecure.

Secure Access to Routers

Access requirements to a given router may include:

- Pingability by the service provider personnel
- Pingability by the customer personnel (restricted to routers to which access is required)
- Interactive access by the service provider personnel (SSH, telnet)
- SNMP read/write access by the service provider personnel
- SNMP read access by the customer personnel, if required
- Privileged mode operation by the service provider personnel

Interactive access to the routers may be accomplished using SSH as a recommended best practice. The security and encryption inherent in SSH make it the only access protocol that should be used within any network environment where there is any risk of compromise (for example, it should be used everywhere except in a limited lab environment).

NOTE   Use of SSH should be a service provider decision, depending on the likelihood of someone sniffing the backbone circuits.

The best practice recommendation is to use Authentication, Authorization, and Accounting (AAA) network security services to provide the primary framework for setting up the access control on a router access server.

NOTE   **Recommendation**

The best practice recommendation is to implement password administration for SNMP (SNMPv3 particularly has enhanced security features as discussed in the IETF RFCs 2272, "Message Processing and Dispatching for the Simple Network Management Protocol (SNMP)" and 2274, "User-based Security Model (USM) for version 3 of the Simple Network Management Protocol (SNMPv3)."

In general, with respect to a PE-CE link operation, the benefits gained by allowing ICMP echo mechanisms outweigh the risks associated therein. However, some rate limiting for the ICMP traffic would address this concern to a certain degree.

Example 5-1 depicts a configuration for SSH access to a router. To enable SSH, first configure both a host name and domain name. Then use the command **crypto key generate rsa** to create a key pair, which is required for SSH, as shown in Example 5-2. After the key creation, SSH will automatically be enabled, and some default SSH commands will appear.

Example 5-1   *SSH-Controlled Access to a Router*

```
            hostname top
            #required for SSH

            username cow secret 5 $1$9uVj$iPPDLOS.VE73x/Z3XChLc.
            aaa new-model
aaa authentication login default tacacs+ local enable
aaa authorization exec default tacacs+ local if-authenticated
aaa authorization commands 15 default tacacs+ local if-authenticated
            #simple AAA login control forcing verification of
            username/password pair as above

            ip domain name barstool.com
            #domain name required for RSA key generation

            access-list 13 permit 1.13.13.13
            access-list 13 deny any log
            #access-list permitting host 1.13.13.13 and denying/logging
             all else

            line vty 0 4
            access-class 13 in
            #access list limiting access to vty's

            transport input ssh

            #only SSH incoming connections permitted
```

After configuring what is shown in Example 5-1, it is necessary to generate the RSA keys, as Example 5-2 shows.

Example 5-2 *Key Generation for SSH*

```
router(config)#crypto key generate rsa
The name for the keys will be: top.cisco.com
Choose the size of the key modulus in the range of 360 to 2048 for your
  General Purpose Keys. Choosing a key modulus greater than 512 may take
  a few minutes.

How many bits in the modulus [512]:
% Generating 512 bit RSA keys ...[OK]

top(config)#
2d04h: SSH: host key initialized
2d04h: %SSH-5-ENABLED: SSH 1.5 has been enabled
2d04h: SSH: successfully generated server key
```

Within an MPLS VPN environment, the configuration constructs for telnet access have been altered to apply them to VRF instances. For example, when applying an access class to a set of VTYs, the parameter "vrf-also" is required. Failure to include this modifier will cause all telnet attempts from a CE to be refused. As such, application of a simple access list to the VTY ports will prevent access to the router, as previously recommended, and with the **log** keyword included in the explicit deny, inappropriate attempts will be logged.

A configuration example for denying CE telnet access may be found in Example 5-3.

Example 5-3 *Controlling Telnet access*

```
Line vty 0 4
        login
        password 884f2A
        access-class dog in
#applies access-list dog to inbound telnet requests
ip access-list standard dog
        permit 1.13.13.2
        deny any log
#creates a named ACL "dog" which permits access from host
1.13.13.2 denies and logs all other attempts
```

The operations of other access service functions, such as rsh, rcp, and tftp, are not changed when used within an MPLS VPN environment. That is, access control remains as it has been prior to MPLS VPNs, and such controls should be applied using the appropriate access control lists (ACLs) and authentication mechanisms. Note that these services would not normally be enabled on a PE or CE router—the security implications are unacceptable, and the management requirements for these functions are minimal.

NOTE   The safest way to copy files from and to a router is the Secure Copy (SCP) feature, which is available on every IOS image that supports SSH. SCP uses the same strong security mechanisms as SSH in terms of encryption and authentication and is the recommended transfer method. To use SCP, type the following, for example:

```
copy scp: flash:
```

NOTE   **Disabling ifindex persist Feature**

Some service providers have found it quite necessary for SP performance management systems to have this capability enabled and also that SNMP communities should always be protected by an ACL, even when the community "password" is hard to guess. Reason: The ACL code is very efficient while starting to process SNMP, and its ASN.1 coding is CPU intensive and could be used for a DoS against the route processor.

Disabling Unnecessary Services for Security

Many of the built-in services in Cisco IOS are not needed in a SP backbone environment. These features should be turned off in your default configuration because they are not needed and they represent a security risk. Turn them on only if there are explicit requirements.

Some of these will be preconfigured in IOS to be turned off by default, but service providers should ensure they are explicitly turned off in configuration files:

- **no service finger**—Disables the process, which listens for "finger" requests from remote hosts. Only SP personnel normally access the backbone routers, and there are other and better means of tracking who is logged in. Besides, **finger** is a known security risk in the Internet, due to its divulgence of detailed information of people logged into a system.

- **no service pad**—Simply not required. It refers back to the days of X.25 networking, and in recent versions of IOS has become the default.

- **Small TCP and UDP servers**—Those with port numbers below 10—typical services include "echo" and "discard" ports, the former echoing all packets sent to it, the latter throwing away all packets sent to it. If they are enabled and active, they could be used to carry out successful denial of service attacks—their use will divert CPU resources away from other processes, which will cause problems for the connected networks and the Internet service dependent on that router.

- **bootp service**—Provides support for systems that find their configuration using the **bootp** process. This is commonly used in LANs (X-terminals use **bootp**, for example) and never on the WAN. It should be disabled.

- **Cisco Discovery Protocol (CDP)**—Used for some network management functions, but is dangerous in that it allows any system on a directly connected segment to learn that the router is a Cisco device and to determine the model number and the Cisco IOS software version being run. This information may in turn be used to design attacks against the router. CDP information is accessible only to directly connected systems. The CDP protocol may be disabled with the global configuration command **no cdp running**. CDP may be disabled on a particular interface with **no cdp enable**.

- **Network Time Protocol (NTP)**—Not especially dangerous, but any unneeded service may represent a path for penetration. If NTP is actually used, it is important to explicitly configure a trusted time source and to use proper authentication because corrupting the time base is a good way to subvert certain security protocols. If NTP isn't being used on a particular router interface, it should be disabled with the interface command **no ntp enable**. Note that usually NTP is an important service, for example to get precise timestamps on logging messages.

- **ICMP unreachables**—Disabled with the command **no ip unreachables**. Normally, an interface responds with an ICMP unreachable message back to the sender, if a packet is dropped on that interface. This can be abused to deny service to an interface. Therefore, where the generation of ICMP unreachables is not required, it is recommended to disable the generation or to rate-limit the generation of ICMPs. Note also that the Null0 interface generates ICMP unreachables, such that this command should also be applied to Null0.

- **ICMP redirect message**—Instructs an end node to use a specific router as its path to a particular destination. In a properly functioning IP network, a router sends redirects only to hosts on its own local subnets. No end node will ever send a redirect, and no redirect will ever be traversed more than one network hop. However, an attacker may violate these rules; some attacks are based on this. It is a good idea to filter out incoming ICMP redirects at the input interfaces of any router that lies at a border between administrative domains, and it is not unreasonable for any access list that is applied on the input side of a Cisco router interface to filter out all ICMP redirects. This causes no operational impact in a correctly configured network.

NOTE   This filtering prevents only redirect attacks launched by remote attackers. It is still possible for attackers to cause significant trouble using redirects if their host is directly connected to the same segment as a host that's under attack.

The IP protocol supports *source routing* options that allow the sender of an IP datagram to control the route that datagram will take toward its ultimate destination and, generally, the route that any reply will take. These options are rarely used for legitimate purposes in real networks. Some older IP implementations do not process source-routed packets properly, and it may be possible to crash machines running these implementations by sending the datagrams with source routing options. Also note that source-routed packets allow the circumventing of ACLs, for example where the ACL is looking into the source and destination header field, only while ACLs are effectively irrelevant for source-routed packets. A Cisco router with **no ip source-route** set never forwards an IP packet carrying a source routing option. You should use this command unless you know that your network needs source routing.

NOTE	There are many other types of filters or schemas that need to be implemented in order to prevent attacks or security leaks, such as a close-group design, which does not allow its own address access from the Internet; additionally, a customer can only have access from the defined prefixes.

Table 5-1 lists the ports that should be blocked in a router unless there is a specific requirement.

Table 5-1   *Ports in Use on a Router*

Port	Service
1 (TCP and UDP)	tcpmux
7 (TCP and UDP)	echo
9 (TCP and UDP)	discard
11 (TCP)	Systat
13 (TCP and UDP)	daytime
15 (TCP)	Netstat
19 (TCP and UDP)	chargen
37 (TCP and UDP)	time
43 (TCP)	Whois
67 (UDP)	Bootp
69 (UDP)	Tftp
93 (TCP)	Supdup
111 (TCP and UDP)	Sunrpc
135 (TCP and UDP)	Loc-srv
137 (TCP and UDP)	Netbios-ns
139 (TCP and UDP)	Netbios-ssn
177 (UDP)	Xdncp
445 (TCP)	Netbios (DS)

continues

Table 5-1   *Ports in Use on a Router (Continued)*

Port	Service
512 (TCP)	Rexec
515 (TCP)	Lpr
517 (UDP)	Talk
518 (UDP)	Ntalk
540 (TCP)	Uucp
1900, 5000 (TCP and UDP)	Microsoft UpnP SSDP
2049 (UDP)	Nfs
6000 – 6063 (TCP)	X Windows System
6667 (TCP)	Irc
12345 (TCP)	NetBus
12346 (TCP)	NteBus
31337 (TCP and UDP)	Back orifice

In the same way, the ports listed in Table 5-2 should be blocked for external users.

Table 5-2   *Ports to Block to External Users*

Port	Service
79 (TCP)	Finger
161 (TCP and UDP)	Snmp
162 (TCP and UDP)	Snmp trap
513 (TCP)	rlogin
513 (UDP)	Who
514 (TCP)	rsh, rcp, rdist, rdump
514 (UDP)	syslog
550 (TCP and UDP)	new who

NOTE   For a service provider, IP packets should not be permitted from outside of the network except the strictly necessary ports for key network protocols such as routing. The concept of "infrastructure ACLs" enforces this notion. It is discussed later in this chapter in the section "Infrastructure Access Lists (iACLs)."

IP Source Address Verification

Egress and ingress filtering are a critical part of a service provider's router configuration strategy. Ingress filtering applies filters to traffic coming into a network from outside. This can be from a service provider's customers and/or from the Internet at large. The goal is to verify the source address of incoming packets to prevent source address spoofing. Egress filtering applies a filter for all traffic leaving a service provider's network.

Both filtering techniques help protect a service provider's resources and customer's networks, enforce policy, and minimize the risk of being the network chosen by hackers to launch an attack on other networks. Service providers are strongly encouraged to develop strategies using egress and ingress filtering to protect themselves from their customers and the Internet at large.

NOTE   RFC 2827, "Network Ingress Filtering: Defeating Denial of Service Attacks which employ IP Source Address Spoofing," (May 2000) provides general guidelines for all service providers on ingress and egress filtering.

12000 Protection and Receive ACLs (rACLs)

Data received by a gigabit switch router (GSR) can be divided into two broad categories: traffic that passes through the router via the forwarding path and traffic that must be sent via the receive path to the gigabit router processor (GRP) for further analysis. In normal operations, the vast majority of traffic simply flows through a GSR in route to other destinations. However, the GRP must handle certain types of data, most notably routing protocols, remote router access, and network management traffic such as Simple Network Management Protocol (SNMP). In addition to the aforementioned traffic, other Layer 3 packets might require the processing flexibility of the GRP. These would include certain IP options and certain forms of Internet Control Message Protocol (ICMP) packets.

A GSR has several data paths, each servicing different forms of traffic. Transit traffic is forwarded from the ingress line card (LC) to the fabric and then to the egress card for next hop delivery. In addition to the transit traffic data path, a GSR has two other paths for traffic requiring local processing: LC-to-LC CPU and LC-to-LC CPU to fabric to GRP. Generally, GSRs should be protected against three scenarios, which may result from DoS attacks directed at a GRP of the router:

- Routing protocol packet loss from a normal-priority flood
- Management session (telnet, Secure Shell [SSH], SNMP) packet loss from a normal-priority flood
- Packet loss from a spoofed high-priority flood

rACLs affect traffic sent to the GRP because of receive adjacencies. *Receive adjacencies are* Cisco Express Forwarding adjacencies for traffic destined to the IP addresses of the router, such as the broadcast address or addresses configured on the interfaces of the router. Receive ACLs are part one of a multipart program range of mechanisms to protect the resources in a router Control Plane Policing (CoPP), as explained later in this chapter, and are a recommended best practice for rate limiting on the 12000 platform.

Syntax

A receive ACL is applied with the following global configuration command to distribute the rACL to each LC in the router as in Example 5-4.

Example 5-4 *Global Configuration Command to Distribute rACL to Each LC*

```
[no] ip receive access-list num
```

In this syntax, *num* is defined as follows.

```
1-199 IP access list (standard or extended)
1300-2699 IP expanded access list (standard or extended)
```

Basic Template and ACL Examples

The sample ACL shown in Example 5-5 provides a simple outline and presents some configuration examples that can be adapted for specific uses. The ACL illustrates the required configurations for several commonly required services/protocols. For SSH, telnet, and SNMP, a loopback address is used as the destination. For the routing protocols, the actual interface address is used. The choice of router interfaces to use in the rACL is determined by local site policies and operations. For instance, if loopbacks are used for all BGP peering sessions, then only those loopbacks need to be permitted in the **permit** statements for BGP. These are nicely explained at Cisco.com.

Example 5-5 *Basic ACL Template*

```
!--- Permit BGP.

access-list 110 permit tcp host bgp_peer host loopback eq bgp
!--- Permit OSPF.

access-list 110 permit ospf host ospf_neighbor host 224.0.0.5
!--- Permit designated router multicast address, if needed.

access-list 110 permit ospf host ospf_neighbor host 224.0.0.6
access-list 110 permit ospf host ospf_neighbor host local_ip
!--- Permit Enhanced Interior Gateway Routing Protocol (EIGRP).

access-list 110 permit eigrp host eigrp_neighbor host 224.0.0.10
access-list 110 permit eigrp host eigrp_neighbor host local_ip
!--- Permit remote access by telnet and SSH.
```

Example 5-5 *Basic ACL Template (Continued)*

```
access-list 110 permit tcp management_addresses host loopback eq 22
access-list 110 permit tcp management_addresses host loopback eq telnet
!--- Permit SNMP.

access-list 110 permit udp host NMS_stations host loopback eq snmp
!--- Permit Network Time Protocol (NTP).

access-list 110 permit udp host ntp_server host loopback eq ntp
!--- Router-originated traceroute:
!--- Each hop returns a message that time to live (ttl)
!--- has been exceeded (type 11, code 3);
!--- the final destination returns a message that
!--- the ICMP port is unreachable (type 3, code 0).

access-list 110 permit icmp any any ttl-exceeded
access-list 110 permit icmp any any port-unreachable
!--- Permit TACACS for router authentication.

access-list 110 permit tcp host tacacs_server router_src established
!--- Permit RADIUS.

access-list 110 permit udp host radius_server router_src log
!--- Permit FTP for IOS upgrades.

access-list 110 permit tcp host image_server eq ftp host router_ip_address
access-list 110 permit tcp host image_sever eq ftp-data host router_ip_address
```

NOTE

As with all Cisco ACLs, there is an implicit **deny** statement at the end of the access list, so any traffic that does not match an entry in the ACL will be denied. Also note that one may need to open more "reply" packets, such as DNS packets from DNS servers, with newer IOS versions such as 25S or 27S, as the IOS may be using high port numbers ≥ 11000 when sending out TCP and UDP packets. For example, one ISP implements the following lines:

```
access-list 110 permit tcp address mask any gt 10000
access-list 110 permit udp address mask any gt 10000
```

One needs this in order to get BGP functioning in some cases. When configured on two core routers, the preceding example would permit TCP from port 179 to port 179 only.

Some other useful ports as examples:

UDP+TCP port 646 for LDP:

```
access-list 110 permit tcp address mask any eq 646
access-list 110 permit udp address mask any eq 646
```

APS, HSRP, and RTR/SAA:

```
access-list 110 permit udp address mask eq 1972 any eq
access-list 110 permit udp any eq 1985 host 224.0.0.2 eq 1985
access-list 110 permit udp address mask any eq 1967
access-list 110 permit udp address mask any eq 5000
```

rACLS and Fragmented Packets

ACLs have a **fragments** keyword that enables specialized fragmented packet-handling behavior. In general, noninitial fragments that match the L3 statements (irrespective of the L4 information) in an ACL are affected by the **permit** or **deny** statement of the matched entry. Note that the use of the **fragments** keyword can force ACLs to either deny or permit noninitial fragments with more granularity.

In the rACL context, filtering fragments adds an additional layer of protection against a DoS attack that uses only noninitial fragments (such as FO > 0). Using a **deny** statement for noninitial fragments at the beginning of the rACL denies all noninitial fragments from accessing the router. Under rare circumstances, a valid session might require fragmentation and therefore be filtered if a **deny fragment** statement exists in the rACL.

For example, consider the partial ACL shown in Example 5-6.

Example 5-6   *Filtering Fragments*

```
access-list 110 deny tcp any any fragments
access-list 110 deny udp any any fragments
access-list 110 deny icmp any any fragments
output omitted
```

NOTE   Fragments are further explained at Cisco.com: http://www.cisco.com/en/US/partner/tech/tk827/tk369/technologies_white_paper09186a00800949b8.shtml.

Adding these entries to the beginning of an rACL denies any noninitial fragment access to the GRP, while nonfragmented packets or initial fragments pass to the next lines of the rACL unaffected by the **deny fragment** statements. The preceding rACL snippet also facilitates classification of the attack because each protocol—Universal Datagram Protocol (UDP), TCP, and ICMP—increments separate counters in the ACL. We recommend that you test this feature in the lab prior to deployment.

Deployment Guidelines

We recommend conservative deployment practices. To successfully deploy rACLs, the existing control and management plane access requirements must be well understood. In some networks, determining the exact traffic profile needed to build the filtering lists might be difficult. The following guidelines describe a very conservative approach for deploying rACLs using iterative rACL configurations to help identify and eventually filter traffic.

Some key best practice guidelines include:

1   **Identify protocols used in the network with a classification ACL.**

2 **Deploy an rACL that permits all the known protocols that access the GRP.** This "discovery" rACL should have both source and destination addresses set to **any**. Logging can be used to develop a list of source addresses that match the protocol **permit** statements. In addition to the protocol **permit** statement, a **permit any any log** line at the end of the rACL can be used to identify other protocols that would be filtered by the rACL and that might require access to the GRP.

The objective is to determine what protocols the specific network uses. Logging should be used for analysis to determine "what else" might be communicating with the router.

Note	Although the **log** keyword provides valuable insight into the details of ACL hits, excessive hits to an ACL entry that uses this keyword might result in an overwhelming number of log entries and possibly high router CPU usage. Use the **log** keyword for short periods of time and only when needed to help classify traffic.

3 **Review identified packets and begin to filter access to the GRP.** Once the packets filtered by the rACL in step 1 have been identified and reviewed, deploy an rACL with a **permit any any** statement for the allowed protocols. Just as in step 1, the **log** keyword can provide more information about the packets that match the **permit** entries. Using **deny any any log** at the end can help identify any unexpected packets destined to the GRP. This rACL will provide basic protection and will allow network engineers to ensure that all required traffic is permitted.

The objective is to test the range of protocols that need to communicate with the router without having the explicit range of IP source and destination addresses.

4 **Restrict a macro range of source addresses.** Only allow the full range of your allocated classless interdomain routing (CIDR) block to be permitted as the source address. For example, if you have been allocated 171.68.0.0/16 for your network, then permit source addresses from just 171.68.0.0/16.

This step narrows the risk without breaking any services. It also provides data points of devices/people from outside your CIDR block that might be accessing your equipment. All outside addressed will be dropped.

External BGP peers will require an exception because the permitted source addresses for the session will lie outside the CIDR block.

This phase may be left on for a few days to collect data for the next phase of narrowing the rACL.

5 **Narrow the rACL permit statements to only allow known authorized source addresses.** Increasingly limit the source address to only permit sources that

communicate with the GRP. Note also the assumption for this recommendation is that a source address cannot be spoofed also.

Increasingly limit the source address to only permit sources that communicate with the GRP.

6 **Limit the destination addresses on the rACL (*optional*).** Some service providers may choose to only allow specific protocols to use specific destination addresses on the router. This final phase is meant to limit the range of destination addresses that will accept traffic for a protocol.

Control Plane Policing

A router can be logically divided into three functional components or planes:

- Data plane
- Management plane
- Control plane

The vast majority of traffic generally travels through the router via the data plane; however, the route processor must handle certain packets, such as routing updates, keepalives, and network management. This is often referred to as control and management plane traffic.

The route processor is critical to network operation, so any service disruption to the route processor, and hence the control and management planes, can lead to business-impacting network outages. A denial of service (DoS) attack targeting the route processor, which can be perpetrated either inadvertently or maliciously, typically involves high rates of RP-destined traffic that result in excessive CPU utilization on the route processor itself. Such an attack can be devastating to network stability and availability and may include the following symptoms that can be addressed via the use of Control Plane Policing or CoPP:

- High route processor CPU utilization (near 100%)
- Loss of line protocol keepalives and routing protocol updates, leading to route flaps and major network transitions
- Interactive sessions via the Command Line Interface (CLI) being slow or completely unresponsive due to high CPU utilization
- Route processor resource exhaustion: resources such as memory and buffers unavailable for legitimate IP data packets
- Backing up of packet queues, leading to indiscriminate drops (or drops due to lack of buffer resources) of other incoming packets

CoPP addresses the need to protect the control and management planes, ultimately ensuring routing stability, reachability, and packet delivery. It uses a dedicated control-plane configuration via the modular quality of service (QoS) CLI (MQC) to provide filtering and rate limiting capabilities for control plane packets.

Command Syntax

CoPP leverages MQC to define traffic classification criteria and specify configurable policy actions for the classified traffic. Traffic of interest must first be identified via class maps, which are used to define packets for a particular traffic class. Once classified, enforceable policy actions for the identified traffic are created with policy maps. The control-plane global command allows the CP service policies to be attached to the control plane itself.

There are four steps required to configure CoPP:

Step 1   Define a packet classification criteria. This is shown in Example 5-7.

Example 5-7   *Defining Packet Classification Criteria*

```
router(config)#class-map traffic_class_name

router(config-cmap)#match access-list | protocol | ip prec | ip dscp | vlan
```

Step 2   Define a service policy, as in Example 5-8.

Example 5-8   *Defining a Service Policy*

```
router(config-pmap)#policy-map service_policy_name

router(config-pmap)#class traffic_class_name

router(config-pmap-c)#police cir rate conform-action transmit exceed-action drop
```

Step 3   Enter control-plane configuration mode, as in Example 5-9.

Example 5-9   *Enter Control Plane Configuration Mode*

```
router(config)#control-plane
```

Step 4   Apply QoS policy, as in Example 5-10.

Example 5-10   *Apply QoS Policy*

```
service-policy    {input | output} service_policy_name

input   Assign policy-map to the input of an interface

output2    Assign policy-map to the output of an interface
```

Developing a CoPP Policy

Prior to developing the actual CoPP policy, required traffic must be identified and separated into different classes. One recommended methodology involves stratifying traffic into distinct groups based on relative importance. In the example discussed in this section, traffic is grouped into five different classes, as listed next. The actual number of classes needed might differ and should be selected based on local requirements, security policies, and a thorough analysis of the customer's baseline "normal" traffic.

- Critical
  - Traffic that is crucial to the operation of the router and the network.
  - Examples: Routing protocols such as Border Gateway Protocol (BGP) and Open Shortest Path First (OSPF).
  - Local site policy should dictate what traffic is deemed critical.
- Important
  - Necessary, frequently used traffic that is required during day-to-day operations.
  - Examples: Traffic used for remote network access and management, such as telnet, Secure Shell (SSH), Network Time Protocol (NTP), and Simple Network Management Protocol (SNMP).
- Normal
  - Traffic that is expected but not essential to network operation.
  - Examples: ICMP echo request (ping)
  - Normal traffic used to be particularly hard to address when designing control-plane protection schemes, as it should be permitted but should never pose a risk to the router. With CoPP, this traffic can be permitted but limited to a low rate
- Undesirable
  - Explicitly identifies "bad" or malicious traffic that should be **dropped** and denied access to the route processor.
  - Particularly useful when known traffic destined to the router should always be denied and not placed into a default category. Explicitly denying traffic allows the end user to collect rough statistics on this traffic via show commands and therefore offers some insight into the rate of denied traffic.
- Default
  - All remaining traffic destined to the route processor that has not been identified.
  - MQC provides the default class so the user can specify the treatment to be meted out to traffic not explicitly identified in the other user-defined classes. It is desirable to give such traffic access to the route processor but at a highly reduced rate.
  - With a default classification in place, statistics can be monitored to determine the rate of otherwise unidentified traffic destined to the control plane. Once this traffic is identified, further analysis can be performed to classify it, and if needed the other CoPP policy entries can be updated to account for this traffic.

Using the classification scheme defined above, commonly required traffic is identified with a series of ACLs:

- ACL 120: Critical traffic
- ACL 121: Important traffic
- ACL 122: Normal traffic
- ACL 123: Explicitly denies unwanted traffic (slammer worm traffic in this example)

The ACLs will then build classes of traffic that are used to define the policies.

In Example 5-11, the router IP address for control/management traffic will be 10.1.1.1.

Example 5-11 *Sample Basic ACLs for CoPP Classification*

```
! Sample basic ACLs for CoPP classification
! In this network, critical was defined at routing protocols: BGP and OSPF
access-list 120 remark CoPP ACL for critical traffic
! Allow BGP from a known peer to this router's BGP TCP port
access-list 120 permit tcp host 192.168.1.1 host 10.1.1.1 eq bgp
! Allow BGP from a peer's BGP port to this router
access-list 120 permit tcp host 192.168.1.1 eq bgp host 10.1.1.1
access-list 120 permit tcp host 192.168.2.1 host 10.1.1.1 eq bgp
access-list 120 permit tcp host 192.168.2.1 eq bgp host 10.1.1.1
! Permit OSPF
access-list 120 permit ospf any host 224.0.0.5
access-list 120 permit ospf any host 224.0.0.6
access-list 120 permit ospf any any
! Important is defined as traffic that is required for access to and management of
the router
access-list 121 remark CoPP Important traffic
! Permit return traffic from TACACS host
access-list 121 permit tcp host 10.2.1.1 host 10.1.1.1 established
! SSH access to the router from a subnet
access-list 121 permit tcp 10.2.1.0 0.0.0.255 host 10.1.1.1 eq 22
! telnet access to the router from a specific subnet
access-list 121 permit tcp 10.86.183.0 0.0.0.255 any eq telnet
! SNMP access from the NMS host to the router
access-list 121 permit udp host 10.2.2.2 host 10.1.1.1 eq snmp
! Allow the router to receive NTP packets from a known clock source
access-list 121 permit udp host 10.2.2.3 host 10.1.1.1 eq ntp
! In this classification scheme, normal traffic is traffic that we expect to see
destined to
the router and want to track and limit
access-list 122 remark CoPP normal traffic
! Permit router-originated traceroute
access-list 122 permit icmp any any ttl-exceeded
access-list 122 permit icmp any any port-unreachable
! Permit receipt of responses to router-originated pings
access-list 122 permit icmp any any echo-reply
! Allow pings to router
access-list 122 permit icmp any any echo
! This ACL identifies traffic that should always be blocked from accessing the route
processor.
```

continues

Example 5-11 *Sample Basic ACLs for CoPP Classification (Continued)*

```
Once undesirable traffic flow is identified, an ACE entry classifying it can be added
and mapped
to the undesirable traffic class. This can be used as a reaction tool.
access-list 123 remark explicitly defined "undesirable" traffic
! Permit, for policing, all traffic destined to UDP 1434
access-list 123 permit udp any any eq 1434
```

NOTE   ACL 123 is a "permit" entry for classification and monitoring purposes. This traffic will then be dropped as a result of the CoPP policy.

CoPP Deployment Guidelines

To successfully deploy CoPP, the existing control and management plane access requirements must be well understood. Determining the exact traffic profile required to build the filtering lists can be difficult. Following is a summary of the previous section:

- Start the deployment by defining liberal policies that allow most traffic through to the route processor (RP).
- Use **show policy-map** and **show access-lists** to figure out your traffic patterns.
- Use the statistics gathered in step 2 above to tune up your policies.

The following guidelines describe a very conservative approach for deploying CoPP using iterative ACL and policy configurations to help identify and eventually filter traffic:

Step 1. Determine Classification Scheme for Your Network

As described in the earlier section, a classification scheme can simplify the CoPP policy development. Enumerate the known protocols that access the route processor and divide them into categories:

- Example: critical, important, normal, undesirable, and default traffic classes for policy development.
- Select a scheme suited to the individual environment, which may require a greater or lesser number of classes.

Step 2. Classification ACLs and Policies

Develop an ACL that permits all known protocols requiring access to the route processor. Cisco recommends the use of distinct ACL numbers for each type of traffic defined in Step 1, in order to ease management. These "discovery" ACLs should have both the source and destination addresses set to "any". The final entry in the last ACL4 should be a **permit IP any any**. This will match traffic not explicitly permitted by other entries in the other ACLs.

Once the ACLs have been configured, apply them to a corresponding set of class maps using descriptive names, if possible. These class maps should be applied to a policy map that permits all traffic, regardless of classification. A default policy is not required at this stage of policy development.

The **router(config-pmap)** #class *traffic_class_name* command can ascertain which entries in the ACL are in use, as well as the number of packets permitted by the final ACL entry (that is, the **match ip any any** ACE). The objective is to identify the protocols used by a given network.

Ideally, the classification performed in Step 1 identified all required traffic destined to the router. Realistically, not all required traffic will be identified prior to deployment, and the **permit ip any any** access list entry will log a number of packet matches. Some form of analysis will be required to determine the exact nature of the unclassified packets. This extra classification step can be accomplished using several techniques: general ACL classification, as described in "Characterizing and tracing packet floods using Cisco Routers, packet analyzers, or using Receive ACLs (Cisco 7500 Series Router and Cisco 12000 Series Internet Router only)."

Once classified, the traffic can be either handled accordingly.

The **router(config-pmap-c)# police cir <rate> conform-action transmit exceed-action drop** command should be used to collect data about the actual policies in place: packet count and rate information will help develop a baseline for increasingly granular policy.

Step 3. Review Identified Packets and Begin to Filter Access to the Route Processor

Once the packets permitted by the ACLs in Step 2 have been identified and reviewed, a set of ACLs, updated if necessary, with a **permit any any** statement for the allowed protocols should be deployed. The **permit any any** in the final ACL should be removed. The key change in this step is the addition of the class-default policy: this default will apply to all traffic not otherwise identified by an ACL.

The objective is to test the range of protocols that need to communicate with the router without filtering the explicit range of IP source and destination addresses.

As with Step 2, **show** commands should be used to review the affect of the policy, particularly the rate data reported by the **router(config)#control-plane** command.

Step 4. Restrict a Macro Range of Source Addresses

Only allow the full range of the allocated CIDR block to be permitted as the source address. For example, if the network has been allocated 172.68.0.0/16, then permit the source address from just 172.68.0.0/16 where applicable.

This step limits the risk without breaking any services. It also provides data points of devices/people from outside the CIDR block that might be accessing the equipment.

The eBGP peer will require an exception; the permitted source addresses for the session will lie outside the CIDR block. This phase might be left on for a few days to collect data for the next phase of narrowing the ACL entries.

Step 5. Narrow the ACL Permit Statements to Only Allow Known Authorized Source Addresses

Increasingly limit the source address to only permit sources that communicate with the route processor. For instance, only network management station (NMS) workstations should be permitted to access the SNMP ports on a router. Note that filtering for the source address is recommended when one can safely assume that the source address cannot be spoofed.

Step 6. (Optional): Limit the Destination Addresses

Ideally, only allow specific protocols to use specific destination addresses on the router. This final phase is meant to limit the range of destination addresses that will accept traffic for a protocol. For instance, BGP peering typically occurs via loopback addresses, while BGP traffic can be permitted only to the loopback interface.

Risk Assessment

Care must be taken to ensure that the CoPP policy does not filter critical traffic such as routing protocols or interactive access to the routers. Filtering this traffic could prevent remote access to the router, thus requiring a console connection. For this reason, lab configurations should mimic the actual deployment as closely as possible.

We recommend that customers test this feature in their lab prior to deployment.

CoPP Summary

Infrastructure attacks are becoming increasingly common, highlighting the need for infrastructure protection. Control Plane Policing (CoPP) provides a hardware-independent mechanism for defining and implementing router protection schemes of varying sophistication. In its most basic form, CoPP can be used to permit or deny traffic destined to the router's processor. As operational experience grows, so does the complexity of the policy. The rate limiting features provide extremely flexible policy implementation.

CoPP deployment provides several key benefits:

- Protects against DoS attacks targeted toward the network infrastructure.
- Eases deployment: CoPP leverages the existing MQC infrastructure, which allows customers to preserve the existing interface configurations and add global commands to address the aforementioned security goals.
- Provides a consistent implementation strategy across all Cisco hardware.
- Increases the reliability, security, and availability of router services.

AutoSecure

Cisco AutoSecure is a Cisco IOS Security Command Line Interface (CLI) command. Customers can deploy one of its two modes, depending on their individual needs:

- Interactive mode—Prompts the user with options for enabling and disabling services and other security features.
- Noninteractive mode—Automatically executes the Cisco AutoSecure command with the recommended Cisco default settings.

Cisco AutoSecure performs the following functions:

- Disables the following Global Services
  - Finger
  - PAD
  - Small servers
  - Bootp
  - HTTP service
  - Identification service
  - CDP
  - NTP
  - Source routing
- Enables the following Global Services
  - Password-encryption service
  - Tuning of scheduler interval/allocation
  - TCP synwait-time
  - TCP-keepalives-in and tcp-kepalives-out
  - SPD configuration
  - No ip unreachables for null 0
- Disables the following services per interface
  - ICMP
  - Proxy-Arp
  - Directed Broadcast
  - Disables MOP service
  - Disables icmp unreachables
  - Disables icmp mask reply messages.

- Provides logging for security
  - Enables sequence numbers and timestamps
  - Provides a console log
  - Sets log buffered size
  - Provides an interactive dialogue to configure the logging server ip address.
- Secures access to the router
  - Checks for a banner and provides facility to add text to automatically configure:
    - Login and password
    - Transport input and output
    - Exec-timeout
    - Local AAA
  - SSH timeout and SSH authentication-retries to minimum number
  - Enable only SSH and SCP for access and file transfer to and from the router
  - Disables SNMP if not being used
- Secures the forwarding plane
  - Enables Cisco Express Forwarding (CEF) or distributed CEF on the router, when available
  - Antispoofing
  - Blocks all IANA-reserved IP address blocks
  - Blocks private address blocks if customer desires
  - Installs a default route to NULL 0 if a default route is not being used
  - Configures TCP intercept for connection-timeout, if TCP intercept feature is available and the user is interested
  - Starts interactive configuration for CBAC on interfaces facing the Internet when using a Cisco IOS Firewall image
  - Enables NetFlow on software-forwarding platforms

NOTE Prior to deploying Cisco AutoSecure, please check your network management application requirements. Some applications require services that may be disabled by Cisco AutoSecure.

Also refer to Cisco.com for current updates on this capability, which has caused problems in certain cases (http://www.cisco.com/en/US/customer/products/sw/iosswrel/ps5207/products_field_notice09186a00803e13e9.shtml).

Denial of service, spoofing, and other forms of attacks are on the increase on the Internet. Many of these attacks can be thwarted by judiciously using ingress filtering (filtering of packets originating from your network) and egress filtering (filtering of packets arriving from the Internet), hence the importance of filtering.

CE-Specific Router Security and Topology Design Considerations

The one key point to emphasize when referring to the customer edge (CE) router is that it is an untrusted device from the service provider's perspective. However, the customer's concerns include the following:

- Reliable transfer of data and routes, unhindered to all appropriate endpoints
- Ensuring that data and routes are not leaked to other service provider customers
- Ensuring that the service provider is attaining committed service-level agreements (SLAs) in terms of availability and throughput
- Expeditious troubleshooting of a network problem by the SP
- Expeditious problem analysis by the customer

Clearly, the type of physical network that is selected to interconnect the CE to the PE offers differing levels of resilience to intrusion and redirection. A serial point-to-point facility is difficult to subvert, and intrusions are usually noticeable. When this type of serial connection is interrupted, alarms are raised quickly and the two endpoints are difficult to masquerade.

Private virtual circuit (PVC)–based networks, such as Frame Relay and ATM, are somewhat less resistant in that they are generally controlled by software-based virtual circuit switching and can be readily misswitched or duplicated. However, even these facilities typically use a serial point-to-point connection between the CE and the telecommunications central office (telco), making intrusion difficult outside of the telco realm.

Ethernet-based facilities are most readily compromised in that it is relatively easy to insert a promiscuous monitoring device somewhere in the path. Note that the physical links from the CE to the central office remain directly cabled, and consequently intrusion still generally requires telco access.

Of course, it is possible to insert equipment into these physical plants, but the level of expertise required to identify the correct facility, access the physical structures, and unobtrusively insert illicit systems is very high and not readily performed by any but a determined and well-funded attacker.

NOTE   So what is the security recommendation for a CE-to-PE circuit?

One comment about Local Loop Security, such as a point-to-point connection between the CE and the PE where the underlying transport is SDH, which is typically *not* point-to-point on the physical map: The deployment of 1+1 protection in metropolitan area networks automatically duplicates the traffic depending on the configuration itself. Ethernet installations, for example, may be based on Ethernet switch connections at customer locations that are organized in rings going from a Customer A site to a Customer B site to a Customer C site, and so on. These switches consequently have physical access to the Ethernet trunks. It is therefore essential to be cognizant of the physical security plant factors when implementing a CE-to-PE link.

The more significant issues with shared physical-interface accesses (PVC-based or VLAN-based) would be managing the offered traffic loads so that one VPN cannot impact the operational characteristics of other VPNs being terminated on the same port. To guarantee the performance of the VPNs per SLA agreements, it is necessary to either provision much greater bandwidth on the access port than the expected load or to manage the bandwidth available using policing and shaping mechanisms. Typically, this is done by offering a limited set of performance options (say four or five classes) to customers when they request the service.

Policing controls are then applied to the interfaces based on these predefined classes of service to meet the expectations of the customer. In an unmanaged VPN, where different entities control the CE and PE, and consequently neither can be guaranteed to stay within the expected operational characteristics, these controls would need to be applied to both routers to ensure that offered loads do not impact the applicable networks.

MPLS VPNs offer a few network topology design options to address varying customer deployment needs:

- **Central services topology**—In this scenario, either the customer or the SP is providing a service at a centralized site, which can then be accessed by various VPN entities. For example, the SP may be providing a storage area network (SAN) facility or perhaps an IP telephony CallManager service. This necessitates judicious use of MPLS VPN route targets to provide connectivity to these facilities without leaking access between VPNs. Note that the servers providing such support must be carefully managed so that access to these devices themselves will not compromise the various VPNs.

- **Hub and spoke topology**—In this design, a particular customer site is designated as the focal point for user traffic and is also likely to provide corporate services to other sites. Examples may be server farms or Internet access. These types of implementations have security needs as well.

- **Any to any topology**—When traffic profiles indicate that sites need to freely communicate with one another, any-to-any connectivity may be appropriate. This is the simplest topology to implement from an MPLS VPN perspective in that the import/export policies of route targets are the same at all sites within a given VPN.

An example of security concerns for the above topologies is controlling services, which may be specific to particular corporate groups or providing firewall/NAT mechanisms for Internet access such as assuring that access to a customer's VPN is not compromised. However, MPLS introduces no additional concerns with respect to managing corporate traffic flows in a hub-and-spoke design and, as such, typical network planning approaches can still be applied.

Managed CE Security Considerations

In a VPN managed by a service provider, the SP also manages the CE equipment. That is, the SP's control extends all the way out to a point of presence within the customer's Interior Gateway Protocol (IGP). This section recommends best-practice deployment guidelines for the customer edge implementation. When a service provider manages a customer edge, as such, the SP has full control of the CE configuration, including:

- Access to the router itself for configuration and fault diagnostics
- Interaction with the rest of the customer's IGP or routing instance
- Interaction with the SP's PE routing mechanism; that is, the routing instance between the CE and PE
- Gathering customer statistics as required for reporting

This model provides the SP with the greatest degree of control over the potential impact of customer operations on the SP's network itself as well as greater control over issues that may arise affecting other SP customer virtual private networks (VPNs). The SP has a single backbone infrastructure for multiple sets of customers.

Conversely, this arrangement implies some degree of trust on the part of the customer, as follows:

- Customer permits another company (the SP) to have access to its IGP
- Customer trusts the SP to map its network communications solely to endpoints approved by the customer
- Customer assumes that the SP will provide the majority of fault analysis and resolution activity (since its own access is somewhat limited) because the service is managed by the SP

We emphasize, however, that the CE is always untrusted, and therefore the service provider must secure its network against attacks that may originate from the CE. In a managed service, the service provider network management station requires access to the CE, and therefore the service provider network management station must also implement security measures such that the network operations center is not compromised.

Unmanaged CE Security Considerations

There may be environments where the customer demands a call for some degree of sharing of responsibility between the SP and itself. In these situations, the span of control with respect to these parameters may shift from one direction to the other. A customer may have an unmanaged VPN that is distinguished by the notion that the CE router is owned and controlled by the customer. While the term *unmanaged VPN* is, strictly speaking, a misnomer (and perhaps indicative of a more SP-centric perspective), it is widely accepted to mean a network where the customer manages the CE router itself rather than the SP. In this scenario, the demarcation point between the SP and the customer is usually the remote end (the customer premise end) of the local loop where the service provider offers or manages the leased line as well customer premises. The customer has full control of the CE router's configuration and interacts with the SP's network over some mutually agreed arrangement between the SP and the customer.

The SP may have some exposure of the SP network operation to the customer's configurations of the CE router. As such, the SP needs to take additional steps to ensure that the SP network operations are not disturbed by changes in the customer network environment or CE router setups.

However, this operative mode may be more palatable to customers who desire to maintain the following:

- Complete control of their IGP
- Additional information access to fault analysis and troubleshooting
- Minimized exposure of the customer network to the SP

From the SP's perspective, the unmanaged VPN environment changes the span of control significantly. This approach impacts the SP in a number of ways, including the following:

- The need to protect the Layer 3 interconnect between the CE and PE
- The possible requirement to protect the Layer 2 interconnect (if shared)

The requirement for a clear definition of SLA-impacting responsibilities due to changes in the span of control and the need to closely interact with customers in the event of problems requires additional level of security awareness at the PE router because the CE is no longer under its explicit control.

CE Data Plane Security

Generally for the CE router, securing the data plane is pivotal for overall security. The Unicast Reverse Path Forwarding (uRPF) lookup feature should be enabled on each interface of the PE routers' CE-facing interfaces and on the CE routers' PE-facing interfaces. uRPF attempts to verify that the source of an incoming packet is accessible via the interface from which it was received (by checking the CEF tables) prior to switching the packet through. uRPF is currently available in two general operating modes:

- **Loose**—In this mode, if the incoming packet's source address is reachable via any interface in the router, the packet is forwarded. Loose mode is primarily applicable in network cores.

- **Strict**—In this mode, the packet must enter via the exact interface through which the source address would be reached prior to forwarding. Strict mode is intended for use at the edges of a given network.

Since PE and CE routers implement the network edge in an MPLS/VPN context, strict mode would be the appropriate choice. However, if the connections are dual-homed, then the uRPF mechanism must be relaxed somewhat by using loose mode.

In the next section, we review provider edge security recommendations as part of the CE relationship for security. An essential aspect of CE security is to consider the overall service relationship to the provider, such as managed vs. unmanaged and the associated topological factors, whether operating in hub and spoke, full mesh, or the Internet access provisioning model.

PE-Specific Router Security

In this section, we discuss PE-specific security considerations. The key point is that the PE is a trusted device and, as such, must be installed in a secure location. A PE must *never* be located in an insecure location such as a customer premise. If, for example, MPLS is required on a CE, Carrier's Carrier (CsC) should be implemented. The PE has trusted interfaces toward the core and untrusted interfaces toward the CE. These interfaces need to be secured, for example, by blocking all traffic from the outside to the PEs and the rest of the core, with the exception of routing. We discuss the interface security details in the section "Infrastructure Access Lists (iACLs)" later in this chapter.

The service provider's concerns can be generalized to the following issues:

- Protection of the backbone infrastructure in terms of availability, accessibility, load, manageability, and so on

- Ensuring that committed service level agreements (SLAs) are maintained

- Ensuring that billing support functions are uncompromised

- Maintaining segregation between different customer domains

- Verifying that customers are receiving the services that they are entitled to—no more and no less

The provider edge (PE) is within the SP domain and could have multiple customer relationships; for example, multiple customer VPNs may be provisioned on a single PE. From a security point of view, assuring complete privacy between various customers is of utmost importance for the service provider.

Hardening the control and data plane for a PE is required as a security best practice guideline. To manage forwarding information between the PE and CE, some sort of Layer 3 routing must be performed. There are, in essence, two options: static routing and dynamic routing. The pros and cons of each are well understood in Layer 3 routing environments and apply equally to an MPLS VPN network. However, because an MPLS VPN PE-CE connection involves a relationship between separate corporate entities, due consideration must be given to the security and stability implications of such interconnections.

For example, the concerns of interconnecting two entities may include:

- The PE or CE may be subject to floods of routes from its neighbor.
- Instabilities in the routing protocol processes may adversely affect CPU utilization.
- Invalid routes injected into either network space may cause traffic flows resulting in suboptimal or insecure paths.

These issues are no different than those faced by most service providers today, although generally, SPs do not utilize IGPs in their interconnection points, relying solely on BGP for this purpose. MPLS VPN customers may desire the use of mechanisms other than BGP, and as a result consideration needs to be given to the requirements this may impose.

PE Data Plane Security

For data plane security, as in the CE, the use of Unicast Reverse Path Forwarding (uRFP) is recommended also for the PE. The Unicast Reverse Path Forwarding (uRPF) lookup feature should be enabled on each interface of the PE routers' CE-facing interfaces and on the CE routers' PE-facing interfaces.

NOTE   There is a potential risk of transit traffic compromising a router such as a PE. The service provider network engineer could use the following example for IP options:

```
ip options ignore/drop
```

The **ignore** command option allows the operator to process transit packets with IP options set, but with drop packets that are on the router's receive path. This provides some mitigation of direct IP option-based attacks without impacting packets with IP options destined to customers. Customers should check with Cisco.com for updates when using this command and others referenced in this chapter.

PE-CE Connectivity Security Issues

Various QoS mechanisms can be used to protect the PE and CE router interfaces from undue traffic volumes. A higher than expected traffic flow may be caused by a deliberate DoS assault, or it may simply be the result of a misconfigured device somewhere within the network. However, as these mechanisms are inserted directly into the forwarding path, they do have an impact on packet forwarding rates, especially on software-based platforms. As such, these features should be applied with care and due consideration given to the environment where they are to be applied. The concept of a *traffic anomaly*—that is, understanding the customer and SP traffic patterns and detecting deltas in these patterns— is important in order for the service provider to determine whether or not a spike in traffic is due to a DoS or DDoS attack.

Similarly, the customer may wish to provide some degree of access to the CE router in order to enhance the SP's ability to troubleshoot a network problem. In the case of a managed CE, the same set of questions would be applicable. Generally speaking, one should not permit access to a given router beyond the minimally required set for good network operations and maintenance. Because the PE is generally a device supporting multiple customers' connections, and because there is no per-vrf segmentation of resource views, access to router statistics should be limited to SP personnel only. From the opposite perspective, the customer should also refrain from providing interactive access to systems under their direct control to the SP.

P-Specific Router Security

Provider (P) devices are trusted; that is, these devices do not interface to any untrusted platforms. Consequently, the P exposure is rather limited. Provider devices must be fully secured, using measures as described under the section "Generic Router Security Measures," earlier in this chapter. The key security point is that if a P node is compromised (for example, via internal exploits), the security of the PEs and the attached VPNs may also be compromised as a consequence.

NOTE   Best practice access for P nodes, as for any other router, is out-of-band security, and it must be tightly secured because access is often possible via the public telephone system.

Like with PE routers, P routers must be located in physically secure locations to avoid password recovery using a console connection.

Securing the Core

In this section, we discuss security considerations for the core network as a whole. That is, once all routers are secured independently, securing the network—which includes network-wide security measures such as infrastructure access lists (iACLs)—must be done by the SP network manager.

Infrastructure Access Lists (iACLs)

In this subsection, we emphasize that the core routers do not need to be accessible from the outside (with few exceptions, such as routing). If you block all packets from reaching the core routers, you are able to avert most attack forms.

In an effort to protect routers from various risks—both accidental and malicious—infrastructure protection ACLs should be deployed at network ingress points. These IPv4 and IPv6 ACLs deny access from external sources to all infrastructure addresses such as router interfaces; at the same time, the ACLs permit routine transit traffic to flow uninterrupted and provide basic RFC 1918, RFC 3330, and antispoof filtering.

Data received by a router can be divided into two broad categories—traffic that passes through the router via the forwarding path and traffic destined for the router via the receive path for route processor handling. In normal operations, the vast majority of traffic simply flows through a router in route to its ultimate destination. However, the route processor (RP) must handle certain types of data directly, most notably routing protocols, remote router access (such as Secure Shell [SSH]), and network management traffic such as Simple Network Management Protocol (SNMP). In addition, protocols such as Internet Control Message Protocol (ICMP) and IP options might require direct processing by the RP. Most often, direct infrastructure router access is required only from internal sources. A few notable exceptions include External Border Gateway Protocol (eBGP) peering, protocols that terminate on the actual router (such as generic routing encapsulation [GRE] or IPv6 over IPv4 tunnels), and potentially limited ICMP packets for connectivity testing such as echo-request or ICMP unreachables and time-to-live (TTL) expired messages for traceroute. Please bear in mind that ICMP is often used for simple denial of service (DoS) attacks and should only be permitted from external sources if necessary.

All RPs have a performance envelope in which they operate. Excessive traffic destined for the RP can overwhelm the router, causing high CPU usage and ultimately resulting in packet and routing protocol drops that cause a denial of service. By filtering access to infrastructure routers from external sources, many of the external risks associated with direct router attacks are mitigated. Externally sourced attacks can no longer access infrastructure equipment; the attack is simply dropped on ingress interfaces into the autonomous system (AS).

The filtering techniques described in this document are intended to filter data destined for network infrastructure equipment. Do not confuse infrastructure filtering with generic filtering; the infrastructure protection ACL has a singular purpose: to control on a granular level what protocols and sources can access critical infrastructure equipment.

Network infrastructure equipment encompasses the following:

- All router and switch management addresses, including loopback interfaces
- All internal link addresses: router-to-router links (point-to-point and multiple access)
- Internal servers or services that should not be accessed from external sources

In this subsection, transit traffic refers to all traffic not destined for the infrastructure. The implementation of iACLs is the foundation block for other security mechanisms such as rACL and CoPP mechanisms.

Techniques

Infrastructure protection can be achieved using a variety of techniques, such as the following:

- **Individual router ACLs**—Routers can also be protected by defining ACLs that permit only authorized traffic to the router's interfaces, denying all others except for transit traffic, which must be explicitly permitted. This ACL is logically similar to an rACL but does affect transit traffic and therefore can have a negative performance impact on a router's forwarding rate.

NOTE   Note, however, that in an MPLS network where Penultimate Hop Popping (PHP) may be functioning but an explicit null could be activated for LDP, a labeled packet is not filtered by IP ACLs, so a hop-by-hop router filter mechanism may not be appropriate here. Instead, the use of individual router ACLs is recommended for the network engineer. Additionally, routers deploying 6PE possess a construct where an incoming IPv6 packet is always labeled only emphasizing the importance of individual router ACL implementation rather than a hop-by-hop construct.

- **Edge filtering via infrastructure ACLs**—ACLs can be applied to the edge of the network; in the case of a service provider (SP), this would be the edge of the AS. This ACL will explicitly filter traffic destined for infrastructure address space. Deployment of edge infrastructure ACLs requires that you clearly define your infrastructure space and the required/authorized protocols that access this space. The ACL is applied at ingress to your network on all externally facing connections, such as peering connections, customer connections, and so on.

NOTE   There is an important difference between the use of rACLs and the edge or individual router ACLs: The first is the **explicit permit** type that terminates with a **deny any any**, while the latter is an **explicit deny** with a **permit any any** at the end. Theoretically, the first is more secure, and we recommend deploying both types because of the differences in command principles.

ACL Examples

The IPv4 and IPv6 access lists shown in Examples 5-12 and 5-13 provide simple yet realistic examples of typical entries required in a protection ACL. These basic ACLs need to be customized with local, site-specific configuration details. In dual IPv4 and IPv6 environments, both types of access lists should be deployed.

Example 5-12 *IPv4 Example*

```
!--- Antispoofing entries are shown here.

!--- Deny special-use address sources.
!--- Refer to RFC 3330 for additional special-use addresses.

access-list 110 deny ip host 0.0.0.0 any
access-list 110 deny ip 127.0.0.0 0.255.255.255 any
access-list 110 deny ip 192.0.2.0 0.0.0.255 any
access-list 110 deny ip 224.0.0.0 31.255.255.255 any
!--- Filter RFC 1918 space.

access-list 110 deny ip 10.0.0.0 0.255.255.255 any
access-list 110 deny ip 172.16.0.0 0.15.255.255 any
access-list 110 deny ip 192.168.0.0 0.0.255.255 any
!--- Deny your space as source from entering your AS.
!--- Deploy only at the AS edge.


access-list 110 deny ip YOUR_CIDR_BLOCK any
!--- Permit BGP.

access-list 110 permit tcp host bgp_peer host router_ip eq bgp
access-list 110 permit tcp host bgp_peer eq bgp host router_ip
!--- Deny access to internal infrastructure addresses.

access-list 110 deny ip any INTERNAL_INFRASTRUCTURE_ADDRESSES
!--- Permit transit traffic.

access-list 110 permit ip any any
```

NOTE   We recommend that the network engineer validate all examples in a test lab environment that reflects the appropriate service provider network reference architecture. Example 5-12 could result in performance issues associated with a 12000 Engine 2 line card because filtering on the source port is performed on the Line Card CPU in software. One ISP uses the following command example as a workaround:

```
access-list 110 permit tcp host bgp peer host router ip gt 10000
```

Example 5-13 *IPv6 Example (IPv6 access-list must be applied as an extended, named access-list)*

```
!--- Configure the access-list.
ipv6 access-list iacl
!--- Deny your space as source from entering your AS.
!--- Deploy only at the AS edge.

 deny ipv6 YOUR_CIDR_BLOCK_IPV6 any
!--- Permit multiprotocol BGP.
```

Example 5-13 *IPv6 Example (IPv6 access-list must be applied as an extended, named access-list) (Continued)*

```
permit tcp host bgp_peer_ipv6 host router_ipv6 eq bgp
permit tcp host bgp_peer_ipv6 eq bgp host router_ipv6
!--- Deny access to internal infrastructure addresses.
deny ipv6 any INTERNAL_INFRASTRUCTURE_ADDRESSES_IPV6
!--- Permit transit traffic.

permit ipv6 any any
```

NOTE   The **log** keyword can be used to provide additional detail about source and destinations for a given protocol. Although this keyword provides valuable insight into the details of ACL hits, excessive hits to an ACL entry that uses the **log** keyword increase CPU utilization. The performance impact associated with logging varies by platform. Also, using the **log** keyword disables Cisco Express Forwarding (CEF) switching for packets that match the access-list statement. Those packets are fast switched instead.

Developing a Protection ACL

In general, an infrastructure ACL is composed of four sections:

- Special-use address and antispoofing entries that deny illegitimate sources and packets with source addresses that belong within your AS from entering the AS from an external source

NOTE   RFC 3330 defines IPv4 special-use addresses that might require filtering. RFC 1918 defines an IPv4 reserved address space that is not a valid source address on the Internet. RFC 3513 defines the IPv6 addressing architecture. RFC 2827 provides ingress filtering guidelines.

- Explicitly permitted externally sourced traffic destined to infrastructure addresses
- **deny** statements for all other externally sourced traffic to infrastructure addresses
- **permit** statements for all other traffic for "normal" backbone traffic in route to noninfrastructure destinations

The final line in the infrastructure ACL will explicitly permit transit traffic: **permit ip any any** for IPv4 and **permit ipv6 any any** for IPv6. This entry ensures that all IP protocols are permitted through the core and that customers can continue to run applications without issues.

The first step when developing an infrastructure protection ACL is to understand the required protocols. Although every site has specific requirements, certain protocols are commonly deployed and will be well understood. For instance, external BGP to external peers needs to be explicitly permitted. Note that because both sides can initiate a BGP session (a session to TCP port 179), both directions must be permitted in the iACL. Any other protocols that require direct access to the infrastructure router will need to be explicitly permitted as well. For example, if you terminate a GRE tunnel on a core infrastructure router, then protocol 47 (GRE) also needs to be explicitly permitted. Similarly, if you terminate an IPv6 over IPv4 tunnel on a core infrastructure router, then protocol 41 (IPv6 over IPv4) also needs to be explicitly permitted.

To help identify the required protocols, a classification ACL should be used. The classification ACL is composed of **permit** statements for the various protocols that could be destined for an infrastructure router. Using the **show access-list** command to display a count of access control entry (ACE) hits will identify required protocols. Suspicious or surprising results should be investigated and well understood prior to creating **permit** statements for unexpected protocols.

For example, the IPv4 ACL shown in Example 5-14 would help determine whether GRE, IPsec (ESP), and IPv6 tunneling (IP Protocol 41) need to be permitted.

Example 5-14 *IPv4 ACL to Permit GRE, Ipsec, and IPv6 Tunneling*

```
access-list 101 permit GRE any infrastructure_ips
access-list 101 permit ESP any infrastructure_ips
access-list 101 permit 41 an infrastructure_ips
access-list 101 permit ip any infrastructure_ips log
!--- The log keyword provides more details
!--- about other protocols that are not explicitly permitted.

access-list 101 permit ip any any

interface int
 ip access-group 101 in

This IPv6 ACL can be used to determine if GRE and IPsec (ESP) need to be permitted.
ipv6 access-list determine_protocols
 permit GRE any infrastructure_ips_ipv6
 permit ESP any infrastructure_ips_ipv6
 permit ipv6 any infrastructure_ips_ipv6 log
!--- The log keyword provides more details
!--- about other protocols that are not explicitly permitted.

 permit ipv6 any any

interface int
 ipv6 traffic-filter determine_protocols in
```

In addition to required protocols, infrastructure address space needs to be identified because this is the space the ACL will be protecting. Infrastructure address space includes any addresses that are used for the internal network and should rarely, if ever, be accessed by external sources such as router interfaces, point-to-point link addressing, and critical infrastructure services. Since these addresses will be used for the destination portion of the infrastructure ACL, summarization is critical and, wherever possible, these addresses should be grouped into classless interdomain routing (CIDR) blocks.

Using the protocols and addresses identified, the infrastructure ACL can be built to permit the protocols and protect the addresses. In addition to direct protection, the ACL should also provide a first line of defense against certain types of invalid traffic on the Internet:

- RFC 1918 space should be denied.
- Packets with a source address that falls under special-use address space, as defined in RFC 3330, should be denied.
- Antispoof filters should be applied. (Your address space should never be the source of packets from outside your AS.)

This newly constructed ACL should be applied inbound on all ingress interfaces.

iACL Risk Assessment

When deploying infrastructure protection ACLs, remember to consider two key areas of risk:

- Ensure that the appropriate **permit/deny** statements are in place. For the ACL to be effective, all required protocols must be permitted and the correct address space must be protected by the **deny** statements.
- ACL performance varies from platform to platform. Before deploying ACLs, review the performance characteristics of your hardware.

NOTE   Note that the best practice recommendation is to implement rACL, CoPP, and iACLs in order to secure core infrastructure routers.

As always, we recommend that you test this design in the lab prior to deployment. Also, do not forget to update the ACLs when changes to the core are made, specifically when more address space is added.

Deployment Examples

We provide deployment examples for both IPv4 and IPv6 in the following subsections.

IPv4

The IPv4 example shown in Example 5-15 shows an infrastructure ACL protecting a router based on the following addressing:

- The service provider's address block is 169.223.0.0/16.
- The service provider's infrastructure block is 169.223.252.0/22.

- The loopback for the router is 169.223.253.1/32.

- The router is a peering router and peers with 169.254.254.1 (to address 169.223.252.1).

The infrastructure protection ACL shown in Example 5-15 was developed based on this information. The ACL permits external BGP peering to the external peer, provides antispoof filters, and protects the infrastructure from all external access.

Example 5-15 *IPv4*

```
!
no access-list 110
!
! !!!!!!!!!!!!!!!!!!!!!!!!!!!!!!!!!!!!!!!!!!!!!!!!!!!!!!!!!!
!--- Phase 1 - Antispoofing Denies
!--- These ACEs deny fragments, RFC 1918 space,
!--- invalid source addresses, and spoofs of
!--- internal space (space as an external source).


!
!--- Deny fragments to the infrastructure block.

access-list 110 deny tcp any 169.223.252.0 0.0.3.255 fragments
access-list 110 deny udp any 169.223.252.0 0.0.3.255 fragments
access-list 110 deny icmp any 169.223.252.0 0.0.3.255 fragments
!--- Deny special-use address sources.
!--- See RFC 3330 for additional special-use addresses.

access-list 110 deny ip host 0.0.0.0 any
access-list 110 deny ip 127.0.0.0 0.255.255.255 any
access-list 110 deny ip 192.0.2.0 0.0.0.255 any
access-list 110 deny ip 224.0.0.0 31.255.255.255 any
!--- Filter RFC 1918 space.

access-list 110 deny ip 10.0.0.0 0.255.255.255 any
access-list 110 deny ip 172.16.0.0 0.15.255.255 any
access-list 110 deny ip 192.168.0.0 0.0.255.255 any
!--- Deny our internal space as an external source.
!--- This is only deployed at the AS edge.

access-list 110 deny ip 169.223.0.0 0.0.255.255 any
!!!!!!!!!!!!!!!!!!!!!!!!!!!!!!!!!!!!!!!!!!!!!!!!!!!

!--- Phase 2 - Explicit Permit
!--- Permit only applications/protocols whose destination
!--- address is part of the infrastructure IP block.
!--- The source of the traffic should be known and authorized.


!
!--- Note: This template must be tuned to the network's
!--- specific source address environment. Variables in
!--- the template need to be changed.
```

Example 5-15 *IPv4 (Continued)*

```
!--- Permit external BGP.

access-list 110 permit tcp host 169.254.254.1  host 169.223.252.1  eq bgp
access-list 110 permit tcp host 169.254.254.1  eq bgp host 169.223.252.1
!
!!!!!!!!!!!!!!!!!!!!!!!!!!!!!!!!!!!!!!!!!!!!!!!!!!!!!!!!!!!!!!!
!--- Phase 3 - Explicit Deny to Protect Infrastructure


access-list 110 deny ip any 169.223.252.0 0.0.3.255
!
!!!!!!!!!!!!!!!!!!!!!!!!!!!!!!!!!!!!!!!!!!!!!!!!!!!!!!!!!!!!!!!
!--- Phase 4 - Explicit Permit for Transit Traffic


access-list 110 permit ip any any
```

IPv6

The IPv6 example shown in Example 5-16 shows an infrastructure ACL protecting a router based on the following addressing:

- The service provider's address block is 3FFE:B00:C18:::/48.

- The router is a peering router and peers with 3FFE:B00:C19:2:1::F (to address 3FFE:B00:C18:2:1::1).

The infrastructure protection ACL shown in Example 5-16 was developed based on this information. The ACL permits external multiprotocol BGP peering to the external peer, provides antispoof filters, and protects the infrastructure from all external access.

Example 5-16 *IPv6*

```
no ipv6 access-list iacl
ipv6 access-list iacl
!!!!!!!!!!!!!!!!!!!!!!!!!!!!!!!!!!!!!!!!!!!!!!!!!!!!!!!!!!!!!!
!--- Phase 1 - Antispoofing and Fragmentation Denies
!--- These ACEs deny fragments and spoofs of
!--- internal space as an external source.
!--- Deny fragments to the infrastructure block.

 deny tcp any 3FFE:B00:C18:3::/64 fragments
 deny udp any 3FFE:B00:C18:3::/64 fragments
 deny icmp any 3FFE:B00:C18:3::/64 fragments
!--- Deny our internal space as an external source.
!--- This is only deployed at the AS edge.

 deny ipv6 3FFE:B00:C18:::/48 any
!!!!!!!!!!!!!!!!!!!!!!!!!!!!!!!!!!!!!!!!!!!!!!!!!!
!--- Phase 2 - Explicit Permit
!--- Permit only applications/protocols whose destination
```

continues

Example 5-16 *IPv6 (Continued)*

```
!--- address is part of the infrastructure IP block.
!--- The source of the traffic should be known and authorized.

!--- Note: This template must be tuned to the network's
!--- specific source address environment. Variables in
!--- the template need to be changed.

!--- Permit multiprotocol BGP.

 permit tcp host 3FFE:B00:C19:2:1::F host 3FFE:B00:C18:2:1::1 eq bgp
 permit tcp host 3FFE:B00:C19:2:1::F eq bgp host 3FFE:B00:C18:2:1::1
!!!!!!!!!!!!!!!!!!!!!!!!!!!!!!!!!!!!!!!!!!!!!!!!!!!!!!!!!!!!!
!--- Phase 3 - Explicit Deny to Protect Infrastructure

 deny ipv6 any 3FFE:B00:C18:3::/64
!!!!!!!!!!!!!!!!!!!!!!!!!!!!!!!!!!!!!!!!!!!!!!!!!!!!!!!!!!!!!
!--- Phase 4 - Explicit Permit for Transit Traffic

 permit ipv6 any any
```

Routing Security

This section identifies how to secure routing protocols and includes the use of Message Digect-5 (MD-5) for MPLS control plane protocols such as Label Distribution Protocol (LDP). We specifically illustrate PE-CE routing protocol examples from a security perspective and introduce a Time-To-Live (TTL) security mechanism for BGP (Generalized TTL Security Mechanism [RFC 3682]). We also discuss mechanisms such as setting prefix limitations in order to monitor further for traffic anomalies.

Neighbor Router Authentication

How does a provider really know that the routing updates are from one of the provider's internal backbone routers and that the route really came from a neighboring router on the provider's backbone? It is difficult to validate this situation unless route authentication is used. Theoretically, routing information can be spoofed and injected into a service provider's backbone. The horror of experiencing a normal 50 K route object's jump to 200 K or 500 K and then observing these routes propagate all over the SP backbone has been a subject of numerous security meetings. Service providers are strongly encouraged to prevent their routers from receiving fraudulent route updates by configuring neighbor router authentication.

Neighbor router authentication occurs whenever routing updates are exchanged between neighbor routers that are in the control of the service provider. This authentication ensures that a router receives reliable routing information from a trusted source. Without neighbor authentication, unauthorized or deliberately malicious routing updates could compromise the security of your network traffic. A security compromise could occur if an unfriendly party diverts or analyses your network traffic. For example, an unauthorized router could send a fictitious routing update to convince your router to send traffic to an incorrect destination. This diverted traffic could be analyzed to learn confidential information about your organization or merely used to disrupt your organization's ability to effectively communicate using the network. Neighbor router authentication prevents any such fraudulent route updates from being received by your router. You should configure any router for neighbor authentication if that router meets all of these conditions:

- The router uses any of the routing protocols previously mentioned.
- It is conceivable that the router might receive a false route update.
- If the router were to receive a false route update, the service provider network might be compromised.

Configure a router for neighbor authentication and configure the neighbor router for neighbor authentication.

When neighbor authentication has been configured on a router, the router authenticates the source of each routing update packet it receives. This is accomplished by the exchange of an authenticating key (sometimes referred to as password) that is known to both the sending and receiving router. There are two types of neighbor authentication used: plain text authentication and Message Digest Algorithm Version 5 (MD5) authentication. Both forms work in the same way, with the exception that MD5 sends a "message digest" instead of the authenticating key itself. The message digest is created using the key and a message, but the key itself is not sent, preventing it from being read while it is being transmitted. Plain text authentication sends the authentication key itself over the wire.

Using MD5 authentication, however, is a recommended security best practice.

CAUTION   As with all keys, password, and other security secrets, it is imperative that the SP closely guard authenticating keys in neighbor authentication. The security benefits of this feature are reliant on the SP maintaining all authenticating keys confident. Also, when performing router management tasks via SNMP, do not ignore the risk associated with sending keys using nonencrypted SNMP.

Note also that with SNMP access for customers there is a risk of overloading the CPU with SNMP walks. The service provider recommendation is to use an SNMP proxy for customer access. MD5 authentication works similarly to plain text authentication, except that the key is never sent over the wire. Instead, the router uses the MD5 algorithm to produce a "message digest" of the key (also called a *hash*). The message digest is then sent instead of the key itself.

Hash provides an additional layer of security in addition to encryption. The hash system does not provide absolute security. MD5, is the most common hashing system for today's cryptography. MD5 processes the input text in 512-bit blocks, divided into 16 32-bit sub-blocks. The output of MD5 is a set of 4 32-bit blocks, which are concatenated to form a single string of 128-bit hash value.

MD5 for Label Distribution Protocol

The Label Distribution Protocol (LDP) for the P components use Message-Digest 5 (MD5) authentication in order to protect against label spoofing. Enable all LDP sessions for MD5 authentication. This recommendation also applies for CsC environments where a PE router is providing CE routers with labels for IGP routes in the VPN MD5 for LDP:

```
mpls ldp neighbor 194.22.15.2 password 7 ****** (scrambled)
```

NOTE   MD5 can only be supported for LDP, not TDP.

The best practice recommendation is to use LDP and not Tag Distribution Protocol (TDP), which is Cisco proprietary.

In environments using the Cisco proprietary Tag Distribution Protocol (TDP) globally, LDP can be enabled on a per-circuit basis if authentication is required.

In case of LDP sessions for CsC, the **vrf keyword** is added to the **mpls ldp neighbor** command of the PE router.

From PE for CsC:

```
mpls ldp neighbor vrf Reading 192.168.2.25 password 7 **** (scrambled)
```

From CE for CsC:

```
mpls ldp neighbor 192.168.2.26 password 7 **** (scrambled)
```

For PE-PE authentication, enable MD5 authentication on the multiprotocol BGP sessions between PE routers. This requires only **the neighbor password** command:

```
router bgp 10
no synchronization
bgp log-neighbor-changes
neighbor 194,22,15.2 remote-as 10
neighbor password 7 ******************** (scrambled)

Same for route reflectors (vpnv4 route exchange)
```

TTL Security Mechanism for BGP

The BGP Support for TTL Security Check feature introduces a lightweight security mechanism to protect Exterior Border Gateway Protocol (eBGP) peering sessions from CPU utilization-based attacks using forged IP packets. Enabling this feature prevents attempts to hijack the eBGP peering session by a host on a network segment that is not part of either BGP network or by a host on a network segment that is not between the eBGP peers.

You enable this feature by configuring a minimum Time-To-Live (TTL) value for incoming IP packets received from a specific eBGP peer. When this feature is enabled, BGP will establish and maintain the session only if the TTL value in the IP packet header is equal to or greater than the TTL value configured for the peering session. If the value is less than the configured value, the packet is silently discarded and no Internet Control Message Protocol (ICMP) message is generated. Note that the value corresponds to the "hop" count, where the minimum TTL calculated value is 255.

BGP must be configured in your network, and eBGP peering sessions must be established.

This feature needs to be configured on each participating router. It protects the eBGP peering session in the incoming direction only and has no effect on outgoing IP packets or the remote router.

Restrictions for BGP Support for TTL Security Check

This feature is designed to protect only eBGP peering sessions and is not supported for iBGP peers and iBGP peer groups.

When configuring the BGP Support for TTL Security Check feature to support an existing multihop peering session, you must first disable the **neighbor ebgp-multihop** router configuration command by entering the **no neighbor ebgp-multihop** command before configuring this feature with the **neighbor ttl-security** router configuration command. These commands are mutually exclusive, and only one command is required to establish a multihop peering session. If you attempt to configure both commands for the same peering session, an error message will be displayed in the console.

The effectiveness of this feature is reduced in large-diameter multihop peerings. In the event of a CPU utilization-based attack against a BGP router that is configured for large-diameter peering, you may still need to shut down the affected peering sessions to handle the attack.

This feature is not effective against attacks from a peer that has been compromised inside your network. This restriction also includes BGP peers that are not part of the local or external BGP network but are connected to the network segment between the BGP peers (for example, a switch or hub that is used to connect the local and external BGP networks).

This feature does not protect the integrity of data sent between eBGP peers and does not validate eBGP peers through any authentication method. This feature validates only the locally configured TTL count against the TTL field in the IP packet header.

The BGP Support for TTL Security Check feature introduces a lightweight security mechanism to protect eBGP peering sessions from CPU utilization-based attacks. These types of attacks are typically brute force denial of service (DoS) attacks that attempt to disable the network by flooding the network with IP packets that contain forged source and destination IP addresses.

This feature protects the eBGP peering session by comparing the value in the TTL field of received IP packets against a hop count that is configured locally for each eBGP peering session. If the value in the TTL field of the incoming IP packet is greater than or equal to the locally configured value, the IP packet is accepted and processed normally. If the TTL value in the IP packet is less than the locally configured value, the packet is silently discarded and no ICMP message is generated. This is designed behavior; a response to a forged packet is unnecessary.

Accurately forging the TTL count in an IP packet is generally considered to be impossible. It is possible to forge the TTL field in an IP packet header. However, accurately forging a packet to match the TTL count from a trusted peer is not possible unless the network to which the trusted peer belongs has been compromised.

This feature supports both directly connected peering sessions and multihop eBGP peering sessions. The BGP peering session is not affected by incoming packets that contain invalid TTL values. The BGP peering session will remain open, and the router will silently discard the invalid packet. The BGP session, however, can still expire if keepalive packets are not received before the session timer expires.

Configuring the TTL Security Check for BGP Peering Sessions

The BGP Support for TTL Security Check feature is configured with the **neighbor ttl-security** command in router configuration mode or address family configuration mode. When this feature is enabled, BGP will establish or maintain a session only if the TTL value in the IP packet header is equal to or greater than the TTL value configured for the peering session. Enabling this feature secures the eBGP session in the incoming direction only and has no effect on outgoing IP packets or the remote router. The *hop-count* argument is used to configure the maximum number of hops that separate the two peers. The TTL value is determined by the router from the configured hop count. The value for this argument is a number from 1 to 254.

Configuring the TTL Security Check for Multihop BGP Peering Sessions

The BGP Support for TTL Security Check feature supports both directly connected peering sessions and multihop peering sessions. When this feature is configured for a multihop peering session, the **neighbor ebgp-multihop** router configuration command cannot be configured and is not needed to establish the peering session. These commands are mutually exclusive, and only one command is required to establish a multihop peering session. If you attempt to configure both commands for the same peering session, an error message will be displayed in the console.

To configure this feature for an existing multihop session, you must first disable the existing peering session with the **no neighbor ebgp-multihop** command. The multihop peering session will be restored when you enable this feature with the **neighbor ttl-security** command.

This feature should be configured on each participating router. To maximize the effectiveness of this feature, the *hop-count* argument should be strictly configured to match the number of hops between the local and external network. However, you should also consider path variation when configuring this feature for a multihop peering session.

Benefits of the BGP Support for TTL Security Check Feature

The BGP Support for TTL Security Check feature provides an effective and easy-to-deploy solution to protect eBGP peering sessions from CPU utilization-based attacks. When this feature is enabled, a host cannot attack a BGP session if the host is not a member of the local or remote BGP network or if the host is not directly connected to a network segment between the local and remote BGP networks. This solution greatly reduces the effectiveness of DoS attacks against a BGP autonomous system.

How to Secure BGP Sessions with the BGP Support for TTL Security Check Feature

This section contains the following procedures:

- Configuring the TTL-Security Check (required)
- Verifying the TTL-Security Check Configuration (optional)

Configuring the TTL-Security Check

To configure the BGP Support for TTL Security Check Feature, perform the steps in this section.

To maximize the effectiveness of this feature, we recommend that you configure it on each participating router. Enabling this feature secures the eBGP session in the incoming direction only and has no effect on outgoing IP packets or the remote router.

Restrictions

The **neighbor ebgp-multihop** command is not required when this feature is configured for a multihop peering session and should be disabled before configuring this feature.

The benefit of this feature is reduced in large-diameter multihop peerings. In the event of a CPU utilization-based attack against a BGP router that is configured for large-diameter peering, you may still need to shut down the affected peering sessions to handle the attack.

This feature is not effective against attacks from a peer that has been compromised inside of the local and remote network. This restriction also includes peers that are on the network segment between the local and remote network.

CE-PE Routing Security Best Practices

This section focuses on PE-CE IGP and addressing best practice security recommendations. You need to use what you learned in the previous sections as building blocks for this section.

PE-CE Addressing

The physical facility between the PE and CE remains an exposure with respect to access to the networks, data flows, and attack points. This link should be secured to the extent feasible while supporting application requirements and maintenance efforts.

The use of unnumbered links for addressing is frequently seen as a means to enhance the security of the PE, and to some extent the CE, because there is no exposed Layer 3 address to attack. If such an approach is desired, consideration must be given to the implications on the routing protocol being used between the PE and CE.

For example, if eBGP is the protocol in use, peering will need to be linked to loopback (or other) addresses and multihop must be enabled for the eBGP session. This control allows eBGP sessions to maintain over a number of hops by setting the Time-To-Live (TTL) appropriately. Unfortunately, the use of this modifier allows for remote eBGP connection attempts from any number of hops not necessarily just as defined in the sourcing configuration.

One of the most used troubleshooting tools in the IP network space is the ICMP Echo (ping) test. The use of unnumbered links removes the ability of the network operator to ping the directly connected interface as a fault analysis methodology. This may be seen as sufficient cause to support numbered interfaces. Further protection may also be available by encrypting the traffic flowing over the link using either payload encryption mechanisms or full link encryptors.

If the data being passed over the network is considered an extreme risk then such protection may be appropriate as discussed earlier in this chapter. Note also that use of overlapping address space for different VPNs is permitted and implemented today and is fundamental to BGP-VPN mechanisms for MPLS VPN.

Static Routing

Clearly, static routing provides the most stable and controlled scenario for the PE-CE interconnect. With static route definitions, there are no opportunities for errant routes to be introduced other than by typing them directly into the configurations. Also, there is less CPU impact with static routes because there is no dynamic routing process to run (other than the SP iBGP). In addition, because the CE and PE are both using explicitly configured routes, the security of the interconnection is improved—monitoring the intervening path will not provide any information as to what routes are accessible beyond the router.

Dynamic Routing

Alternatively, using a dynamic routing protocol reduces the amount of configuration effort on both the PE and CE routers. Also, changes within the customer's network addressing are readily accommodated and alternate pathing is more easily deployed. If a dynamic protocol is to be used between the PE and CE routers, then eBGP is the recommended choice due to its inherent stability, scalability, and control features. In any case, the use of a dynamic protocol mandates the use of an authentication mechanism between the two routers for security purposes.

In order to provide a degree of security in a dynamically routed PE-CE environment with respect to the peer relationships across the PE-CE links, MD5 authentication (Message Digest 5 Hashed Message Authentication Code [HMAC]) should be enabled between the peers. This mechanism uses a highly resistant hash algorithm in the handshake between the peers to provide some assurance that the peer is in fact the intended neighbor. The use of a preshared secret on the PE and CE routers provides support for the one-way encrypted hash message used to authenticate the peers. As such, coordination is required between the PE and CE management entities if they are separately controlled.

MD5 should be used as opposed to the other, less resilient hashing mechanisms available.

This mechanism is available for all the PE-CE routing protocols currently supported, including the following examples.

Key Chaining

Cipher block chaining (CBC) is a mode of operation for a block cipher (one in which a sequence of bits are encrypted as a simple unit or a block with a cipher key applied to the entire block). CBC uses what is known as an initialization vector (IV) of a certain length. One of its key characteristics is that it uses a chaining mechanism that causes the decryption of a block of cipher text to depend on all the preceding cipher blocks.

eBGP PE-CE Routing

With BGP between PE and CE, authentication is defined on a per-neighbor basis. Also, BGP does not currently support the use of key chains. Key-chaining of MD5 hashes is not yet supported with BGP.

Example 5-17 illustrates BGP authentication.

Example 5-17 *BGP AUTHENTICATION*

```
router bgp 13
        address-family ipv4 vrf Peabody1
        neighbor 1.1.1.1 remote-as 14
        neighbor 1.1.1.1 password 5 1Sherman2
```
continues

Example 5-17 *BGP AUTHENTICATION (Continued)*

```
                          # establishes use of MD5 password "1Sherman2" for this neighbor
                          address-family ipv4 vrf Dudley1
                          neighbor 2.2.2.2 remote-as 15
                          neighbor 2.2.2.2 password 5 77doright2
                          # establishes use of MD5 password "77doright2" for this neighbor
```

NOTE   With BGP, ensure that MD5 authentication is enabled at both ends of the router pair.
          A router without MD5 authentication definitions will result in a keepalive timeout
          observed from the routers with MD5 configured as per the BGP authentication explained
          in RFC 1771.

EIGRP PE-CE Routing

EIGRP authentication is defined in an interface-specific manner and can be instantiated
using either clear text or MD5 passwords. As previously stated, MD5 is the recommended
usage. Authentication must be enabled for the autonomous system (AS) in question, as
illustrated in Example 5-18.

Example 5-18 *EIGRP Authentication*

```
            router eigrp 13
                    address-family ipv4 vrf Bullwinkle1
                    autonomous-system 14
                    network 1.0.0.0
                    # define the vpn known as "Bullwinkle1" as operating under the
                    eigrp autonomous system 14

                    address-family ipv4 vrf Rocky1
                    autonomous-system 15
                    network 1.0.0.0
                    # define the vpn known as "Rocky1" as operating under the eigrp
                    autonomous system 15

            interface Ethernet0/0
            ip vrf forwarding Bullwinkle1
            ip address 1.1.1.1 255.0.0.0
            no ip directed-broadcast
            ip authentication mode eigrp 14 md5
            # defines authentication mode for eigrp AS 14
            # to be MD5
            ip authentication key-chain eigrp 14 eigrp14
            # sets the key chain name for eigrp AS 14 to the
            # string "eigrp14"

            interface Ethernet0/1
            ip vrf forwarding Rocky1
            ip address 1.1.1.1 255.0.0.0
            no ip directed-broadcast
```

Example 5-18 *EIGRP Authentication (Continued)*

```
                    ip authentication mode eigrp 15 md5
                    # defines authentication mode for eigrp AS 15
                    # to be MD5
                    ip authentication key-chain eigrp 15 eigrp15
                    # sets the key chain name for eigrp AS 15 to the
                    # string "eigrp15"

                    key chain eigrp14
                            key 1
                            key-string 5 1natashafatale3
                    # creates a 'chain' known as "eigrp14" of 1 key, with the   # MD5
                    password set to "1natashafatale3"
                    key chain eigrp15
                            key 1
                            key-string 5 3Borisbadenov1
                    # creates a 'chain' known as "eigrp15" of 1 key, with the   # MD5
                    password set to "3Borisbadenov1"
```

The key-chain software feature allows the user to define a set of keys bound into a chain
that can then be applied to an authentication operation. The ability to define a set of keys,
rather than just one, allows for easier key migration on the basis of some predetermined
interval. Note the key number in this command construct is just an index rather than the
"key" variable used in an MD5 context.

OSPF PE-CE Routing

OSPF also establishes authentication requirements on a per-interface basis. Additionally,
authentication must be enabled for the area within the AS where authentication will be
performed.

As with BGP, OSPF does not currently use the key chain methodology. Example 5-19
illustrates an OSPF authentication configuration.

Example 5-19 *OSPF Authentication*

```
                    router ospf 52 vrf Donald
                    network 1.0.0.0 0.255.255.255 area 52
                    area 52 authentication message-digest
                    # enables use of authentication within this ospf area for # ospf
                    process 52

                    interface Ethernet0/0
                    ip vrf forwarding Donald
                    ip address 10.1.1.2 255.255.255.0
                    no ip directed-broadcast
                    ip ospf authentication message-digest
                    # establishes authentication for the neighbor across this interface

                    ip ospf message-digest-key 13 md5 5 1Daisy3
```
continues

Example 5-19 *OSPF Authentication (Continued)*

```
                    # defines "1Daisy3" as the MD5 password to be used on this link
                    router ospf 42 vrf Mickey
                    network 1.0.0.0 0.255.255.255 area 42
                    area 42 authentication message-digest
                    # enables use of authentication within this ospf area for # ospf
                    process 42
                    interface Ethernet0/1
                    ip vrf forwarding Mickey
                    ip address 10.1.1.2 255.255.255.0
                    no ip directed-broadcast
                    ip ospf authentication message-digest
                    # establishes authentication for the neighbor across this interface
                    ip ospf message-digest-key 13 md5 5 2minn1e7
                    # defines "2minn1e7" as the MD5 password to be used on this link
```

RIPv2 PE-CE Routing

RIP version 2 supports neighbor authentication in a similar fashion to EIGRP. Example 5-20 shows a configuration for RIPv2 authentication.

Example 5-20 *RIPv2 Authentication*

```
                interface Ethernet0/0
                ip vrf forwarding Daffy1
                ip address 1.1.1.1 255.0.0.0
                no ip directed-broadcast
                ip rip authentication mode md5
                #enables MD5 authentication over this rip interface
                ip rip authentication key-chain Daffy1
                #sets "Daffy1" as the key chain to be used for this link
            key chain Daffy1
                    key 1
                    key-string 5 13Sylvester1
                #creates a 'chain' known as "Daffy1" of 1 key, with the # MD5 password
                set to "13Sylvester1"
```

PE-CE Routing Summary

The following summarizes PE-CE routing security, in order of security preference:

- **Static**—If no dynamic routing is required (no security implications)
- **BGP**—For redundancy and dynamic updates and inherent security features for BGP
- **IGPs**—If BGP is not supported (limited security features such as MD-5)

Prevention of Routes from Being Accepted by Nonrecognized Neighbors

In the PE-CE dynamic routing space, the interconnections may be across multi-access media or may be misconnected in such a way that erroneous peers may be introduced. In order to prevent routes being accepted from nonrecognized neighbors, it is recommended that MD5 authentication be used between PEs and CEs that utilize dynamic protocols. If, however, this is not acceptable in a given environment, there is still a need to control the peering associations. Within BGP, this is inherently accomplished through the "neighbor" construct.

When EIGRP or RIP implemented, this functionality is not yet available for PE-CE interfaces. Without MD5, the only protection against unwanted routes would be the autonomous system numbers, which is a very weak mechanism from a protection perspective. In this environment, the **distance** command may be used to control acceptable route sources, as shown in Example 5-21.

Example 5-21 *Distance Command*

```
      router eigrp 666
              address-family ipv4 vrf VPN_20399
              redistribute bgp 65000 metric 1000 100 100 1 500
              network 140.0.0.0
              distance 90 140.0.200.2 0.0.0.0
              #defines an administrative distance of 90 (default) for eigrp
              routes
              #received from address 140.0.200.2
              distance 255 0.0.0.0 255.255.255.255
              #sets all other sources of routing to a value of unknown/untrusted
              autonomous-system 1
              exit-address-family

      #NOTE: EIGRP requires that acceptable sources must precede the "255"
      source as
       #shown above
       router rip
       version 2

       address-family ipv4 vrf VPN_20399
       version 2
       redistribute bgp 65000
       network 140.0.0.0
       distance 255
       #sets all sources of routing info to a value of 255      unknown/untrusted
       distance 120 140.0.200.2 0.0.0.0
       #sets an administrative distance of 120 (default) for rip routes
       received from
       #140.0.200.2
              no auto-summary
              exit-address-family
```

BGP Maximum-Prefix Mechanism

Within an MPLS VPN environment, it is conceivable that through deliberate action or accidental misconfiguration, an excessive number of routes may be propagated from one routing peer to another. This behavior could readily impact the recipient router CPU, and if great enough, could lead to memory consumption sufficient to cause the router to disable

CEF (and thereby all MPLS forwarding) or reload. This exposure exists for both the CE router and the PE router and, as such, should be controlled on both to the extent possible.

At this time, only BGP supports the concept of a maximum number of permitted prefixes. Within BGP, the **maximum-prefix** construct allows a user to define a maximum number of routes to be accepted from this peer. Once this maximum has been reached, the router can be configured to either issue a warning message or to restart the offending peer, with the interval to restart being configurable. In addition, a threshold may be defined where warning messages are issued prior to reaching the maximum.

Example 5-22 shows the configuration of BGP prefix limits.

Example 5-22 *BGP Prefix Limit Configuration*

```
router bgp 13
no synchronization
bgp log-neighbor-changes
no auto-summary

address-family ipv4 vrf VPN_20499
neighbor 140.0.250.2 remote-as 500
neighbor 140.0.250.2 activate
neighbor 140.0.250.2 maximum-prefix 45 80 restart 2
defines a 45 prefix maximum for routes delivered from this neighbor,
with a warning message issued at 80% of 45, and the BGP session
restarted on exceeding 45, with a 2 minute interval for retry
no auto-summary
no synchronization
exit-address-family
```

The following code reflects the console logging that occurs as the number of routes from a BGP peer reaches the threshold set for warning messages, and the subsequent peer restart once the actual maximum has been reached:

```
6d22h: %BGP-4-MAXPFX: No. of prefix received from 140.0.250.2 (afi 2) reaches 37,
max 45
6d22h: %BGP-3-MAXPFXEXCEED: No. of prefix received from 140.0.250.2 (afi 2): 46
exceed limit 45

6d22h: %BGP-5-ADJCHANGE: neighbor 140.0.250.2 vpn vrf VPN_20499 Down BGP
Notification sent
6d22h: %BGP-3-NOTIFICATION: sent to neighbor 140.0.250.2 3/1 (update malformed)
0 bytes  FFFF FFFF FF
```

Once the maximum number of routes on the connection has been exceeded, the status of the BGP peer will indicate that it has been idled due to the prefix count limit having been overrun:

```
ESR3#sh ip bgp v a s | i 140.0.250.2
140.0.250.2   4   500     149   130   0   0   0 00:01:01 Idle (PfxCt)
```

For PE best practice considerations, implementing routing neighbor update authentication (MD5) and maximum-prefix for BGP updates are recommended for service provider implementations.

Internet Access

In Chapter 4, we discussed implementation details regarding security best practices for Internet access. We highlight some of these key points from Chapter 4 in this section as it pertains to overall core security.

In network environments where both private network and Internet access are provided by one infrastructure, the security considerations applicable to the MPLS VPN assume the added significance of the Internet component's impact or potential impact on the SP backbone and the CE connections. Not only are two corporate entities involved in the network service's provisioning, but the Internet and its millions of connections and users are now closely coupled with the corporate data networks.

This necessitates stringent adherence to the SP security best practices to ensure the security and reliability of the backbone. In addition, it is essential to address network design issues to guarantee that corporate (once private) network data is not adversely impacted by the vagaries of the Internet data flows. Of course, it is also conceivable that high volumes of corporate data (say large image transfers or data backups) could also impact the infrastructure to an extent that Internet traffic may suffer.

However, typically, Internet traffic is viewed as "best effort" traffic with little or no expected service levels and, as such, as long as user performance is not unduly hindered, this should not be a major issue. As the usage profiles of the Internet change to support traffic that has more stringent latency or jitter restrictions, more attention may be required with respect to general traffic performance.

Of greater importance are intrusion-oriented security concerns and DoS attacks, which are more likely to be sourced from the Internet than the corporate space and must be addressed to mitigate impact to the VPN traffic flows. At an overview level, there are three basic approaches to providing Internet and MPLS VPN services to a given set of customers:

- Totally distinct networks
- Shared core network with separate PE and CE components and connections
- Shared resources end to end

Clearly, the provisioning of totally separate networks ensures that the only Internet-driven security vulnerabilities will be through the customer's own interconnect points within the customer network. However, this is a very costly approach for the service provider, which will be reflected in the costs passed on to the consumer of such services.

Resource Sharing: Internet and Intranet

In general, it is recommended that the VPN service network interconnects and the Internet access be run over separate links and to separate routers (not the VPN-supporting routers), rather than attempting to homogenize them over a single facility.

That is, the SP should provision separate PEs for VPN versus Internet access even if the backbone P routers are convergent.Also, the interconnections between the VPN (intranet) and Internet PEs should be unique and preferably be terminated on separate CE routers. This allows for the greatest degree of configuration flexibility (thereby policy control) and will reduce the concern that Internet-launched DoS attacks will have an immediate impact on the VPN performance. Internet traffic can also be directed through DMZ facilities at centralized customer sites where firewall-based control and intrusion detection systems can be readily deployed. Internet access can then be provided to other sites with default routing propagated through the corporate VPN.

The use of default routing to direct traffic through the DMZ ensures that corporate security policies are applied to traffic that traverses the Internet, and additionally provides a single connection point where problems can be identified and controlled. Also, this approach minimizes the memory usage on the PE and CE routers that would be considerable if the entire Internet table were propagated.

Sharing End-to-End Resources

Sharing end-to-end resources ensures that the network deployment costs are minimized, at least from a hardware and facilities perspective.

However, this approach is fraught with considerable security risks. It is essential that both services (MPLS VPN and Internet access) are tightly controlled so as to avoid any adverse interactions. In this scenario, the SP backbone, the PE router, the interconnection facility between the CE and PE, and the CE router itself are shared resources with respect to both the VPN and Internet traffic flows. The CE router needs to implement some mechanism to groom VPN and Internet traffic into different channels. The Internet traffic must be directed through a firewall device before remerging with the corporate traffic. Policy-based routing or Multi-lite VRF may be utilized to perform the traffic direction. Indeed, some security perspectives suggest the use of doubled firewalls to try to provide an additional level of protection.

Additional Security

No matter which approach you choose for providing Internet and MPLS VPN services, the use of intrusion detection systems (IDSs) is highly recommended to provide early warnings and information leading to quicker resolution of Internet-driven attacks.

Clearly, firewalling should be viewed as a necessary component of any Internet access, whether accomplished by any of the following means:

- Firewall at central site with centralized Internet access
- Firewall at each CE site
- Firewalling through an SP service offering, either through stacked or shared approaches

Addressing Considerations

Many current implementations of customer networks have been based on the use of private address space. Interconnecting to the Internet requires the use of global addresses that generally necessitate some form of network address translation (NAT). In addition to firewalls, this NAT functionality can be implemented either through shared services provided at a central customer site or by the SP.

LAN Security Issues

In this section we discuss LAN security issues as they pertain to core security. We also illustrate LAN factors for peering constructs.

In the case of a LAN-based Layer 2 interconnect, the PE router will need to maintain ARP entries for all of the end system addresses that are reachable beyond that interface.

The number of entries may be considerable depending on the size of the connected site, and it can considerably impact router CPU and memory. It is generally viewed that an excess of 20,000 ARP entries can lead to issues on the connected router and, as such, it may be desirable to segment such a large campus.

As well, because there is no Layer 3 "CE" router in this scenario, there are no reasonable mechanisms available to ensure that the only accesses into the VPN from this interface are those authorized to do so. That is, given some large number of hosts on this Layer 2 domain, it is difficult, if not impossible, to create access controls that can ensure that only the appropriate traffic sources exist—the Layer 2 domain must be a "trusted" network space. This must be an operational consideration of the entity controlling the Layer 2 network—be it the customer or the SP. Intrusion into the network at this point will give access to much if not all of the entire VPN (depending on VLAN arrangements).

Also, because this is a Layer 2 environment, there are no Layer 3 opportunities for controlling denial of service (DoS) issues beyond the PE edge. If an assault or intrusion reaches the Layer 2 space, it must be dealt with at that level. For example, a broadcast-oriented attack would have an immediate impact on all nodes within the same Layer 2 domain.

The SP must also determine the degree of interaction it wants to perform with respect to L2 operations—spanning tree termination, Cisco Discovery Protocol (CDP) functions, quality of service (QoS), trusted ports, and so on.

LAN Factors for Peering Constructs

A third party in the same VLAN (such as Internet Exchange Point, or IXP) can insert spoofed packets into VPNs, thus introducing a risk scenario for a service provider.

Note that within a VLAN, attacks are easy (these will be further discussed in Chapter 7) via ARP spoofing (hacking tool *hunt, arpspoof*); CAM overflow (hacking tool *macof*); DoS against Spanning Tree, and DoS storms (for which a hacking tool exists). An example of a solution includes, for 1 and 2, port security.

Few service providers do this normally, so this attack is not difficult; and to disable Spanning Tree on the router port, hard code Root Bridge is a factor here.

For labeled packets on a VLAN, the data plane attributes are that any label combination can be sent, by any station in the VLAN, and for Carriers Carrier, the top label (LSP) is checked by the PE.

NOTE For both CsC and Inter-AS deployments, implement only on private peerings due to vulnerabilities highlighted above. For Inter-AS and CsC (when labeled packets are exchanged), do *not* use a shared VLAN.

Best recommendation: Dedicated connection

Second best recommendation: Dedicated VLAN

IPsec: CE to CE

The use of CE-CE IPsec may be implemented if required by the end customer. MPLS VPNs forward user information over the network in the same format as it is received from the CE, as with any other data-transparent transport network (ATM, Frame Relay, or HDLC).

NOTE Note that the use of IPsec between CE routers is transparent to the MPLS core and has therefore no influence on the security of the core. As such, it is possible, though perhaps requiring considerable effort and access, to monitor traffic as it passes through the network. This may not be acceptable for highly sensitive information such as financial data or confidential materials. If inherent protection of the data from monitoring is desired, it is necessary to use some sort of encryption technique.

Various data-encryption mechanisms have been available for some time, including software- and hardware-based encryption and the most typically used within the IP world—IPsec.

Full link encryptors may be used as long as they are inserted in the lines between the routers such that the original data stream, in particular the header information, is available for the routers to perform their forwarding decisions. As such, information is "in the clear" on the cables between the encryptor/decryptor and the attached router.

However, a more typical approach in an IP environment is to use the IPsec mechanisms, which encrypt the data and still produce an output IP packet that can be switched by the routers. In addition, IPsec also can provide support for verification of the endpoints of the data flow, thus providing a high degree of certainty that the information is actually being received by the intended party.

IPsec PE-PE

The applicability of IPsec between PEs is when the core may not be pure MPLS, but rather IP based. The principle behind the use of IPsec between PEs is to protect against misbehaving transit nodes.

However, with PE-PE IPsec, snooping on the link is possible. Recall that your weakest link is between the PE and CE.

The best practice is to implement CE-CE IPsec when required, or consider an alternative technology implementation such as MPLS over L2TPv3, which we will discuss in the next section.

Table 5-3 compares security aspects between IPsec CE-CE and IPsec PE-PE.

Table 5-3   *Nonapplication: Customer Security*

Hacker wants to. . .	IPsec CE-CE	IPsec PE-PE
Read VPN traffic	Protects fully	Protects partially
Insert traffic into VPN	Protects fully	Protects partially
Join a VPN	Protects fully	Doesn't protect
DoS a VPN/the core	Doesn't protect	Doesn't protect

MPLS over IP Operational Considerations: L2TPv3

In addition to running MPLS with label-based forwarding in the core, there are quite a few options for the deployment of MPLS over IP, such as:

- MPLS directly over IP
- MPLS over "Full" GRE/IP
- MPLS over "Simple" GRE/IP
- MPLS over L2TPv3 w/BGP Tunnel Subsequent Family Address Identifier(SAFI)
- Each of the above with IPsec

On an MPLS core with label-based forwarding it is not possible to insert spoofed packets from the outside of the core because labeled packets are not accepted on outside interfaces (Inter-AS presents an exception here; see Chapter 3 for details). If IP-based forwarding is used on the core, however, this architectural separation no longer exists. Additional security measures must be taken to protect packet spoofing from the outside.

MPLS over GRE, for example, relies 100 percent on L3 ACLs on outside-facing interfaces to protect the VPNs from spoofed data. In this scenario, a service provider IP address can be discovered or easily guessed. The GRE header contains constant, well-known values, and the MPLS VPN label is 20 bits of variant data that must be guessed by the hacker.

How quickly can a hacker guess a correct 20-bit MPLS label? The hacker can launch an attack as follows:

- 100 packet-per-second attack rate
- 100 active VPN labels (routes) on a PE

Answer:

It takes only 1 minute, 45 seconds to find a valid VPN label! However, this attack form has some serious limitations:

- The hacker does not know which VPN has been intruded.
- While the VPN label is being guessed, it is hard to insert significant traffic into a VPN; usually this attack is limited to a single or few packets entering.
- In addition to guessing a valid VPN label, it is necessary to craft a valid and meaningful IP packet underneath the guessed label. This means the hacker must either guess or find out about IP addressing in the VPN.

The hacker does not see any return traffic because the reverse direction does not work. However, even single packets can be a security threat, for example in the spreading of worms. In order to avoid becoming a transit point for packets inserted into a customer VPN, IP ACLs alone are not a robust solution because they are hard to maintain 100 percent correct on all entry points. IPsec may be used with any MPLS over IP tunnel type; this is a very secure solution, but may be rather expensive to deploy; however, this is a decision for the customer to make. What is still required is an additional layer of protection to make spoofing far more difficult than it is today with GRE, but without the overhead of IPsec.

Figure 5-1 illustrates a blind insertion attack for VPN access.

Figure 5-1   *VPN Services over IP Tunnels: Blind Insertion Attack for VPN Access*

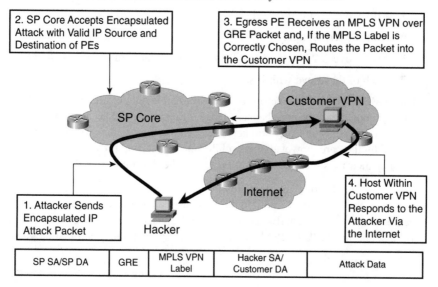

MPLS over L2TPv3

L2TPv3 provides an efficient method to make simple packet spoofing attacks harder. Protection occurs at the most important point, right before entering the customer VPN.

There is no requirement for encryption hardware to use MPLS over L2TPv3.

Rather than checking an IP source or destination address, L2TPv3 "seeds" each packet with a random value selected by each PE and advertised to other PEs in the VPN via the BGP Tunnel SAFI. This function is somewhat analogous to an ACL, but easier to manage and hard for a hacker to guess.

To spoof VPNs over L2TPv3 tunnels, we assume the following: The L2TPv3 session ID may be known, as it could be predictable or even hard-coded to a constant for some services in order to optimize forwarding.

How quickly can a hacker guess a correct 64-bit L2TPv3 cookie? The hacker can launch an attack as follows:

- 10 Mbps attack rate
- Any VPN labels is considered valid

Answer: 60,000 years!

Therefore, if an MPLS core uses IP-based traffic forwarding and if IPsec between the PEs is too expensive to deploy, then the best alternative for MPLS over IP is the use of L2TPv3.

Table 5-4 compares these security factors amongst the various MPLS over IP types.

Table 5-4   *VPN Services over IP Tunnels: Review of Capabilities*

	Static IP	Static GRE Overlay	Dynamic Multipoint GRE	L2TPv3 w/SAFI
Encapsulates MPLS over IP	Yes	Yes	Yes	Yes
Tested in a large active deployment	?	Yes	?	Yes
Avoids full mesh via scalable, dynamic, p2mp tunnels	No	No	Yes	Yes
Avoids blackholes by advertising tunnel capabilities	No	No	No	Yes
Encapsulation facilitates highspeed lookup and distributed processing assist	No	No	No	Yes
Simple, scalable, antispoofing protection built-in	No	No	No	Yes

Securing Core and Routing Check List

The following provides a brief checklist of the recommendations detailed within this overall chapter:

- Use static routing between PE and CE if possible.
- If dynamic routing is required between PE and CE, secure the peering using MD5:
    - Use eBGP as the dynamic routing protocol if possible.
    - Configure "maximum prefix" limits per VRF and per neighbor.
    - Establish "dampening" parameters.
    - If MD5 is not possible, use **distance** to mark all but the peering router as unreliable.
    - Only use EIGRP/OSPF/RIP as PE-CE routing protocol if static/eBGP routing are not available and only if PE-CE links are point-to-point.
    - Minimize and secure access to PE and CE routers.
    - Limit access to devices within the span of control of the operating entity; that is, customers do not access SP routers, and SP does not access customer routers.
    - Define ACLs and apply "access-group" to VTYs.
    - Use AAA and centralized servers to control access.
    - Protect access to console and auxiliary ports.
    - Use CoPP and AutoSecure.
    - Use SSH for access to router VTYs.
    - If SSH not availablem then use ACLs to control telnet access.
    - Limit SNMP access to specific servers through ACLs.
    - Provide only read-only SNMP access.
    - Use receive ACLs where possible.
    - Use iACLs to secure the core.
    - Log, log, log
    - Implement uRPF on all edge routers
    - Use "strict" mode wherever possible.
    - Use "loose" mode if strict cannot be applied.
    - Apply QoS/policing to PE/CE interfaces to control offered loads.
    - Implement DMZs using IDS and firewalls to protect networks from intrusions as discussed in the previous chapter.
    - Run CE-to-CE IPsec where data sensitivity or environment demands.

— Use MD5 for LDP in the core.

— Use MPLS over L2TPv3 when considering an MPLS over IP deployment scenario for best practice security.

See Appendix A for a detailed configuration example of a provider edge router.

Figure 5-2 depicts the requisite best practice functions for each of the network components, such as P, PE, and CE.

Figure 5-2 *Securing the MPLS Core*

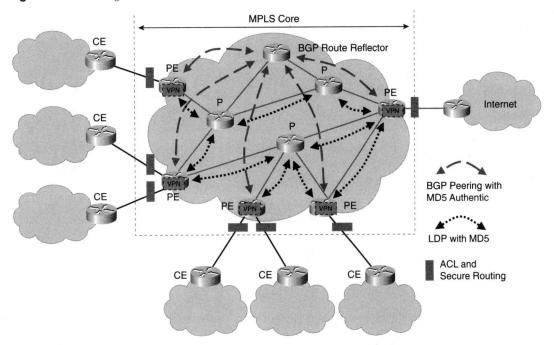

Summary

In this chapter, we provided an operational overview of security considerations for each MPLS VPN component—for example, P, PE and CE. Using a building block approach in order to understand essential service and topological factors that affect security mechanisms, we have recommended best practice guidelines for each MPLS VPN service component. We introduced topics and basic configurations, such as Layer 2, which we will further discuss in Chapters 7 and 9. Finally, we summarized the best practices into an implementation checklist and supplied actual configuration examples that highlight principles discussed in this chapter.

Part III

Practical Guidelines to MPLS VPN Security

In this chapter, you learn about the following:

- Where IPsec can be used in an MPLS VPN environment and what the benefits are
- Where PE-PE IPsec is applicable
- How IPsec remote access works

CHAPTER 6

How IPsec Complements MPLS

When the idea of MPLS VPNs was first discussed, there was a strong notion of competition between MPLS VPNs and IPsec VPNs. Many people voiced concern that MPLS VPN technology does not add significant advantages over IPsec VPNs and, indeed, that it is inferior in some respects: by default, MPLS VPNs do not provide confidentiality on the network, for example.

Today, there is at least a strong market perception that MPLS VPNs are useful. Indeed, both MPLS VPNs and IPsec VPNs have significant deployments, and that suggests that both types have their benefits, albeit in different scenarios. The benefits of MPLS VPNs are primarily on the service provider side, where this technology allows highly scalable VPN architectures, with integrated QoS support. The VPN customer benefits indirectly through lower prices because the service provider can offer a VPN service more cheaply. IPsec VPNs have their main benefit in customer network security: data in transit are encrypted, authenticated, and integrity is maintained.

We will not engage here in an argument about which of the VPN technologies is better or more suitable for a given network. Instead, we will provide technical arguments on how the two VPN technologies can be used together. Both have advantages for different target groups—the VPN customer and the service provider. The combination of the two can result in a very compelling overall VPN architecture.

The first section of this chapter gives an overview of various deployment scenarios of IPsec together with MPLS. The subsequent sections give more detail on each of them. Finally, some practical decision guidelines are given on how to decide which way of mapping IPsec onto MPLS is the best for a given case.

IPsec Overview

IPsec is a technology that offers security services across an IP network:

- Confidentiality through the use of encryption
- Authenticity through the use of peer and message authentication
- Integrity through the use of message integrity checks
- Anti-replay, by using authenticated sequence numbers, to guarantee freshness of a message

One of the key advantages of IPsec is that its security services are all applied in Layer 3, the network layer, just as with IP. This way, the security services remain independent of the underlying transport mechanism as well as the protocols and applications used on top of the stack.

NOTE   IPsec addresses most typical security requirements, such as confidentiality, as just discussed. An important requirement that IPsec does not provide an answer to, however, is availability. The use of IPsec typically does not make networks less vulnerable to DoS attacks.

IPsec can, in principle, be applied end to end, for example, between a client and a server. IPsec *transport mode* can be used for this. However, the most widespread use of IPsec today is between specific IPsec gateways—in a company network, for example. In that case, traffic within an office (a trusted zone) is usually in clear, with the IPsec gateways securing the traffic over the public network. In this case, *tunnel mode* is used to tunnel packets securely from one office to the other. Figure 6-1 shows both transport mode and tunnel mode with their typical applications.

NOTE   In colloquial language, IPsec "encrypts" packets. Here we use the term "secure" instead because encryption is only one of several features of IPsec.

Figure 6-1   *IPsec Transport Mode and Tunnel Mode*

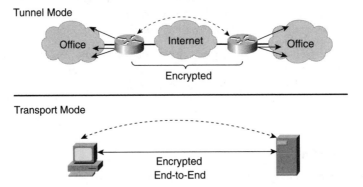

With those two connection modes, there are two ways to map clear-text IP packets into an IPsec packet. In tunnel mode, the entire clear-text IP packet is secured, and a new IP header is prepended, followed by an IPsec header that identifies the logical connection between the IPsec gateways. In transport mode, the original IP header is preserved, and the IPsec header is inserted before the secured IP packet. Figure 6-2 displays these two packet formats.

Figure 6-2   *IPsec Packet Formats*

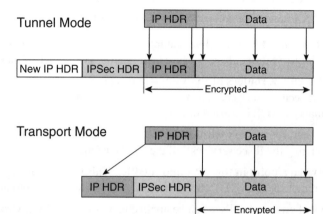

A single IPsec tunnel connects two sites. By adding more tunnels, a VPN can be constructed between the IPsec gateways. This can be done in a full mesh topology, a hub-and-spoke topology, or any mixture of the two. Figure 6-3 shows basic VPN topologies that can be built using IPsec.

Figure 6-3   *IPsec VPN Topologies*

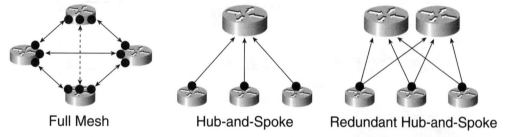

When securing a network—for example, let's say a bank network with two central offices and 100 branch offices—the key design criterion is where to place the IPsec gateways. In most designs, the offices of the bank each would be considered a trusted zone, with the communication infrastructure between them being untrusted from the VPN customer's point of view. In such a design, the IPsec gateways must be inside the trusted zones for the overall VPN to remain protected with the IPsec services.

When designing an IPsec overlay network, two main topics must be discussed:

- Where should the IPsec tunnels be applied?

- How should the tunnels be established?

For both questions, there are a number of options. So, we'll first discuss the location of the IPsec termination points; later, we'll discuss the way tunnels are established between those sites.

Location of the IPsec Termination Points

In an MPLS VPN environment, IPsec can be applied at various points of the network:

- **Within the VPN sites**—For example, end-to-end IPsec security. (This case will not be discussed further here because here security is completely independent of MPLS.)

- **Between CE routers of the VPN**—In this case, the MPLS core is also not involved in the security services. The trust of this solution depends on whether the party who manages the CE is trusted or not.

- **Between PE routers within the MPLS VPN core**—Here, the service provider is managing the IPsec services and the VPN customer has no visibility of it.

- **Between a point in the VPN and the PE**—This is a special case and is usually used for remote access of PC clients (for example, teleworkers) into an MPLS VPN.

Figure 6-4 shows where IPsec can be applied in an MPLS VPN environment.

Figure 6-4 *IPsec Termination Points in an MPLS VPN Environment*

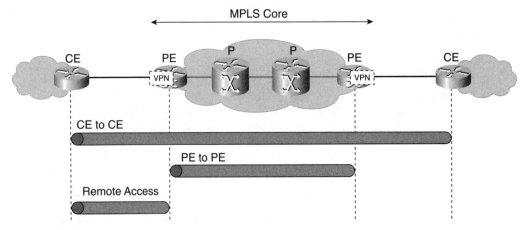

Different termination points provide different security properties. A fundamental principle is that the IPsec gateway must be within a trusted zone and operated by a trusted party.

In the following sections, the various options to provide IPsec on an MPLS VPN infrastructure are discussed in detail. This is followed by an overview of the options, with a discussion of where the different scenarios are applicable.

CE-CE IPsec

If IPsec is used between the CEs, the entire path between the CEs is protected—the access lines (between CE and PE), as well as the entire MPLS core consisting of PEs, Ps, and lines. The assumption for this model is that the CE is located in the trusted zone—that is, the office building with access control and physical security. The operator of the gateway must be trusted: either it is an employee of the VPN customer, or the outsourcing partner is trusted. The outsourcing partner could be the service provider. Figure 6-5 outlines the CE-CE IPsec model.

Figure 6-5   *IPsec from CE to CE*

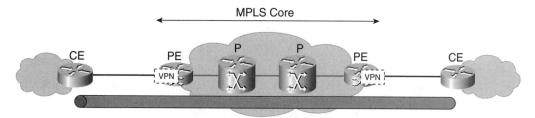

CE-CE IPsec is an appropriate solution for securing the VPN customer's traffic across an untrusted infrastructure. Two key requirements are typically the reason for using CE-CE IPsec:

- Traffic must be secured whenever it is outside a trusted zone (office). This includes the access lines, the core lines, but also potential sniffing directly on core devices. This requirement can come from the company's security policy, but it could also be a legal requirement, such as when personal data are transmitted over public networks.

- The MPLS VPN service provider is not trusted. As discussed in Chapter 3, "MPLS Security Analysis," in a standard MPLS VPN network the customer must trust the service provider. The service provider can make any VPN insecure by misconfiguring a PE router, for example. If the VPN customer protects all data in transit with IPsec CE-CE, however, this trust can be very limited. Not even misconfiguration is an issue because all packets are verified to come from a trusted source.

NOTE   **Recommendation**

If encryption is required or the service provider is not trusted (misconfiguration and related issues), then IPsec between CEs under the operational control of the VPN customer is the recommended way to secure the VPN.

IPsec CE-CE protects against the following threats (note in brackets the service that provides the feature):

- Eavesdropping anywhere between the CEs. Note that the most critical part to protect is typically the access line: it is usually easier to find and record traffic on the access line than in the core. (confidentiality)

- Insertion of bogus packets into the network. (authenticity)

- Change of packets in transit. (integrity)
- Replay of legitimate, recorded packets (anti-replay)

By protecting against these basic threats, IPsec CE-CE also provides implicit protection in the following cases:

- Insertion of a bogus CE into the VPN: this cannot happen because the bogus CE would not be able to authenticate against a legitimate CE.
- Leakage of other VPNs' traffic into the secured VPN: if through misconfiguration traffic from another VPN were redirected to a CE, this traffic would be discarded because the packets cannot be authenticated.
- Leakage of traffic from the secured VPN into another, nontrusted VPN: traffic from the secured VPN in transit would be encrypted, and the nontrusted VPN would not be able to see the clear-text traffic.

IPsec CE-CE does not protect against the following threats:

- **Denial of service (DoS) from outside the trusted VPN into the VPN**—IPsec does not improve the availability of a service. In fact, it has been argued that IPsec gateways themselves might become a target for DoS attacks. While this is theoretically true, availability is a difficult issue for any type of service, and IPsec does not make an exception here.
- **Threats within the trusted zone**—An example would be a worm outbreak within the VPN that would be carried over the IPsec tunnels, just as legitimate traffic.

Overall, CE-CE IPsec provides an ideal means of securing an MPLS VPN beyond the standard security of MPLS networks. It is the technique of choice for providing additional security such as traffic encryption to an MPLS VPN.

Opponents to MPLS would, at this point, argue that because IPsec provides all necessary VPN functions and indeed more than standard MPLS (encryption, for example), MPLS is not really required. In considering this argument, two topics have to be discussed separately: security and packet transport. Even if IPsec would be sufficient, the IPsec packets have to be transported from one CE to another. In most cases, MPLS VPN services are cheaper for this type of service than general IPsec service for all office sites. It should also be noted that at the time of this writing most MPLS VPN services were not additionally secured with IPsec, meaning that most MPLS VPN customers do trust their service providers and do not require encryption over the wide area network.

The reason why CE-CE IPsec is not that widely implemented today was until recently, to a large extent, due to the complexity of implementing an IPsec overlay network: there were scalability issues that made large IPsec deployments complex. New deployment models, such as DMVPN and GD01 significantly improve scalability. Later in this chapter, we discuss the various types of IPsec deployments and their scalability.

To work around the scalability issues of CE-based IPsec VPNs, some consultants have proposed the usage of PE-based IPsec services. This would make IPsec a network service; however, there are potential security problems with this model.

PE-PE IPsec

Quite often, PE-PE IPsec is seen as a way to avoid the VPN customer having to set up CE-based IPsec. Some consultants position this as an architecture similar in security but much easier to implement, especially for the customer. Figure 6-6 displays PE-based IPsec services.

Figure 6-6   *IPsec from PE to PE*

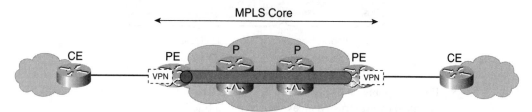

The perception is that the main threat for VPN security is eavesdropping on the MPLS core. In practice, this is not correct: it is much easier for an attacker to find a local loop close to an office building and to sniff traffic on this line than it is to do the same on the MPLS core.

NOTE   **Recommendation**

If the purpose of the IPsec deployment is VPN security, then PE-based IPsec does not address all the requirements: specifically, the local loop (CE-PE) is not secured.

The Internet Draft "Use of PE-PE IPsec in RFC2547 VPNs" (draft-ietf-l3vpn-ipsec-2547-03.txt) describes how IPsec can be used to encrypt data between PEs. This document is clear about the aforementioned issue: "IPsec Security Associations that associate ingress PE routes with egress PE routers do not ensure privacy for VPN data."

In this mode, the LSPs in the MPLS core are replaced with IPsec tunnels. Therefore, it is also an alternative for running RFC 2547bis networks over a non-MPLS infrastructure. Figure 6-7 shows the encapsulation used:

1 The VPN label is prepended to the VPN packet as in normal MPLS; however, IPsec can only secure IP packets, not labeled packets.

2 Therefore, the labeled packet is first encapsulated in *Generic Routing Encapsulation (GRE)*.

3 The GRE packet can then be secured with IPsec. Because the endpoints of the GRE tunnel are the same as for the IPsec tunnel, transport mode can be used, and this reuses the GRE header.

Figure 6-7 *IPsec Encapsulation for PE-PE Security*

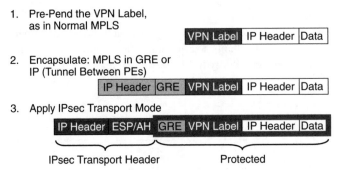

IPsec PE-PE provides adequate protection for the following threats:

- Eavesdropping on lines between the PEs or P routers—specifically, if the MPLS core is routed over untrusted areas such as the public Internet.

- Misbehavior of P routers, which can lead to packets being changed or routed to the wrong egress PE.

It does not, however, provide VPN security.

There are a few security-related special cases where PE-PE IPsec is applicable and usable.

In the United States, ILEC market state carriers hold local VPN connections on their PE routers. To connect to another VPN site in another state, the carriers need to traverse a public network. PE-PE IPsec is an adequate technology for securing this transit. In this case, however, the MPLS core as such cannot be assumed to be a closed, trusted zone. Using IPsec provides this security, and it is largely transparent to the VPN customers because they perceive that they are connected to an overall trusted MPLS VPN core.

In a European country, the government was connecting various ministries to a national government backbone. At the time, there was no MPLS service available, so the government built a network of leased lines and connected routers to them. Because the government wanted to provide VPNs to the ministries, it built its own MPLS core, connected by those leased lines. The PEs were all located in secure government buildings, but the lines were not secure, so PE-PE IPsec encryption was also chosen in this special case. Note that this deployment is not comparable to normal service provider MPLS VPN deployments because in this case the "Provider Edge" routers are really customer edge equipment and, therefore, from a logical point of view, IPsec is applied from customer site to customer site. This deployment model does provide customer security.

The alternative would be to run IPsec between CEs, but this situation would be more complex because typically the number of CEs is significantly higher than the number of PEs.

Except in special cases, PE-PE IPsec currently is not much used for security reasons. It is clearly not a generic solution for VPN security. CE-CE IPsec should be used in those cases.

Apart from using IPsec between CE-CE and PE-PE, there is a third form of using IPsec: as a way of remotely accessing a VPN.

Remote Access IPsec into an MPLS VPN

In enterprise networks, teleworkers connect to their home networks via VPN: this used to be dialup; however, today most traveling employees use IPsec to connect from wireless hot spots, hotels, and conference buildings to their offices. In the traditional setup, an enterprise provisions a VPN concentrator in its own network. If an enterprise is already a customer on an MPLS VPN service, it is easy to outsource the IPsec remote access to the service provider. Figure 6-8 shows this setup.

Figure 6-8   *IPsec Remote Access into MPLS VPN*

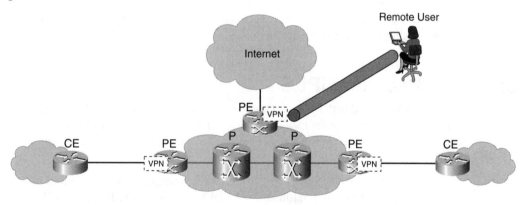

The IPsec tunnel from the remote user is terminated on the PE router, where, based on the user's identity, he or she is mapped into the VPN. The PE router therefore fulfills two tasks: IPsec remote access termination and MPLS PE.

In this application, IPsec serves mainly as a secure access method into the VPN of the user. The protection of IPsec secures the data on transport over any untrusted infrastructure, such as public wireless hot spots or the Internet.

All options for using IPsec have their special applications, pros and cons. The various ways to apply IPsec are summarized in Table 6-1.

Table 6-1   *Summary of IPsec Applications on MPLS*

Protection Against	CE-CE	PE-PE	Remote Access
Eavesdropping on core	Yes	Yes	—
Eavesdropping on access line	Yes	No	—
Receiving traffic from outside a VPN	Yes	No	—
Sending VPN traffic outside the VPN	Yes	No	—
Intrusion via fake CE	Yes	No	—
Access security	—	—	Yes
DoS against the VPN	No	No	—

Table 6-1 illustrates that all three IPsec models have completely different applicability and therefore are not mutually replaceable: CE-CE IPsec protects a VPN against threats from the outside; PE-PE IPsec has very special and limited applications, as described in the previous section; and IPsec remote access is a very special use of IPsec, rather than a generic security solution, in that it protects only the access into the VPN and not general VPN traffic.

Now it should be clear where to implement the IPsec endpoints. The next consideration is how the IPsec tunnels are established. There are various ways to deploy IPsec tunnels, and the next section discusses these options.

Deploying IPsec on MPLS

The models discussed in the previous section describe where IPsec tunnels are established (for example, PE-PE), but not how the tunnels get established, which is the second design consideration when deploying IPsec networks. The main options for IPsec tunnel establishment are

- **Static IPsec**—In this model, every IPsec node is configured statically with all its IPsec peers, the authentication information, and the security policy. This is the oldest way of configuring IPsec. It is hard to configure because each IPsec node requires significant configuration; but because this is the oldest way of configuring IPsec, it is supported on most platforms today. Static IPsec is described in RFC 2401–2412. It can be applied CE-CE and PE-PE.

- **Dynamic IPsec**—In hub-and-spoke environments, the hub can be configured without specific information for each spoke; only the spokes know how to reach the hub, and an IPsec tunnel is established only if the spoke can authenticate itself. Remote access IPsec uses a similar idea, but authentication is usually done on an AAA server. Dynamic IPsec is supported today also, and can be used for CE-CE as well as PE-PE.

- **Dynamic Multipoint VPN (DMVPN)**—This model works with the principle of the *Next Hop Resolution Protocol (NHRP)*: Every IPsec node holds information about how to reach a next hop server, which returns the address of the target IPsec node to the originating node. This is a very scalable way to dynamically establish IPsec tunnels on demand. DMVPN works CE-CE and PE-PE.

- **Group Domain of Interpretation (GDOI)**—All the previous models maintain an IPsec security association per peer, even if the peer is found dynamically. This sets limits to the number of nodes that can be within one IPsec domain because every node must keep state for every active peer. GDOI maintains only a single security association for the whole group of IPsec nodes, such as for all nodes within a VPN. This means that all IPsec nodes in a group must share the same encryption/ authentication key. The key is managed by a secure key server. Each node establishes a static IPsec connection to the key server; the rest of the group is dynamic and does not require state. GDOI is described in RFC 3547. GDOI was not yet available at the time of writing this book.

These various IPsec designs can be quite complex, with many suboptions for each model. This book can only give an overview. For more information on IPsec technology, refer to www.cisco.com/go/ipsec/.

NOTE   As explained in Chapter 1, "MPLS VPN Security: An Overview," the overall security of a solution depends on three parts: correct architecture, operation, and implementation. This section discusses the architecture and its features. To make the overall network secure, the IPsec service must also be implemented and operated correctly.

Using Other Encryption Techniques

IPsec is not the only way to secure data in transit. Long before IPsec became widely available, link encryption devices were used for this purpose. Also, SSL has become more widely used recently.

Link encryption has been used for many years, and a variety of solutions exist on the market for specific link layer protocols. The problem is that link encryption only secures a single link and does not provide end-to-end security from a VPN perspective. Link encryption devices, therefore, are not commonly used in MPLS VPN environments.

The *Secure Sockets Layer (SSL)* has received a lot of attention over the last few years. Both IPsec and SSL provide secure transport but at different points in the stack: IPsec acts at the network layer, which means that it is, just like IP, independent of the transport medium and of the applications that run on top. That means that IPsec can be used on an endpoint without making any change to the applications or to the lower layers in the stack. SSL, however, is based on transport layer security and located at Layer 4 in the stack. This is ideal for applications such as the *Hypertext Transport Protocol (HTTP)*, which is located on top of the TCP layer. However, other protocols have to be mapped onto SSL. Figure 6-9 depicts both protocols and their locations in the stack.

Figure 6-9   *IPsec and SSL*

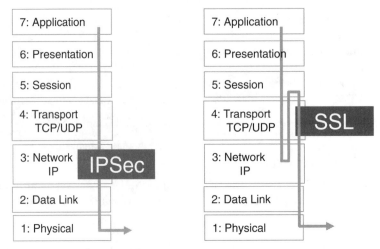

SSL has found application in VPN gateways where limited application support is required, such as when the VPN access is only used to access web pages. The advantage in those scenarios is that SSL does not require a client on the PC.

In MPLS VPN environments, SSL is not used for CE-CE or PE-PE security, but it may be used as a remote access technology. Wherever VPN-level security is required, IPsec is today's key technology, with all its deployment options.

NOTE   There are cases of encryption boxes, which are located in the customer network, behind the CE. These typically fulfill a mixed firewall/encryption function and are sometimes based on SSL. The MPLS network, including the CEs, is not involved in the encryption in this case: it just transports IP packets, which happen to be encrypted.

Summary

IPsec and MPLS VPNs are complementary technologies: MPLS VPNs help service providers scale their VPN networks. This advantage is passed on to the customer as a lower price tag. MPLS offers full VPN separation but no cryptographic security. IPsec helps VPN customers to further secure their VPNs if required. Both technologies work together well.

Before considering specific IPsec solutions over MPLS, the goals should be clearly defined: what are the threats, and what must be protected? With a clear threat model, it is usually easy to find an IPsec deployment model. For example, if the goal is to secure VPN traffic against intrusion, eavesdropping, and misconfiguration of the service provider, the solution must be within the trusted zone of the VPN. This excludes IPsec deployment on PEs. The typical deployment is therefore CE-CE.

There are various options for establishing IPsec tunnels for each of the deployment scenarios. Refer to specific IPsec literature for details; examples are listed in Appendix B.

In this chapter, you learn about the following:

- Generic Layer 2 security as a foundation for Layer 2 over MPLS constructs with an emphasis on Ethernet
- Virtual Private LAN Service (VPLS) security overview
- Virtual Private Wire Service (VPWS) security overview

CHAPTER 7

Security of MPLS Layer 2 VPNs

New architectures allow MPLS to build VPNs interconnecting Layer 2 (L2) networks that transport L2 frames. A Layer 2 VPN comprises switched connections between subscriber endpoints over a shared network. Nonsubscribers do not have access to those same endpoints. Originally designed using network technologies at Layer 2 (Frame Relay, for example), VPNs are now being augmented by packet-based technologies such as IP and MPLS. A shift is underway within service provider networks from circuit-switched to packet-based technology. Virtual Private LAN Service (VPLS) and Virtual Private Wire Service (VPWS) are examples of Layer 2 technologies that make it possible to operate private, multipoint, and point-to-point LANs through public networks. VPWS and VPLS possess different security properties than those within Layer 3 VPNs and will be discussed in this chapter.

Certain aspects of the Layer 2 network architecture have an impact on the mechanisms that can be applied as well as the operational characteristics that need to be addressed. As such, this chapter is structured in consideration of these various schemes. Since many of the recommended practices are applicable across the board, a complete discussion of relevant security recommendations is provided in this chapter.

Generic Layer 2 Security Considerations

Ethernet over MPLS (EoMPLS) is being increasingly deployed in environments where the service provider (SP) does not wish to participate in the management of the customer's Layer 3 routing mechanisms and wishes only to provide a Layer 2 solution similar to traditional Frame Relay and ATM service offerings. Alternatively, some customers may not wish to offload their Layer 3 operations to a service provider, preferring to maintain control over that aspect of their networks themselves. In either of these scenarios, the Layer 2 VPN can meet the applicable network requirements.

In order to protect customer networks, the SP's access network and backbone, and to ensure that service-level expectations can be met, the security considerations of the network must be addressed.

Security in MPLS networks can be viewed from a Layer 2 and Layer 3 perspective. SPs need to concern themselves with securing the network from both layers in order to assure service integrity. In addition, customers need to ensure the security of their own networks, be they L2 implementations or L3-oriented designs. In this section, we introduce generic Layer 2 security issues with a focus on Ethernet, which links Layer 2 with emerging architectures such as Virtual Private LAN Service (VPLS) and Virtual Private Wire Service (VPWS), which will be discussed in the next sections of this chapter.

NOTE   The main security issue behind Layer 2 security is that on a shared Layer 2 medium, for example an Ethernet switch, there is often no control over which side the packets are coming from—whether it be from the customer or other Internet service providers, for example—and consequently, this lack of control permits insertion of traffic from a third party allowing for spoofing of Layer 3 information such as IP addresses. While the control protocols such as routing can be secured via Message Digest-5 (MD-5) mechanisms, the data plane usually is not. So, for example, there may be two CEs connected to a single PE over a shared Ethernet medium, and the security risk is to have all Layer 3 security subverted.

Therefore, it is recommended not to implement this example and to be very cognizant of these issues associated with a shared Ethernet switch example.

C2 Ethernet Topologies

This section discusses the EoMPLS topology solutions that will be addressed in this chapter. From the perspective of the SP to customer interconnect, the three scenarios are as follows:

- **Ethernet single point-to-point connectivity**—Provides a single, port-based Ethernet connection between two physical data ports provided across an MPLS network, which is the foundation for VPWS.

  The port may operate in a direct Ethernet ARPA encapsulation mode or in an 802.1Q encapsulation format, but all traffic entering that physical port will be transported to a remote end without alteration.

  Generally, such a design would be used with a Layer 3 customer network where the typical WAN serial links are replaced with higher speed point-to-point facilities. Alternatively, the customer network may comprise a Layer 2 domain where the customer desires to interconnect various LAN islands into a larger whole using the SP's Layer 2 services. In either case, the Layer 2 VPN network is a transport for customer frames in a similar manner as a set of dedicated links.

- **Multiple Ethernet point-to-point connectivity**—This concept builds on the previous scenario by allowing for subinterface (VLAN)–based point-to-point connections across the WAN cloud. VLANs defined on the physical port may be switched to differing destination endpoints in this model. Typically, the customer network is a Layer 3 entity and the customer is seeking a service from the SP analogous to a traditional Frame Relay or ATM offering.

- **Multipoint mesh connectivity**—While efforts are underway in various vendor communities and standards bodies to provide multipoint L2VPN connectivity, these mechanisms are not yet generally available. The previous two scenarios simply provide one or more point-to-point connections to allow for the desired degree of network meshing. In the future, this meshing (or bridging, if preferred) will use the service provider network resources to provide true multipoint connectivity; that is, from the customer edge's perspective, a single connection into the service provider network that has the appearance of a LAN interconnect (or bridged interconnect) to some or all of the customer's other CE gear. This approach is frequently referred to as transparent LAN services (TLS), which is the foundation for VPLS.

Figure 7-1 summarizes these topology examples, note that hub-and-spoke and ring implementations are options for deployment at the customer locations.

Figure 7-1   *Current Ethernet Architecture Examples*

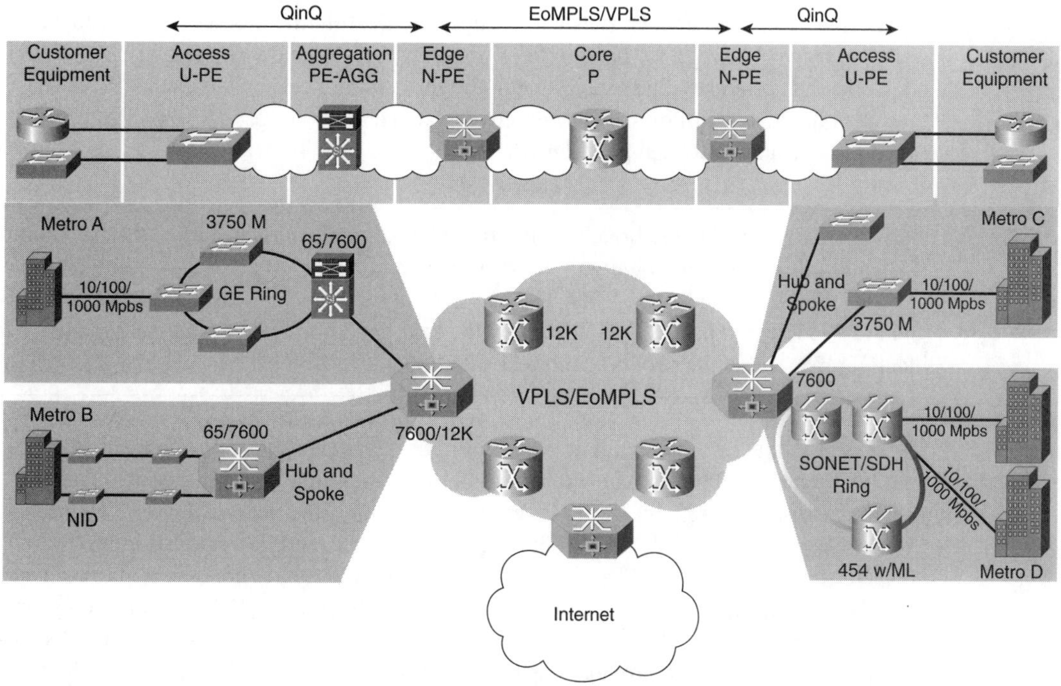

C3 VPLS Overview

Virtual Private LAN Service (VPLS) is a VPN technology that enables Ethernet multipoint services (EMSs) over a packet-switched network infrastructure. VPN users receive an emulated LAN segment that offers a Layer 2 broadcast domain. The end user perceives the service as a virtual private Ethernet switch that forwards frames to their respective destinations within the VPN.

Ethernet is the technology of choice for LANs due to its relative low cost and simplicity. Ethernet has also gained recent popularity as a metropolitan area network (MAN or metro) technology.

A multipoint technology allows a user to reach multiple destinations through a single physical or logical connection. This requires the network to make a forwarding decision based on the destination of the packet. Within the context of VPLS, this means that the network makes a forwarding decision based on the destination MAC address of the Ethernet frame. A multipoint service is attractive because fewer connections are required to achieve full connectivity between multiple points. An equivalent level of connectivity based on a point-to-point technology requires a much larger number of connections or the use of suboptimal packet forwarding.

In its simplest form, a VPLS consists of several sites connected to provider edge devices implementing the emulated LAN service. These provider edge devices make the forwarding decisions between sites and encapsulate the Ethernet frames across a packet-switched network using a virtual circuit or pseudowire. A virtual switching instance (VSI) is used at each provider edge to implement the forwarding decisions of each VPLS. The provider edges use a full mesh of Ethernet-emulated circuits (or pseudowires) to forward the Ethernet frames between provider edges.

NOTE   One security flag is that the broadcast/multicast packet replication occurs in the backbone (PE), and this factor could be high—for example greater than 10 or 20 depending on the number of PEs involved in the VPN. Therefore, what may appear "reasonable" at the U-PE and local loop could have a DoS impact on the backbone itself. This is a deployment planning matter that the network architect should be cognizant of.

VPLS uses a Layer 2 architecture to offer multipoint Ethernet VPNs that connect multiple sites over a metropolitan area network (MAN) or WAN. Other technologies also enable Ethernet across the WAN, including Ethernet over MPLS, Ethernet over Layer 2 Tunneling Protocol Version 3 (L2TPv3), Ethernet over SONET/SDH, and Ethernet Bridging over Any Transport over MPLS (AToM). Even though most VPLS sites are expected to connect via Ethernet, they may connect using other Layer 2 technologies (ATM, Frame Relay, or Point-to-Point Protocol [PPP], for example). Sites connecting with non-Ethernet links exchange packets with the provider edge using a bridged encapsulation. The configuration requirements on the customer edge device are similar to the requirements for Ethernet interworking in point-to-point Layer 2 services.

This section is specific to multipoint constructs. VPLS is designed for applications that require multipoint or broadcast access. Using established VPLS, service providers can create a Layer 2 "virtual switch" over an MPLS core to establish a distributed network access point (NAP). The NAP permits transparent private peering between multiple service providers (SPs) and delivers connections to multiple sites within a specific metro region.

SP-to-SP VPLS can be supported using either Border Gateway Protocol (BGP) or Label Distribution Protocol (LDP). LDP provides more granular control of communication and quality of service between VPLS nodes, more control per node, and is a consistent signaling option to support MPLS, VPLS, or VPWS, whereas BGP communicates the same information to all nodes participating in a VPLS. The hierarchical VPLS architecture includes customer edge devises connected to provider edge routers that aggregate VPLS traffic before it reaches the network provider edge routers, where the VPLS forwarding occurs. In summary, key VPLS architectural attributes include the use of BGP or RADIUS for discovery membership and the use of LDP to establish pseudowires per broadcast domain instance.

C4 VPWS Overview

VPWS makes integration of existing Layer 2 and Layer 3 services possible on a point-to-point basis across a service provider's IP/MPLS network. Implementation examples include Any Transport over MPLS (AToM) and L2TPv3. Both AToM and L2TPv3 support the transport of Frame Relay, ATM, High-Level Data Link Control (HDLC), and Ethernet traffic over an IP/MPLS core.

C5 VPLS and VPWS Service Summary and Metro Ethernet Architecture Overview

The key attribute with VPLS and VPWS is the concept of an Ethernet virtual circuit (EVC). VPLS and VPWS constructs may be summarized as port based and VLAN based. The port-based example is point-to-point for deployment of an Ethernet wire service (EWS) which is deployed with a private line replacement via a router or a bridge. A point-to-point Ethernet service may interconnect with ATM and Frame Relay. Another port-based example is multipoint-to-multipoint for an Ethernet multipoint service (EMS), where each location acts as if it is connecting to a switch.

Ethernet Relay Service (ERS) is an example of a VLAN-based construct where one could have multiple EVCs per port. This service may be used as a Frame Relay replacement, where an EVC is similar to a Frame Relay PVC in function. Ethernet Relay Multipoint Services (ERMS) is another example of a VLAN-based construct for multiple EVCs per port. Finally, at Layer 1, there is the concept of Ethernet Private Line (EPL), such as over SONET/SDH. Figures 7-2 and 7-3 summarize these service examples for Ethernet-based services. Together, these service types comprise the Metro Ethernet Architecture.

Figure 7-2 *Ethernet Baseline Services Matrix*

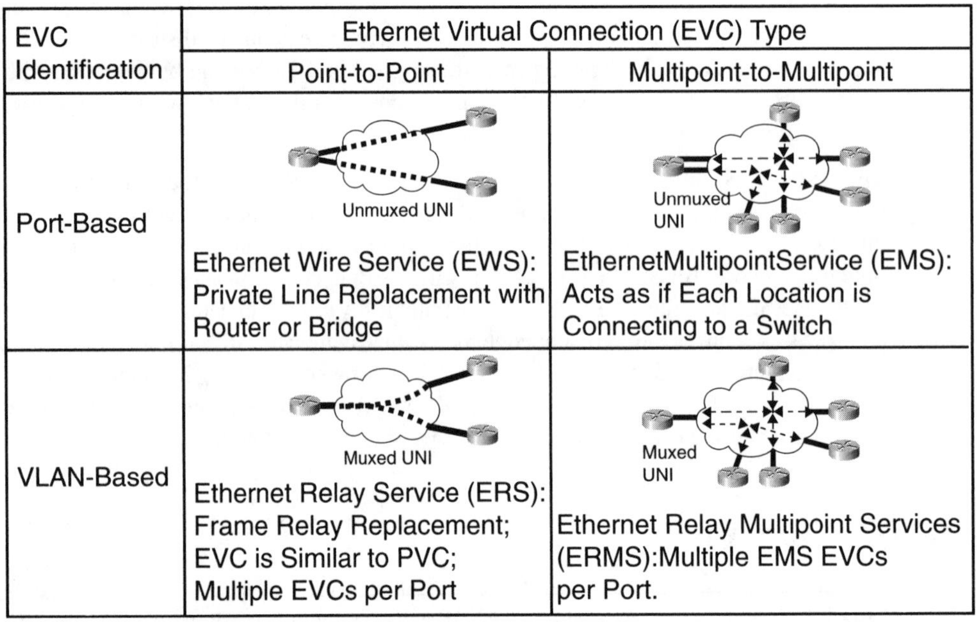

EVC Identification	Ethernet Virtual Connection (EVC) Type	
	Point-to-Point	Multipoint-to-Multipoint
Port-Based	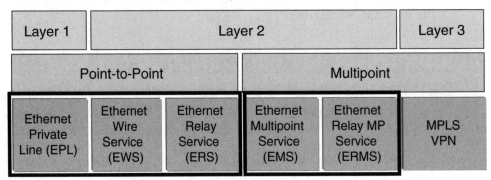 Unmuxed UNI Ethernet Wire Service (EWS): Private Line Replacement with Router or Bridge	Unmuxed UNI EthernetMultipointService (EMS): Acts as if Each Location is Connecting to a Switch
VLAN-Based	Muxed UNI Ethernet Relay Service (ERS): Frame Relay Replacement; EVC is Similar to PVC; Multiple EVCs per Port	Muxed UNI Ethernet Relay Multipoint Services (ERMS):Multiple EMS EVCs per Port.

Figure 7-3 *Cisco Metro Ethernet Services Summary*

Layer 1	Layer 2					Layer 3
	Point-to-Point			Multipoint		
Ethernet Private Line (EPL)	Ethernet Wire Service (EWS)	Ethernet Relay Service (ERS)	Ethernet Multipoint Service (EMS)	Ethernet Relay MP Service (ERMS)		MPLS VPN

The main components of the Metro Ethernet Architecture are as follows:

- Access user PE or access U-PE, which is where the admission control and security policy enforcements occur.

- Aggregation-PE or PE_Agg, which aggregates traffic and enforces congestion management mechanisms.

- Edge Network PE or N-PE, where services such as VPLS and VPWS are fundamentally deployed.

- Provider node or P-node for packet forwarding and implementing traffic engineering.

Figure 7-4 illustrates the Metro Ethernet Architecture model and functional roles.

Figure 7-4   *Metro Ethernet Architecture and Functional Roles*

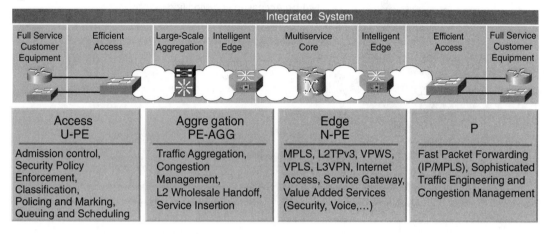

C6 VPLS and VPWS Security Overview

The fundamental security considerations for VPLS and VPWS constructs are to assure the integrity of the U-PE configurations and to prevent DoS and resource starvation attacks against the U-PE, N-PE, and PE-AGG devices. Figure 7-5 shows the untrusted zone, such as floor (of a building) customer switches to an U-PE (or customer UNI to a service provider component). The trust is from a service provider perspective because it is assumed that the U-PE, N-PE, and PE-AGG devices are within the service provider's control. We will introduce types of attacks for these services and the appropriate defenses in this section; the attack details and defense mechanisms will be discussed later in this chapter.

Figure 7-5 depicts the trusted and untrusted zones for VPLS-based service.

Attack mechanisms may be categorized as follows:

- MAC attacks (content-addressable memory or CAM overflow)
- Broadcast/multicast storm attacks
- VLAN hopping or Dynamic Trunking Protocol (DTP) attacks
- Spanning tree attacks
- DHCP rogue server attacks
- Hijack management access

Table 7-1 summarizes these attacks and the appropriate defensive responses. This table is the foundation of our security discussion in this chapter.

Figure 7-5 *Metro Ethernet Security Mode*

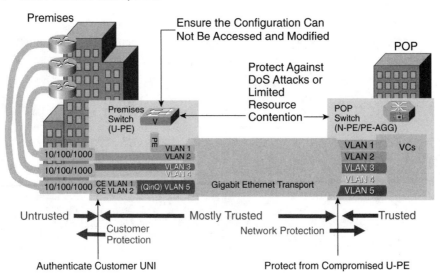

Table 7-1 *VPLS/VPWS Attack Points and Defensive Actions*

Attack	Defensive Features/Actions
MAC attacks (CAM table overflow)	Port security, per-VLAN MAC limiting
Broadcast/multicast storm attacks	Storm control
VLAN hopping, DTP attacks	Careful configuration (disable autotrunking, used dedicated VLAN-ID for trunk ports, set user ports to nontrunking, VLAN 1 minimization, disable unused ports, and so on)
Spanning tree attacks	BPDU guard, root guard, MD5 VTP authentication
DHCP rogue server attack	DHCP snooping (differentiate trusted and untrusted ports)
Hijack management access	Secure variants of management access protocols (not telnet, etc., but SSH and out-of-band management), disable password recovery, encrypted passwords
Proactive defense	Deploy MAC-level port security, wire-speed ACLs, 802.1x

NOTE   A constantly flapping port may cause LDP generating/withdrawing labels and denial of service to the protocol stack.

Note that the IETF (Martini) drafts permit a copy of the VLAN priority fields into the MPLS EXP, and we recommend awareness of this fact.

Physical Interconnection Option Details

The three scenarios previously described can be physically structured in a number of ways:

- Layer 2 end-to-end with no customer VLANs, essentially "port mode" operations. Layer 2 end-to-end with customer VLANs where customer VLANs are transported to customer remote sites, either transparently (ingress/egress VLANs are consistent or customer VLANs are modified by the service provider transport network). Service provider Layer 2 transport of Layer 3 customer edge facing the service provider Layer 2 MPLS network is a router similar to the typical Frame Relay model.

- Service provider Layer 3 interconnect to Layer 2 customer edge is an example of a customer network using a service provider for Layer 3 routing.

D1 SP Interconnect Models

Interconnect models include the following types:

- **Single PE**—The CE device is connected directly to the SP's PE (aka Network-PE [n-PE]), which implements full EoMPLS functionality and provides access facilities, encapsulation/decapsulation, and transport over the core.

- **Distributed PE**—The SP locates an extension of its PE edge device on physical premises that are not directly under SP control (referred to as a "Provider Edge–Customer Located Equipment (PE-CLE)" or "User-PE (U-PE)") and performs part of the EoMPLS interconnect operations—namely, access facilities and some encapsulation mechanism, with the N-PE providing core access.

  This allows the service provider to multiplex many customers' sites over a shared infrastructure—perhaps a fiber ring. In this case, it becomes imperative that the U-PE be very tightly secured because it is exposed in a location where the SP may not be able to monitor access.

NOTE	**Recommendation**
	We recommend that no service provider edge (PE) router be located at a customer premise because such an installation exposes the service provider to unwelcome access. Further, in order to mitigate against control plane spoofing, examples of protocols that should never be exposed to untrusted routers include IGP, BGP, LDP, and RSVP-TE.

The physical structure of the SP access network generally takes the following forms:

- Point-to-point links including hub-and-spoke and tree topologies, where a CE is connected with a point-to-point link directly to an N-PE or to an aggregation PE that grooms some set of links into point-to-point connections to the PE. Security considerations reflect the degree of separation inherent in a point-to-point network layout.

- Ring topology, where customer edge devices are connected to User provider edge (U-PE) devices that are interconnected in a ring formation with an N-PE node providing access to the service provider core.

In this scenario, the shared medium transports a variety of Layer 2 VLANs from a single customer with several physically colocated sites. In addition, this ring may also support VLANs from other customers that the SP can service in that same geographical area. As such, the design needs to address the possibilities of overlapping VLANs, where different customers may have the same VLAN ID and are unwilling to change them. This requires the use of some sort of tag prepending to the packets prior to its forwarding through the shared medium. This can be accomplished either through MPLS tagging of the frames (requiring an MPLS-aware universal provider edge device) or through QinQ VLAN tagging (an additional IEEE 802.1Q VLAN tag is inserted above the customer's VLAN tags).

The QinQ approach is typically used today because the low-cost, MPLS-aware User provider edge devices are still not widely available. As such, the upper VLAN tag that the SP defines must be carefully administered by the SP so that misdirected traffic scenarios do not occur.

D3 Metro Ethernet Model

A typical implementation of an EoMPLS network is the Metro Ethernet Model. In this topology, the service provider extends an Ethernet connection to the customer's network as an access medium to the Layer 2 service being offered. This provides a relatively high bandwidth interconnect at a low price point. However, in consideration of the ease with which Ethernet LAN networks can be compromised if access to the network is gained, it is necessary to be aware of the associated risks and attempt to minimize them.

If intruders can gain access to the Ethernet facilities themselves, an Ethernet hub/repeater can be readily inserted into the network, allowing for complete observation of transit data, man-in-the-middle attacks, and denial of service assaults. As such, steps should be taken to minimize this risk.

Due to the relatively large number of access facilities in a typical service provider network, identifying the appropriate connection to compromise is quite difficult. Ensuring that control traffic exchanges between the customer edge devices are authenticated can greatly reduce the likelihood of man-in-the-middle intrusions. However, simple monitoring of transit traffic is still readily accomplished and if data sensitivity demands it, encryption of the traffic should be considered. The service provider and customer should monitor the status of the interconnect link and investigate any logged circuit anomalies in a proactive manner.

Customer Edge

In this section, we discuss security considerations at the customer edge router as Layer 3 and Layer 2 devices. We illustrate the security factors for both constructs and highlight recommendations for deployment.

CE Interconnection Service Is a Layer 3 Device

In scenarios where customers seek a Layer 2 interconnection service for their Layer 3 networks as would be expected through a Frame Relay/ATM offering, the security approaches are simplest to implement while providing a reasonable degree of control over network access.

The customer needs to follow the Layer 3 best practices as described in Chapter 4, "Secure MPLS VPN Designs." This should include using MD5 signatures for the routing protocol mechanisms traversing the service provider network. In addition, the service provider should provide a MAC address–based filter on the access point to the Layer 2 provider edge. This filter should permit the MAC address of the customer CE router only.

An example is as follows:

```
vacl blah permit aabb.ccdd.eeff
vacl deny all
```

The service provider should further implement traffic load controls on the provider edge router facing the customer's interconnection device. That is, received traffic should be bandwidth limited to the levels as agreed on in the service contract between the customer and the service provider. Bandwidth limiting can be provided by using input policing mechanisms as shownhere:

```
service-policy dogger
        police 3000000

interface ethernet 0/0
        service-policy dogger in
```

In addition, it would be preferable that the service provider also police outbound traffic volumes to protect the customer's network from network anomalies escaping from the service provider core.

The customer should also implement protections on its service provider–facing edge devices to prevent any aberrant traffic loads from impacting its local operations.

Customer Edge Interconnection Service Is a Layer 2 Device

In designs where a customer Layer 2 domain is interconnected by a service provider Layer 2 EoMPLS network, the security considerations are considerably more significant and complex in implementation.

As such, the following configuration components should be addressed for Ethernet VLAN security, VPLS security, and and hijack management access security:

- Secure console/aux access
- Disable password recovery (if possible)
- Ensure that U-PE cannot become spanning tree root (priority configuration)
- Establish broadcast controls on interfaces
- Disable/block Cisco Discover Protocol (CDP), Bridge Protocol Data Units (BPDUs), and Dynamic Trunking Protocol (DTP) on the UNI interfaces
- Ensure VTP operation in transparent mode
- Apply MAC address limits
- Remove VLAN 1 and reserved VLANs from UNI
- Remove unused VLANs from allowed list
- Shut down all unused ports
- Hard-code physical port attributes
- Establish error reporting
- Enable 802.1x as applicable

Hijack Management Security

The interconnect device (CE and especially U-PE) access ports should be strongly secured to prevent unauthorized intrusion into the service provider network. The general recommendations for securing access to Cisco devices can be summarized by protecting access to console ports and implementing router password security mechanisms.

Many of the above recommendations can also be readily applied to large enterprise networks.

Disable Password Recovery

In addition, consideration should be given to disabling password recovery mechanisms inherent in most Cisco hardware. This fail-safe measure allows a user with physical access to the device to power the device off and on and issue a "break" sequence on the console port within 20 seconds of the reboot. This will drop the router into "ROMMON" mode, where the configuration may be viewed and possibly manipulated.

For example, most Cisco routers and switches allow the service provider to disable this recovery mechanism using the following command sequence: **no service password-recovery**.

Once this command is entered, the switch will display the following banner on power-up:

```
The password-recovery mechanism has been triggered, but is currently disabled.
Access to the boot loader prompt through the password-recovery mechanism is
disallowed at this point. However, if you agree to let the system be reset back to
the default system configuration, access to the boot loader prompt can still be
allowed.
Would you like to reset the system back to the default configuration (y/n) ?
```

A "Y" response to this prompt will cause the configuration and VLAN database to be erased. This will prevent unauthorized access to the switch through a password-recovery attack. Note, however, that the configuration will be destroyed and as such the device will be out of service, requiring the service provider to recover the U-PE before user traffic can resume. As such, the service provider must ensure that the configurations are safely stored and must consider that an attack on the device is sufficient reason for a service outage of this magnitude.

NOTE   **Recommendation**

Because the default VLAN used for all ports is 1, it is strongly recommended never to use VLAN 1 in production networks. After a system reset, no port will be connected to a VLAN.

Additionally, access to the console may be disabled with the following approach:

```
line console 0
no exec
```

This will disable access to the device from the console port. CLI-based device management via alternative access mechanisms (SSH) should be ensured prior to issuing this command. It is suggested that this approach only be used where the device in question is located in an unsecured area.

U-PE STP Priority

The U-PE is the service provider's interconnect point to the customer network. As such, it should never become the root of the service provider's Layer 2 network. To ensure that this is the case, the bridge priority of the U-PE should be set to a high number so that it will not overrule the priority of the service provider–desired root bridges (primary and secondary).

```
cons-osr1(config)#bridge 1 priority ?
  <0-65535>  Priority (low priority more likely to be root)
```

In addition, the root guard mechanism can be utilized to protect the switches from receiving BPDUs that suggest that the root bridge has changed. This root guard configuration is applied to ports where the path to the true root bridge should *not* appear.

```
cons-osr1(config-if)#spanning-tree guard  ?
  loop  Set guard mode to loop guard on interface
  none  Set guard mode to none
  root  Set guard mode to root guard on interface
```

The root guard mechanism differs from the BPDU filter approach in the sense that root guard allows connected devices to participate in spanning tree operations as long as they do not attempt to advertise a superior root priority. If such frames are received, the port is disabled, and once the offending messages cease, the port is automatically re-enabled. Root guard should *not* be enabled on the root switch ports directly facing the secondary root.

Apply Broadcast Limiters

The Catalyst switch products can be configured to limit the amount of broadcast traffic load permitted to enter an interface. This can be useful in preventing the propagation of broadcast storms from a particular L2 area to other areas of the network. A sample configuration snippet is shown here:

```
cons-osr1(config-if)#storm-control ?
  broadcast  Broadcast address storm control
  multicast  Multicast address storm control
  unicast    Unicast address storm control

cons-osr1(config-if)#storm-control broadcast ?
  level  Set storm suppression level on this interface

cons-osr1(config-if)#storm-control broadcast level ?
  <0 - 100>  Enter Integer part of level as percentage of bandwidth
```

Disable/Block Layer 2 Control Traffic

The UNI interface between the service provider and its customers should not process unwarranted L2 control traffic.

This would include:

- Cisco Discovery Protocol (CDP)
- Dynamic Trunking Protocol (DTP)
- Spanning Tree Protocol (STP) Bridge Protocol Data Units (BPDUs)

Allowing these control packets to flow freely across a UNI exposes information about the devices on both ends (CDP), allows for the establishment of trunks without manual intervention (DTP), and establishes loop-free pathing through a given set of nodes (STP). While these are useful mechanisms within a contained enterprise environment, they are security exposures in the service provider–Customer interconnect devices and should be disabled/blocked. Examples 7-1, 7-2, and 7-3 show you how to disable/block these protocols.

Example 7-1 *Disable CDP*

```
cons-osr1#sh cdp
Global CDP information:
        Sending CDP packets every 60 seconds
        Sending a holdtime value of 180 seconds
        Sending CDPv2 advertisements is enabled
cons-osr1#conf t
Enter configuration commands, one per line. End with CNTL/Z.
cons-osr1(config)#
cons-osr1(config)#no cdp run
cons-osr1(config)#
cons-osr1(config)#^Z
cons-osr1#sh cdp
% CDP is not enabled
```

Example 7-2 *Disable DTP*

```
cons-osr1(config-if)#switchport ?
  access       Set access mode characteristics of the interface
  autostate    Include or exclude this port from vlan link up calculation
  capture      Set capture mode characteristics of this interface
  dot1q        Set interface dot1q properties
  host         Set port host
  mode         Set trunking mode of the interface
  nonegotiate  Device will not engage in negotiation protocol on this
               interface

interface FastEthernet2/40
switchport
 switchport trunk encapsulation dot1q
 switchport trunk native vlan 999
 switchport trunk allowed vlan 22
 switchport mode trunk
 switchport nonegotiate
```

Example 7-3 *Disable STP*

```
cons-osr1(config-if)#spanning-tree bpdufilter ?
  disable  Disable BPDU filtering for this interface
  enable   Enable BPDU filtering for this interface

cons-osr1 sh run int fas 2/40
Building configuration...

Current configuration : 242 bytes
!
interface FastEthernet2/40
 shutdown
 switchport
 switchport trunk encapsulation dot1q
 switchport trunk native vlan 999
 switchport trunk allowed vlan 22
```

continues

Example 7-3 *Disable STP (Continued)*

```
switchport mode trunk
switchport nonegotiate
spanning-tree bpdufilter enable
```

However, this functionality is implemented in software on the 3550. As an alternative, hardware-based access control lists (ACLs) can be used to filter ingress control protocol data units (PDUs).

For example, the following ACL controls a number of control packets found in switched networks:

```
Extended MAC access list stop_ugly_stuff
    deny    any 0180.c200.0000 0000.0000.001f
    deny    any host 0100.0ccc.cccc
    deny    any host 0100.0ccc.cccd
    deny    any host 0100.0ccd.cdcd
    deny    any host 0100.0ccd.cdce
    deny    any host 0100.0ccc.cdd0
    deny    any host 000c.8580.d000
    permit any any
c3550-b(config)#int fas 0/24
c3550-b(config-if)#mac access-group stop_ugly_stuff in
```

Note the addition of the final **deny** statement in the ACL. This is set to deny packets destined to the unicast MAC address of the switch itself, preventing Layer 2 attacks directed at the switch MAC address. (Note: The MAC address shown is an example.)

VTP Transparent Operation

While use of the VLAN Trunking Protocol can be advantageous within an enterprise environment, it poses security risks in an SP world because VTP allows for the dynamic definition of VLANs amongst switches. Example 7-4 shows how to disable this mode of operation.

Example 7-4 *Disable VLAN Trunking Protocol*

```
cons-osr1(config)#vtp mode ?
  client      Set the device to client mode.
  server      Set the device to server mode.
  transparent Set the device to transparent mode.

cons-osr1(config)#vtp mode trans
Setting device to VTP TRANSPARENT mode.
cons-osr1(config)#^Z
cons-osr1#

cons-osr1# sh vtp st
VTP Version                   : 2
Configuration Revision        : 0
Maximum VLANs supported locally : 1005
```

Example 7-4 *Disable VLAN Trunking Protocol (Continued)*

```
Number of existing VLANs        : 8
VTP Operating Mode              : Transparent
VTP Domain Name                 :
VTP Pruning Mode                : Disabled
VTP V2 Mode                     : Disabled
VTP Traps Generation            : Disabled
MD5 digest                      : 0xCB 0x80 0x9C 0x6C 0x19 0xF8 0x59 0xE3
Configuration last modified by 127.0.0.12 at 2-26-04 15:39:18
```

MAC Address Limits and Port Security

Switches can be configured to permit access from a predefined maximum number of
MAC addresses. This helps to prevent CAM table overflows usually associated with MAC
overflow attacks. The switch can be configured to perform differing operations if the
predefined maximum is exceeded, as follows:

- **Protect mode**—Drops packets with unknown source addresses until you remove a
  sufficient number of secure MAC addresses to drop below the maximum value.

- **Restrict mode**—Drops packets with unknown source addresses until you remove a
  sufficient number of secure MAC addresses to drop below the maximum value and
  causes the SecurityViolation counter to increment.

- **Shutdown mode**—Disables the offending port and generates an SNMP trap. In
  addition, it requires manual intervention to restore the operation.

NOTE   Port security configuration is not permitted on trunk ports in some software releases.

Example 7-5 illustrates a configuration for port security on an Ethernet switch.

Example 7-5 *Port Security*

```
cons-osr1(config-if)#switchport port-security ?
  aging        Port-security aging commands
  mac-address  Secure mac address
  maximum      Max secure addresses
  violation    Security violation mode

cons-osr1(config-if)#switchport port-security maximum ?
  <1-1025>  Maximum addresses

cons-osr1(config-if)#switchport port-security violation ?
  protect   Security violation protect mode
  Restrict  Security violation restrict mode
  Shutdown  Security violation shutdown mode
```

In newer code, global commands allow for the definition of a maximum number of MAC addresses per VLAN (see Example 7-6).

Example 7-6 *MAC Address Limits Per VLAN*

```
cons-osr1(config-if)#mac-address-table limit vlan 666 maximum 13 action ?
  warning      Specifies that the one syslog message will be sent and no
               further action will be taken when the action is violated.
  limit        Specifies that the one syslog message will be sent and/or a
               corresponding trap will be generated with the MAC limit when
               the action is violated.
  limit flood  Enables unknown unicast flooding
  Shutdown     Specifies that the one syslog message will be sent and/or the
               VLAN is moved to the blocked state when the action is violated.
```

Again, the **shutdown** option requires manual intervention if the MAC address limit is exceeded and this parameter becomes activated.

Controlling Reserved VLANs

By default, VLAN 1 is used for control traffic and as a native VLAN for untagged incoming frames. The native VLAN operation of the switches should be mapped to a different VLAN that is not part of the customer domain:

```
c3550-b(config-if)#switchport trunk native vlan ?
  <1-4094>  VLAN ID of the native VLAN when this port is in trunking mode

c3550-b(config-if)#switchport trunk native vlan 999
```

Forcing the tagging of the native VLAN prevents untagged ingress frames from being picked up and forwarded over the native VLAN:

```
cons-osr1(config)#vlan dot1q tag native
```

In addition, VLAN 1 can be removed from trunk ports in hybrid Catalyst software releases:

```
Console> (enable) clear trunk 8/1 1
Removing Vlan(s) 1 from allowed list.
Port 8/1 allowed vlans modified to 2-1005.
```

Alternatively, through the use of VLAN mapping and filtering, access to the control VLAN can be limited.

Removing Unused VLANs

Remove unassigned VLANs from the system configurations to avoid accidental availability of VLANs on ports where they are not required. Example 7-7 shows the removal of unused VLAN configurations.

Example 7-7 *Removal Unused VLANs*

```
cons-osr1(config-if)#switchport trunk allowed vlan none

cons-osr1(config-if)#do sh run int fas 2/40
Building configuration...

Current configuration : 260 bytes
!
interface FastEthernet2/40
Switchport
Switchport trunk encapsulation dot1q
Switchport trunk native vlan 999
Switchport trunk allowed vlan none
Switchport mode trunk
Switchport nonegotiate
spanning-tree bpdufilter enable
spanning-tree guard root
End
```

Note that the **switchport trunk allowed vlan none** configuration statement will not be displayed on the port once some VLANs have been explicitly enabled. Example 7-8 shows this example with VLAN 666 being enabled.

Example 7-8 *Re-enabling VLAN Example*

```
cons-osr1(config-if)#switchport trunk allowed vlan 666

cons-osr1(config-if)#do sh run int fas 2/40
Building configuration...

Current configuration : 259 bytes
!
interface FastEthernet2/40
 switchport
 switchport trunk encapsulation dot1q
 switchport trunk native vlan 999
 switchport trunk allowed vlan 666
 switchport mode trunk
 switchport nonegotiate
 spanning-tree bpdufilter enable
 spanning-tree guard root
 End
```

Hard-Code Physical Port Attributes

In order to reduce the possibility of configuration mismatches or network intruders causing instability, the operational characteristics of the ports in question should be locked down as much as possible. This means hard coding speed, duplex and disabling flow control, as Example 7-9 shows.

Example 7-9 *Hard-Coding Switch Configuration Example*

```
c3550-b(config-if)#speed ?
  10    Force 10 Mbps operation
  100   Force 100 Mbps operation
  auto  Enable AUTO speed configuration

c3550-b(config-if)#dup ?
  auto  Enable AUTO duplex configuration
  full  Force full duplex operation
  half  Force half-duplex operation

cons-osr1(config-if)#int g 1/1
cons-osr1(config-if)#speed ?
  1000         Force 1000 Mbps operation
  nonegotiate  Do not negotiate speed

cons-osr1(config-if)#flowcontrol ?
  receive  Configure receiving flow operation
  send     Configure sending flow operation
```

NOTE   Hard-coding may result in mismatches between the interface unless *all* interfaces are hard-coded. (For example, a switch port configured for full-duplex may result in a workstation failing to detect full-duplex, thus running as half-duplex.)

Establish Network Reporting

The SP and customer should ensure that error occurrences on the network are carefully monitored, and any anomalous events should be investigated. In addition, several additional reporting mechanisms should be enabled on the PE routers, including the following:

```
cons-osr1(config-if)#logg event ?
  bundle-status   BUNDLE/UNBUNDLE messages
  link-status     UPDOWN and CHANGE messages
  spanning-tree   Spanning-tree Interface events
  trunk-status    TRUNK status messages
```

Link status, trunk status, and spanning tree status monitoring should be enabled where appropriate.

Enable 802.1x

Consideration should be given to the use of the 802.1x mechanisms on interconnections where both sides support this functionality. Essentially, 802.1x specifies a supplicant/authenticator operation where the client requests access to the network using Extensible Authentication Protocol over LAN (EAPoL) handshaking. The switch port will not permit data flows from the client other than EAPoL until it has been authorized by an AAA server.

Summary

This chapter provided a detailed reference with respect to security best practices for organizations that either implement Layer 2 MPL VPNs as a service offering or for consumers of such services.

We examined security considerations—both service provider and customer perspectives. This chapter addressed current practices for protecting the network elements, network services, and the data itself from compromises ensuing from unintentional errors as well as deliberate attacks. Finally, we focused on Ethernet over MPLS deployments because these are most complex for Layer 2 constructs.

In this chapter, you learn about the following:

- Operational security considerations
- Network management security considerations
- CE and core infrastructure security considerations

Secure Operation and Maintenance of an MPLS Core

Operation, Administration, and Management (OAM) components require security consideration for MPLS VPN service. Security applicability for OAM is the key topic for this chapter.

The Network Operations Center (NOC) is the most critical organization for both the service provider and the enterprise customer because it is in this organization that service level agreements and security are enforced. Within enterprise organizations that deploy MPLS and are responsible for internal service level agreement (SLA) and security enforcement, a similar NOC structure is usually established. In this chapter, we discuss the security of the management network—for example, access to the NOC in the context of a managed customer premises equipment (CPE) service.

Management Network Security

Security of the management network is critical because breaching the NOC network fundamentally exposes all customer VPNs that are reachable by the NOC. When securing the NOC, recall the principles highlighted in the previous chapters:

- Do not permit packets into your core.
- Secure the routing protocol.
- Design for transit traffic.
- Operate securely.

From a NOC perspective, there are vectors that violate service provider security and control, such as hijacking bandwidth; attacks against infrastructure; distributed denial of service (DDoS) attacks against customers; worms, viruses, and botnets; and reflection attacks.

A NOC team can take steps to establish a service provider security framework that is the foundation for lines of defense in addition to a variety of tools that can be used within this security framework.

Figure 8-1 depicts an example of a service provider security framework that highlights roles, services, planes, and threat vectors. (Examples of roles are endpoints, customer premise equipment, access, aggregation, core, and so on.) These roles are further correlated to services such as voice, video, data, security, hosting, and metro, to name a few. Examples of planes include data, control, management, and services; in Figure 8-1, these are color-coded and aligned with the threat areas such as reconnaissance and DDoS.

Figure 8-1   *SP Infrastructure Security Framework Example*

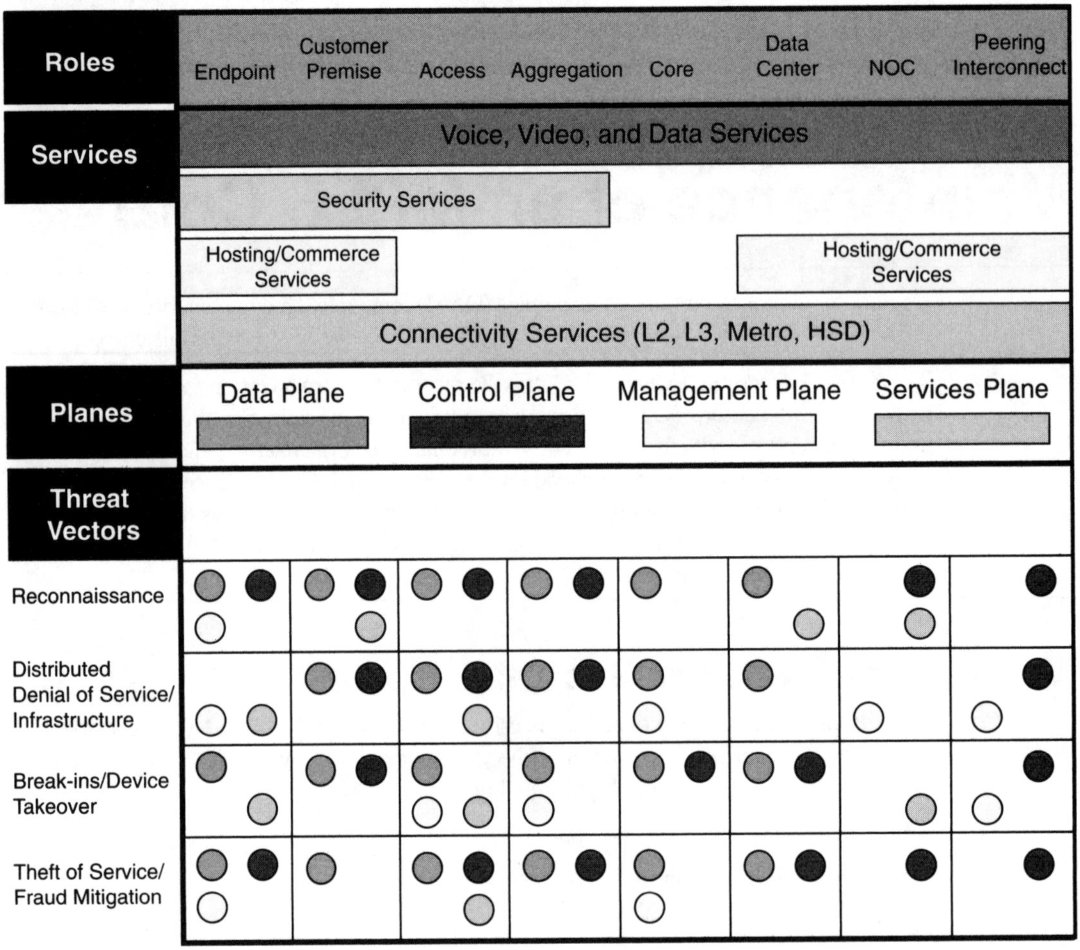

Roles	Endpoint	Customer Premise	Access	Aggregation	Core	Data Center	NOC	Peering Interconnect
Services	Voice, Video, and Data Services							
	Security Services							
	Hosting/Commerce Services					Hosting/Commerce Services		
	Connectivity Services (L2, L3, Metro, HSD)							
Planes	Data Plane		Control Plane		Management Plane		Services Plane	
Threat Vectors								

Reconnaissance
Distributed Denial of Service/ Infrastructure
Break-ins/Device Takeover
Theft of Service/ Fraud Mitigation

Figure 8-2 provides an overview of a security service architecture and maps the architecture with the Cisco-specific toolkit applications that the NOC can use.

With the example of a service provider security framework, we can proceed to explore the operations factors for MPLS security. In OAM, we are fundamentally concerned with the Fault, Configuration, Accounting, Performance, and Security (FCAPS) model. The remainder of this chapter focuses on security.

Securely Managing CE Devices

In providing a managed CPE service, a service provider needs to have access to its customer CPEs. However, all CEs (including customer-owned CEs) should be under the management umbrella. A network management VRF, called the VPN_Network_Management, contains the circuit addresses of all the CE routes. Note that the term *circuit* implies the IP connectivity between these managed customer devices and the NOC. The service provider network management station(s) originates from this VRF. Conversely, each customer VRF should contain the service provider network management station(s) in order to permit bidirectional communication between the management workstation and the CE router. An example of the interaction between the CE router and the service provider network management station is shown in Figure 8-3.

NOTE The CE should all have a unique loopback address from the ISPs management address space. In this example, the PE—CE circuit is part of the customer VPN (and customers may want to have this following *their* address plans. This is an area of negotiation between the service provider and the customer.

Figure 8-2 *Security Service Architecture—Where?*

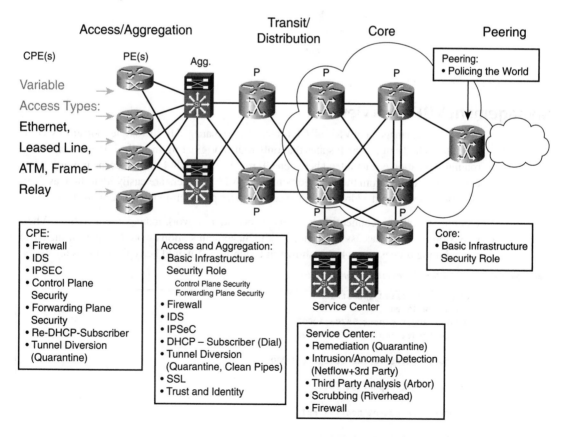

Figure 8-3 *Example Interaction Between CE Router and SP Network Management Station*

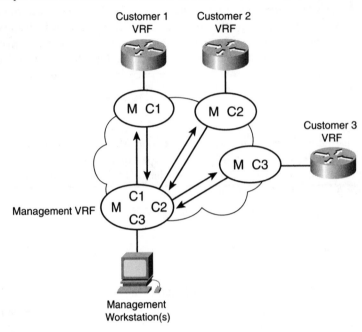

Management VRF Overview

By creating a management VRF, all CE routers can be managed from a single spot; and by virtue of the transitivity rule, which states that only routes originating from the VRF are exported, routing separation is guaranteed between CE routers. Figure 8-4 illustrates the importing and exporting of routes from the management VRF. All CE routers are easily identified, as they all should use a circuit address from the same service provider–managed address space.

Example 8-1 allows connection to a service provider network management station. When provisioning VRFs, access to the network management stations would be part of the basic provisioning process, so what is shown in Example 8-1 would be typical across all VRFs.

Example 8-1 *NOC Station Access to Customer VRFs*

```
ip vrf VPN_Allied_Industries
 rd 64700:10600
 route-target export 64700:10600
 route-target import 64700:10600
 !
 ! Export routes to the Management VRF
 !
 route-target export 64700:1
 !
 ! Import Management host(s) only
 !
 route-target import 64700:10
```

In addition to the normal import/export route-targets for the VRF, two more route-targets are specified. The route-target export 64700:1 exports all routes from this VRF to the management VRF using the extended community attribute 64700:1. The route-target import 64700:10 imports any VPN-IPv4 addresses with the extended community attribute 64700:10, which identifies any management host(s).

Example 8-2 shows a management VRF example. This VRF is configured at the PE that connects to the service provider management subnet. Multiple PEs could provide the network management service for redundancy.

Example 8-2 *Network Management VRF Configuration*

```
ip vrf VPN_Management
 rd 64700:1
 import map IN-Management
 export map OUT-Management
 route-target export 64700:1
 route-target import 64700:1
!
! Only allow CE circuit addresses into VRF
!
ip prefix-list CE-Circuits seq 10 permit 172.24.6.0/16 ge 30
ip prefix-list CE-Circuits seq 10 permit 172.24.7.0/16 ge 30
!and so on...
!
route-map IN-Management permit 10
 match ip address prefix-list CE-Circuits
!
! Set Management Workstation route to 64700:10
!
route-map OUT-Management permit 10
 match ip address 20
 set extcommunity rt 64700:10
!
! Access List to identify management hosts (one line for each host)
!
access-list 20 permit 146.171.66.90 0.0.0.0
...
!
! Set a static route to Management workstation(s)
!
ip route vrf VPN_Management 146.171.66.0 255.255.255.0 <NH Int> <NH IP>
!
! Enter other routes to Management hosts...
```

Management VRF Details

This VRF uses the service provider–specified "well known" RD and RT of 64700:1. In addition to the normal import/export route-targets for the VRF, two route-maps are specified: IN-Management and OUT-Management.

The IN-Management route-map limits any imported addresses to that of the circuit address space. In other words, the address prefix must be a subnet 30 bits long, and it must begin with 172.24.6.0, 172.24.7.0, and so on—the address pools to which all CE circuit addresses belong.

NOTE   In the previous example, all VPN customers must accept that these 172.24.*x.y* networks *cannot* be used by them in the VPN.

This concept is applicable for a certain number of VPNs; for example, when selecting ranges from all three RFC 1918 networks, it helps to minimize the probability of address conflicts. However, with a large number of (larger) VPNs, this concept may be limiting.

Using official addresses could help for scalability, but this is no guarantee because official addresses could be "stolen."

Therefore, the network architect must be aware of these issues when planning the address range for service provider network management access to customer VPNS.

All other routes in the customer VRF are excluded. The service provider could poll a CE hub or switch by simply providing it with 172.24.*x.x* address, which could be included in the VRF.

The management VRF is connected to an interface that could originate from many subnets, in addition to the management subnet. For purposes of example, let's say the management subnet is 146.171.66.0. To guarantee that only the host addresses of management workstations are included in the customer VRF, static routes should be used to identify each management address individually.

The static **route** command specifies the management VRF, the host address, the next hop interface, and the next hop address.

The OUT-Management route-map sets all management host addresses (those that match the access-list 20) to the extended-community attribute of 64700:10, which is then imported into the customer VRF with a corresponding import map.

As an example, the management workstation has an IP address of 146.171.66.90. In the above configuration, a static route is added for each management workstation so we can manage routes down to individual hosts. This prevents CEs from accessing anything else on the management subnet except for the specific hosts.

If these host address routes are redistributed to a CE via a routing protocol such as RIPv2, the CE may re-advertise the route back to the PE in a summarized form even though split-horizon is enabled. (Do not send routes out an interface you received them on.)

For example, if the host route 146.171.66.90 255.255.255.255 is advertised to a CE with auto-summary enabled, that route will be summarized to a B-class address of 146.171.0.0 255.255.0.0 and advertised back to the PE.

The split-horizon process will allow the route to pass because it is not the same as the route that was received.

Two ways to avoid this problem are to

- Turn auto-summary off at the CE
- Use route distribution filtering at the PE

NOTE	We have presented a generic overview of CE management in terms of the link technology implemented. However, there are potentially a variety of emerging applicable configurations, such as Frame Relay, ATM, or VLAN encapsulation on the link, and a VRF on the CE that retains the management (logical) link, thus resulting in a completely separated VPN data link. This solution can avoid address conflict, and the management security is consequently higher due to the VPN separation. We recommend that users commence with a generic solution when launching a Layer 3–based service and consider deploying a solution that results in additional separation of the VPN when deploying a Layer 2–based service.

Securely Managing the Core Network

The configuration for managing the core network is slightly different than managing CE devices because the addresses of the PE routers exist in the global routing table and not in a VRF. There are several ways PE management may be achieved:

- P and PE management via VRF table
- P and PE management via global table

Building on Example 8-2 in the previous section, Figure 8-4 shows an example for P and PE management via VRF table where the P and PE loopback addresses (in the service provider's case, 172.24.4.0) are in the global routing table, while the address of the management workstation is in the VRF. To create connectivity between the MPLS core network and the management workstation, a global static route pointing to the MPLS network loopbacks must be injected into the VRF, and a static route pointing to the management workstation must be injected into the global routing table.

NOTE	One could also provide all Ps and PEs with a second loopback address for management purposes and put the second loopback into the management VPN. In fact, this is a commonly deployed practice today.

For the purposes of this example, let's assume the following:

- The management workstations are connected to FA0/1/0 on a router called TSG000_GTWY_01.
- The IP subnet that the management workstations reside on is 146.171.66.0 255.255.255.0.
- The gateway router is connected to the GSR called TSG000_CLSR_01 via POS0/0/0.

Figure 8-4 *P and PE Management via VRF Table*

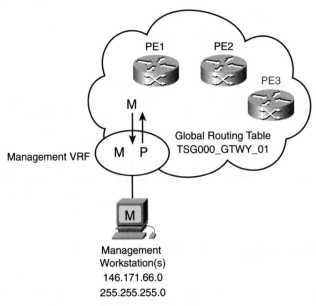

The following configuration illustrates the commands necessary. The first static **route** command injects a route into the VPN_Management VRF (defined previously), indicating that all loopback routes in the 172.24.4.0 space are reachable via the interface pos0/0/0, which happens to point to the GSR. The pos0/0/0 is the interface on the PE (7507) that the downstream P (GSR) router is connected to.

```
ip route vrf VPN_Management 172.24.4.0 255.255.255.0 pos0/0/0
ip route 146.171.66.0 255.255.255.0 fa0/1/0
```

The second static route exists in the global routing table of the P and PE network (outside the VRF) and provides reachability back to the management subnet that is physically connected on fa0/1/0.

NOTE   This return route does not need to be associated with a VRF. A VRF may be configured on an interface, but this does not prevent routes in the global table from also using this interface like a normal routing network that does not use MPLS.

There is a small caveat with this solution: the route for the loopback addresses is pointing to the next hop interface. Why is the next hop not the loopback address of the PE directly connected to the management subnet? If a route is injected into a PE pointing to itself, no recursive lookups will be done for the subsequent routes, so nothing will be reachable. The routes need to point to the next hop for this to work.

The PE that the management VRF is defined on will be reachable, but via the next hop, which will route the packet back to the PE. This is not an elegant solution, but it appears to work. A workaround for managing the directly connected PE is to use a PE–CE circuit address instead for this PE. In this case, it would be the IP address configured on fa0/1/0.

NOTE   We do realize that for a large service provider, provisioning static routes is not optimal, and therefore we assume the use of a provisioning tool such as Cisco IP Solution Center (ISC) to automate these provisioning examples for both Layers 2 and 3 in addition to Metro Ethernet and traffic engineering tunnel deployment in order to accommodate a fuller service management palette required for the service provider.

Another way of managing the core network is to simply connect the management network directly to an interface defined in the global routing table so that it does not have a VRF associated with it. This would be the simplest and most straightforward way to manage the core network, as shown in Figure 8-5.

Figure 8-5   *Managing the Core Network*

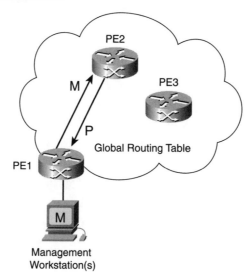

Summary

In this chapter, we showed examples for managing CE and core routers. Note that the MPLS security best practice and design guidelines discussed in the previous chapters must be part of the NOC policies.

In the next chapter, we summarize the MPLS security principles by reviewing case studies.

PART IV

Case Studies and Appendixes

In this chapter, you learn about the following:

- Internet access network address translation implementations
- Multi-lite VRF and Internet access
- Layer 2 LAN best practice

CHAPTER 9

Case Studies

This chapter provides deployment examples and lessons learned, highlighting theoretical discussion points from the previous chapters. We will examine Internet access and the hybrid model for providing both Internet and intranet services on a single provider edge, and will describe examples of applicability for a Multi-lite VPN routing/forwarding instance (VRF). Finally, we will provide examples for Layer 2 access over an MPLS-based network.

Internet Access

This section provides various scenarios for Internet access and points out security considerations for each example. These simple shared Internet access scenarios include the following:

- Network address translation [NAT] via multiple common gateways
- PE to multiple Internet gateways
- NAT via a single common gateway
- Registered NAT by CE
- Internet access via customer-controlled NAT
- Internet access using global routing table
- BGP Internet routing table from service provider of an ISP
- Tier 3 ISP connecting to an upstream tier via a service provider

NAT Via Common Gateways

The network administrator can set up a shared Internet access structure for customers who require a simple method of connecting without having to provide their own cache engines or firewalls. The target customer is someone who does not have an IT infrastructure. NAT is performed at a common gateway point or points managed by a service provider (see Figure 9-1). Although rare, it may be that the entire customer network uses a registered address space, where no NAT function is required and traffic will pass directly through the NAT phase untouched.

Figure 9-1 *Shared Internet Access Multiple NAT Gateways*

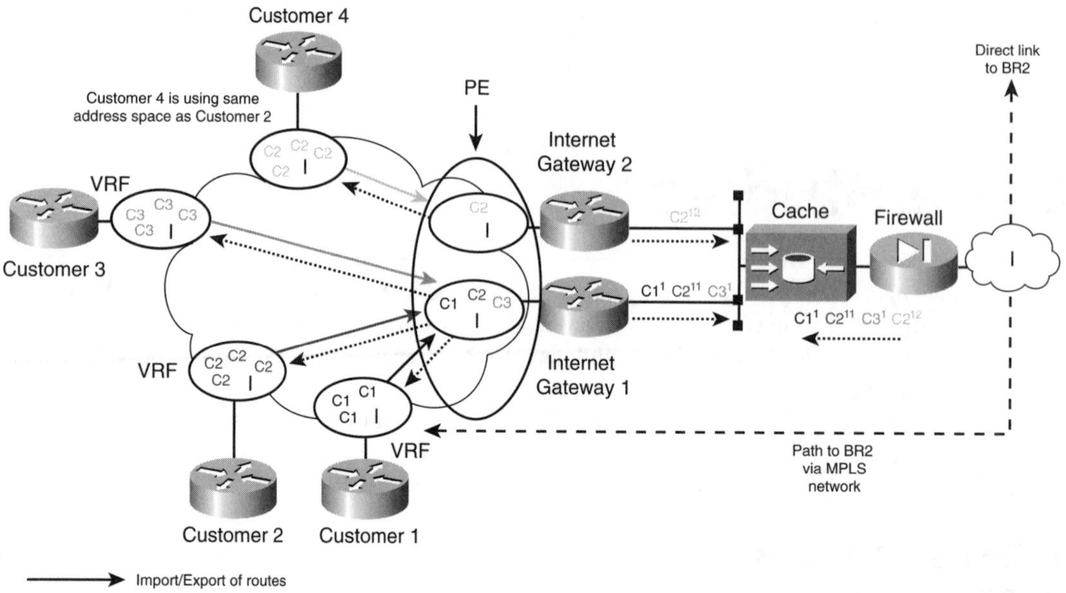

Performing NAT at a central point has the primary advantage of conserving registered address space because all customers share the same common pool. A default Internet route is imported into every subscribing customer VRF; therefore, any traffic from a customer whose destination is not explicitly known will be routed to the Internet gateway router. Corresponding customer routes are imported into the Internet VRF and the provider edge. The Internet gateway will translate the customer traffic to a registered address from an available pool, and then pass the traffic through the cache engine and firewall to the Internet. (Note that address translation can also occur at the firewall.)

The caveat about this design and any central gateway design is that a single gateway can only translate addresses for customers who do not have overlapping addresses. If there is an instance where customers are using the same address space, then there may be a separate gateway performing the translation for each customer that shares a common address space. Multiple gateways, however, can share access to a common firewall.

In practice, connection to the Internet would either connect back to the PE using the global routing space (not a VRF) to access the service provider egress router, or a direct connection would be made to the service provider egress router. In this example, there is a single VRF shared by all customers who do not have overlapping addresses. Customers who do have overlapping addresses will use separate Internet gateways and a VRF. Portions of the registered address pool could also be used on a per-customer basis using access lists or static translations to permit explicit identification of customer hosts from the Internet, such as mail servers or web hosts.

This configuration process would require conduits or holes to be made through the firewall for customer hosts.

PE to Multiple Internet Gateways

The connection between the PE and the Internet gateway could be via Ethernet (Gigabit Ethernet, for example) so hat VLANs can be used. This would allow the support for multiple NAT gateways (to support customers sharing the same address space) via a Cisco Catalyst switch, as shown in Figure 9-2. For example, each would have its own VLAN.

Figure 9-2   *Catalyst Switch for Multiple NAT Gateways*

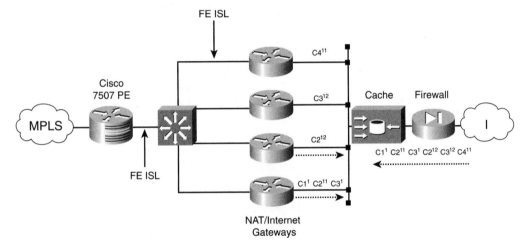

NOTE   A third party in the same VLAN (for example, an Internet exchange point [IXP]) can insert spoofed packets into VPNs and perform man-in-the-middle attacks; therefore, we recommend using Inter-AS and CsC connections only in private peering mode. Even though the Internet gateway is part of the service provider's infrastructure in this context, we emphasize the security concern.

VLANs can be assumed to be separate if:

- The switch is not a low-end model
- Virtual Trunking Protocol (VTP) is disabled on all ports (default)
- Router ports are not trunk ports
- No Inter-Switch Link (ISL) or 802.1q signaling is configured on the router ports.

An Internet service can be created on an Internet gateway router (see Figure 9-3). Dynamic routing can be used to pick up customer routes as they are imported to the Internet VRF. A default route can be configured to point to the cache engine.

Figure 9-3   *Shared Internet Access: Single NAT Gateway*

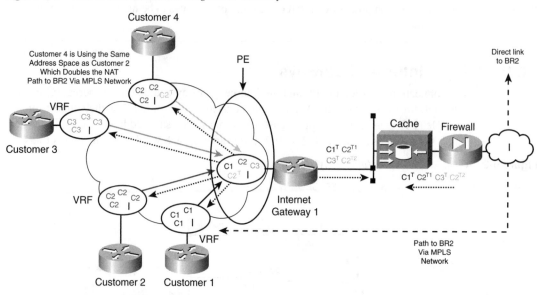

Example 9-1 shows an example of such a configuration.

Example 9-1   *Internet Router Gateway Configuration*

```
!
!Define the registered address pool to use for all customers using the Internet
ip nat pool NAT_Pool1 171.69.233.201  171.69.233.254 netmask  255.255.255.0
ip nat inside source list 1 pool NAT__Pool1
!
!Sub-interface to Internet VRF for customers in the MPLS cloud
!Connects to the PE in the Service Provide x network
interface fastethernet 1/0.18
ip unnumbered loopback0
ip nat inside
!
!LAN subnet to firewall and cache engine
interface fastethernet 1/1
ip address 167.26.17.1 255.255.255.0
ip nat outside
!
access-list 1 permit any
!
!address of cache engine/proxy server
ip route 0.0.0.0  0.0.0.0  167.26.17.10
!
```

Example 9-2 shows an example of a PE connecting to the Internet gateway. (For clarity, the VRF connections for Customer 1 and Customer 2 have been included, but these could most likely be on another PE.) The **VPN_Internet** VRF contains the default route pointing to the gateway. This was picked up by using dynamic routing between the gateway and the PE and redistributing the static route **ip route 0.0.0.0 0.0.0.0 167.26.17.10** in Example 9-1. Each customer VRF will import the Internet route-target 9255:2 and export the route-target 9255:20. Note that the **default-information originate** command must be added to the BGP VRF definition to force BGP to distribute the default route.

The **VPN_Internet** VPN will import the route-targets for all subscribing customers using the route-target 9255:20. In this way, the configuration at the PE remains static and all configuration is done at the customer VRF. (Route-maps could also be used to limit the customer routes imported in the **VPN_Internet** VRF.)

Example 9-2 *Internet PE Configuration*

```
!
!Define Customer1 VRF
ip vrf VPN_Internet
rd 9255:2
route-target export 9255:2
route-target import 9255:20
!
!Define Customer1 VRF
ip vrf VPN_customer1
rd 9255:10760
route-target export 9255:10650
route-target import 9255:10650
route-target import 9255:2
route-target export 9255:20
!
!Define Customer2 VRF
ip vrf VPN_customer2
rd 9255:10750
route-target export 9255:10750
route-target import 9255:10750
route-target import 9255:2
route-target export 9255:20
!
!Link to the Internet Gateway for Internet VRF
interface fastethernet 1/1/0.18
ip vrf forwarding  VPN_Internet
ip unnumbered loopback0

router bgp 9255
address-family ipv4 vrf VPN_Internet
default-information originate

!
```

NOTE   It would be possible to access another customer's network via the gateway because of the default routes. To avoid this problem, policy-based routing should be on all customer traffic to the Internet gateway. All ingress traffic should have its next hop interface forced to be that of the interface connecting directly to the other through the gateway. In other words, all traffic passing through the gateway is always sent to the Internet segment.

Example 9-3 shows the configuration on the Internet gateway to force traffic to the Internet.

Example 9-3 *Forcing Traffic to the Internet*

```
!
!Sub-interface to Internet VRF in the MPLS cloud
!
interface fastethernet 1/0.18
ip unnumbered loopback0
ip nat inside
ip policy route-map TO_Internet
!
interface fastethernet 1/1
Description Cache and Firewall LAN (to Internet)
ip address 167.26.17.1  255.255.255.0
route-map TO_Internet permit 20
set interface fastethernet 1/1
```

NOTE   Given the scenario shown in Figure 9-4, if the target interface goes down, the CE defaults to normal routing that will result in traffic passing into the VPN part of the site and consequently bypassing the security measures. This implementation, therefore, is not recommended for the security risk.

Figure 9-4   *Shared Access Line, Policy-Based Routing*

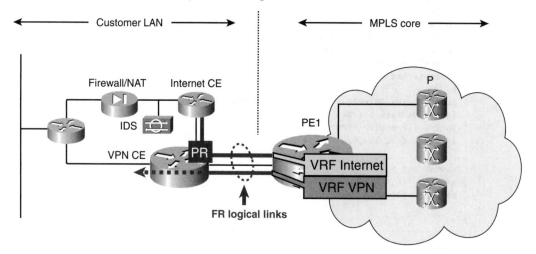

NAT via a Single Common Gateway

When deploying a single Internet gateway where all NAT is performed by one device, and there are customers who have overlapping addresses sharing this device, two stages of translation occur. This process is referred to as *double NAT*.

The first translation occurs at the CE using nonregistered addresses so as not to waste the registered address pool. This translation uniquely identifies customers with overlapping addresses to the gateway, which would then perform the second translation to a registered address for transmission out to the Internet. The motivation behind this scenario is to conserve registered address space.

Registered NAT by CE

The scenario shown in Figure 9-5 is similar to accessing the Internet via a single common gateway, except that the registered NAT is performed at the CE. The firewall and caching functions are still done at a common point. Also, because the customer has its own address range, the common NAT gateway could be completely ignored and the connection could be made directly to the common cache/firewall segment. For example, you could have three customers who have VRFs that only require Internet service. Each customer either already uses registered addresses or performs NAT to registered addresses at the CE. Furthermore, each of these customers may have a customer-owned and maintained WAN behind each of these CE routers where the CE router is viewed as the Internet gateway from the customer's WAN perspective. That is, the default route would point to the CE. The advantage of this scenario is that the customer does not need to manage and maintain firewalls and cache engines.

Figure 9-5   *Shared Internet Access: CE-Registered NAT*

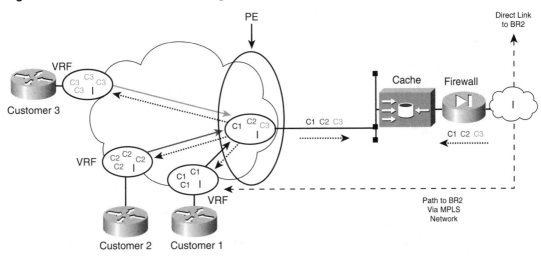

Internet Access via Customer-Controlled NAT

Larger and more security-sensitive customers may wish to provide their own firewall, NAT, and caching services, but want to use the Internet connection provided by a particular service provider. An example of this scenario, which is shown in Figure 9-6, is the case in a hub and spoke environment, where Internet access from all sites of a company pass through a central point such as a corporate data center for security and monitoring purposes.

Figure 9-6 *Internet Access via Customer Hub*

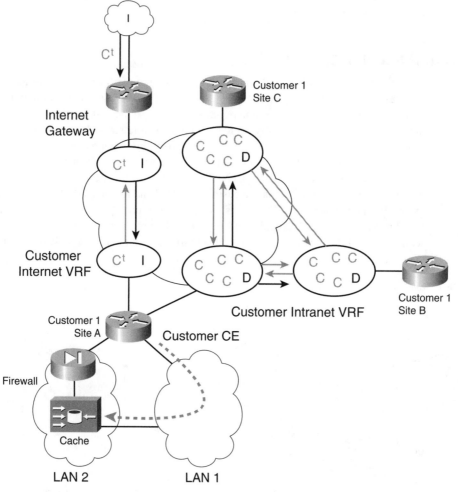

Customers may also desire to provide their own Internet services, such as web hosting, e-mail servers, telnet access, and so on, without requiring intervention from a service provider. Specifically a customer—say Customer 1 Hub Site—could provide caching and firewall services to all Customer 1 sites.

The CE router at the hub site, say Site A (customer or service provider managed) will have two interfaces (Ethernet, ATM, PVCs, and so on):

- One that connects the customer's hosts in the normal manner
- One that connects a cache/firewall segment

The customer site could have two connections from the CE for Internet and intranet traffic, each with its own VRF terminated at the PE.

The default route is injected into the customer Internet VRF at Site A. This default route is then distributed to all VRFs for Customer 1. Note that for this to occur, Multi-Protocol Border Gateway Protocol (MP-BGP) must be configured with the line **default-information-originate** in the address family section pertaining to that VRF. Intranet routes in the customer network are distributed in the normal manner between VRFs. The result is that all customer sites have full mesh/peer connectivity with one another, and Internet access will always be via Site A using the default route.

The Internet VRF in Site A will contain the address of the service provider Internet gateway imported from the Gateway VRF. The registered addresses used by Customer 1 will be exported to the gateway VRF. The registered addresses could be owned by the customer or provided by the service provider where address translation in this case occurs at Site A's firewall. The CE router will direct all routes for the default to the cache engine/proxy server. The firewall will direct traffic back through the CE router to the customer Internet VRF and eventually to the Internet. Policy-based routing is required for this to occur, but again, be aware of the security implications as identified previously in the section, "PE to Multiple Internet Gateways."

NOTE	This example is made more complex due to the fact that there is a single CE router performing both the hub and Internet gateway functions. A simpler method is to directly connect the firewall to the PE, but this requires two physical connections to the service provider network.

The configuration shown in Example 9-4 shows the PE configuration at the customer Hub Site A. The route to the service provider Internet gateway is imported into PUB_Customer1 using route-target import 9255:2 (assuming that there is a corresponding export elsewhere). Similarly, the customer's registered subnet is exported to the Internet gateway VRF to provide a return path for customer traffic using **route-target export 9255:20**. The Internet gateway VRF will have a corresponding **route-target import 9255:20**. The default-route is injected into **VPN_ Customer1** to inform all VRFs how to get to the Internet (via the cache engine). The **default-information-originate** command must be added to the BGP portion of the VRF for the default-route to be redistributed.

Example 9-4 *Customer Internet Hub PE Configuration Example*

```
!
!Define Customer Intranet VRF
ip vrf VPN_Customer1
rd 9255:10650
route-target export 9255:10650
route-target import 9255:10650
!
!Define Customer Internet VRF
ip vrf PUB_Customer1
rd 9255:106500
route-target export 9255:20
!
!Import routes for Service Provider Internet service
route-target import 9255:2

interface Ethernet 3/0
ip vrf forwarding VPN_Customer1
ip address 202.160.223.1  255.255.252

interface Ethernet 3/1
ip vrf forwarding PUB_Customer1
ip address 202.160.223.5  255.255.252


!
!Static route for registered NAT address
ip address vrf PUB_Customer1 171.69.223.208  255.255.255.240  ethernet 3/1
202.160.223.6
!
!Install default route into Intranet
ip route vrf VPN_Customer1 0.0.0.0  0.0.0.0  ethernet 3/0 202.160.221.2

router bgp 9255
address-family ipv4 vrf VPN_Customer1
default-information-originate
```

In Example 9-5, for the CE, any traffic from Ethernet 0 (VPN_Customer1) that does not have an explicit entry into the CE's routing table will be forwarded to the LAN interface of the cache engine, which is reachable via Ethernet 1 (the customer's LAN). This behavior is achieved via the policy-based routing command **set default next-hop** *Cache IP Address*.

Traffic entering Ethernet interface 3 from the firewall will be directed to the PUB_Customer1 VRF via Ethernet 1. The firewall will be responsible for address translation. Traffic returning from the Internet will be directed back via the interface Ethernet 3. No special routing commands are necessary on return traffic because the destination address is always within the 171.69.233.208 255.255.255.240 space, which is only reachable via Ethernet 3.

In Example 9-5, there are a few 10BASE-X interfaces required. If a Fast Ethernet connection or an ATM/Frame Relay connection was used, then subinterfaces in the form of

ISL or PVCs would reduce the physical requirement considerably. Otherwise, intranet traffic will be forwarded to Ethernet 2.

Example 9-5 *Customer Internet Hub CE Configuration*

```
!
!Interface to Intranet VRF
interface Ethernet 0
ip address 202.160.223.2  255.255.255.252
ip policy route-map TO_CacheEngine
!
!Interface to Internet VRF (Public VRF)
interface Ethernet 1
ip address 202.160.223.6 255.255.255.252
!
!Normal Customer LAN
interface Ethernet 2
ip address 192.168.1.94 255.255.255.0
!
!Firewall and Cache subnet
interface Ethernet 3
ip address 171.69.233.209  255.255.255.0
ip policy route-map TO_Internet

route-map TO_Internet permit 10
set default interface Ethernet 1

route-map TO_CacheEngine
set default next-hop Cache IP Address
```

Internet Access Using Global Routing Table

The previous scenarios focused on providing Internet access via a VRF that contains the default route to the Internet gateway. Another method is to use the global routing table to access the Internet gateway (see Figure 9-7):

- A router with connectivity to the Internet is attached the MPLS network. It may or may not inject BGP routes into the global routing table. Note that only the PEs speak BGP; P routers do not run BGP at all.

- Customers requiring access to the Internet will have a default route injected into their VRF pointing to the loopback address of the Internet gateway router. This address resides in the global routing table; therefore, the tag "global" is appended to end of the static **route** command. This forces the static route to look into the global routing table.

- A static route to the customer network must also be injected into the global routing table pointing back to the CE. This static route could then be distributed into BGP for advertising to the Internet.

The premise here is that the customer uses a registered address range that can exist in the service provider's global routing table. If the CE must perform NAT, then a separate subinterface would be required (to translate to), which is essentially the scenario described in the previous section.

Figure 9-7   *CE Access to Full Internet BGP Routing Table*

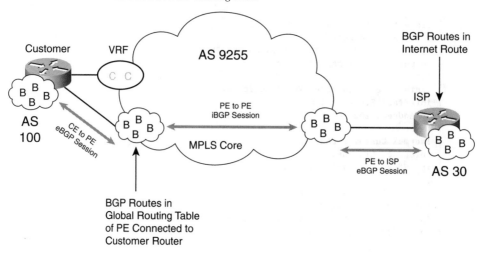

NOTE   This method is not recommended where customers only have private addresses. Consider the following scenario: Customer A and Customer B both use the private address space 192.168.0.0. Customer A subscribes to Internet access via the global routing table (NAT must occur at the Internet gateway). Customer B wants access, but cannot get it because there is a duplication of addresses in the global routing table. To avoid this problem, address translation must be performed at the CE.

BGP Internet Routing Table from the Service Provider of an ISP

There may be customers who need to receive and announce routes from the Internet. (For example, an ISP's service provider may be wholesaling to use the service provider's VPN network or customers may require dual-homed Internet connectivity.)

NOTE   Importing the full BGP Internet routing table into a VRF is not a scalable solution and *must* be avoided.

The PE global routing table—that is, the routing table associated with IGP routes for the core, not any VRF—should be used to propagate Internet BGP routes. To provide Internet routes, a separate connection must be provisioned between the CE and the local PE for a BGP session. At the PE end, the circuit will not terminate in a VRF but will use the global routing table of the PE, which will contain the Internet routes. Therefore, the CE requires two physical/logical connections to the PE if the CE also participates in an MPLS-VPN intranet.

The PE is configured to redistribute Internet BGP routes to the customer CE via a BGP session. Conversely, any BGP routes from the CE that are injected into the global routing table are distributed into the Internet. The Internet routing table does not have to be redistributed to every PE in the MPLS network; only the PEs that are connected to the CEs require this redistribution.

To summarize, a CE that received BGP Internet routes and participates in MPLS VPNs requires two connections to the PE. These may be physical, or logical over a physical connection. Internet routes will appear in the global routing table of PEs as external BGP routes and will *not* have labels assigned to them. The labels associated with the Internet routes will be that of the BGP next hop. Therefore, all Internet routes will share the same label of the next hop BGP router.

NOTE	The BGP table does not need to be carried in the service provider core; it is carried only at the edges where customers require BGP routes.

NOTE	Since the CE has a direct connection to the PE outside a VRF, all global addresses in the service provider's MPLS network could be visible to the CE. Therefore, an access list is necessary on the inbound interface at the PE to deny access to any destination on the MPLS network.

Example 9-6 shows a simple BGP configuration. The CE has two interfaces, atm1/0.100 and atm1/0.200, connected to the PE. The interface atm1/0.100 carries the MPLS VPN traffic, while atm1.0.200 is connected to the MPLS global routing table where the Internet BGP routes reside. An eBGP session is configured over atm1/0.100, as the AS numbers between CE and PE are different.

Example 9-6 *CE BGP Configuration Example for Internet Routes*

```
interface loopback0
ip address 165.21.240.137  255.255.255.255
!
interface atm 1/0.100
description Interface to PE router (for Intranet and Services)
ip address 202.160.223.10  255.255.255.252
!
interface atm1/0.200
description connection to the global table of the PE router
ip address 170.10.0.1 255.255.255.240
!
interface Ethernet 0
```
continues

Example 9-6 *CE BGP Configuration Example for Internet Routes (Continued)*

```
description Connection to Customer LAN/WAN
ip address 170.10.0.1  255.255.255.240
!
router bgp 100
neighbor 202.160.223.9 remote-as 9255
neighbor 202.160.223.9 update-source loopback0
network 170.10.0.0
!
```

NOTE   In this example, for an eBGP neighbor (which is the neighbor peering address), when update-source loopback0 is used, use the lookback IP address of the peering router over a multihop path, which is not a directly connected address, so the neighbor statements may not be required accordingly.

In Example 9-7, there are two BGP sessions defined: an external session to the CE and an internal session to the PE connecting the ISP. An inbound access list is associated with the eBGP session interface to restrict packets from the CE directly accessing the MPLS network. The first line in access-list 102 allows the two BGP peers (CE and PE) to communicate. The second line denies the CE network access to any destination address in the MPLS network. The third line permits Internet traffic to pass through to the ISP.

Example 9-7 *PE BGP Configuration for Internet Routes*

```
!
interface loopback0
ip address 165.21.240.137  255.255.255.255
!
! Define Customer Intranet VRF
ip vrf VPN_Customer1
rd 9255:10650
route-target both 9255:10650
!
interface atm8/0/0.200
Description Connection for eBGP session and Internet Traffic
ip address 202.160.223.9 255.255.255.252
ip access-group in 102
!
access-list 102 permit ip host 202.160.223.9 host 202.160.223.10
access-list 102 deny ip 202.160.223.0 255.255.0.0 any
access-list permit any any
!
router bgp 9255
neighbor 202.160.223.10 remote-as 100 (remote BGP session to CE)
neighbor 202.160.223.10 update-source loopback0
neighbor 165.21.240.134 remote-as 200 (BGP session to PE connecting to ISP)
neighbor 165.21.240.134 update-source loopback0
```

NOTE   In this example for an eBGP neighbor (which is the neighbor peering address), when the update-source loopback0 is used, use the lookback IP address of the peering router over a multihop path, which is not a directly connected address, so the neighbor statements may not be required accordingly.

Because the CE would have a direct connection to the PE outside a VRF, all global addresses in the service provider X MPLS network could be visible to the CE. Therefore, an access list would be necessary on the inbound interface at the PE to deny access to any destination in the MPLS global network.

Tier 3 ISP Connecting to an Upstream Tier via a Service Provider

In this scenario, shown in Figure 9-8, a smaller ISP gains access to the Internet via a larger upstream ISP that is wholesaling Internet access. The tier 3 ISP requires Internet routes. The connectivity between the two ISPs is via the service provider's MPLS network. In this scenario, both ISP connections can be terminated inside a VRF, even though they are exchanging BGP routes. The VRFs do not actually hold the BGP routes; they only hold the routes originating from the tier 3 ISP.

Figure 9-8   *ISP-to-ISP Connection*

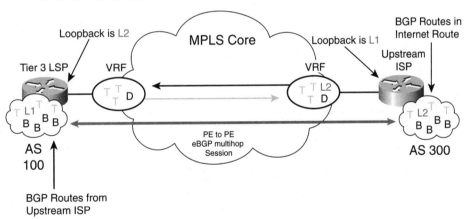

The routing tables in the ISP routers will also contain the loopback address **L1,L2** (entered statically). An eBGP session then can be established between the two CEs (ISP routers). Note that the tier3 ISP VRF does not need to explicitly contain the route to L1, as the default route will provide the connection. The tier 3 ISP will receive the BGP routing table with the next hop of L1, while the wholesale router will receive the tier 3 routes with the next hop of L3.

NOTE	For this solution to be scalable, the tier 3 ISP must not be a transit network for the other ISPs; otherwise, there will be too many routes in the VRF. This ensures that the VRF will only hold originating routes from the tier 3 ISP and not transit routes.
	For example, assume that a tier 3 ISP has three address blocks allocated that the tier 3 ISP wishes to distribute to the Internet. Also, assume that the tier 3 ISP has a second connection to another ISP, hence the requirement for a BGP routing table. These three tier 3 ISP address routes are distributed to the tier 3 VRF. The PE connected to the tier 3 ISP imports a default route, which has been exported from the upstream wholesale ISP VRF. Similarly, the wholesale ISP VRF imports the tier 3 address routes.

Hybrid Model

There are organizations that currently deploy the hybrid service model as depicted in Figure 9-9 and implement a variety of the Internet access scenarios we have discussed. One of the main reasons for implementing the hybrid model is capital expenditure restrictions that preclude full service separation at the physical level, such as the Internet service PE, intranet service PE, and so on.

Figure 9-9   *Key Issue: DoS Through a Shared PE Might Affect the VPN Customer*

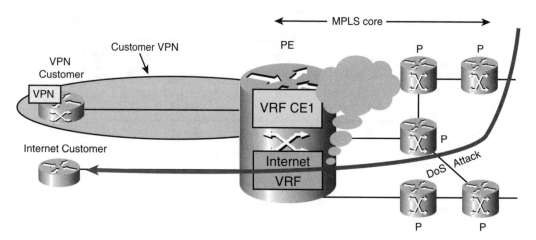

There are tier 1 service providers internationally deploying this model; there are other tier 1 customers that do implement a service separation at the physical level. The important factor is to be cognizant of the design choices and risks, as pointed out in Chapter 4. Additionally, the use of infrastructure ACLS and the development and deployment of high-availability hardware facilitate the implementation of a hybrid service model.

Multi-Lite VRF Mechanisms

Multi-lite VRF is also known as VRF-lite and extends the concept of VRFs to the customer. The Multi-VRF CE architecture uses the VRF concept to support multiple overlapping and independent routing tables (and forwarding tables) per customer and is not a feature but an application based on VRF implementation. Any routing protocol that is supported by normal VRF can be used in a Multi-lite VRF implementation. The CE supports traffic separation between customer networks, and there is no MPLS functionality on the CE and no label exchange between the CE and PE. Figure 9-10 depicts a typical Multi-lite VRF scenario using subinterface access to the PE.

Figure 9-10 *Multi-lite VRF*

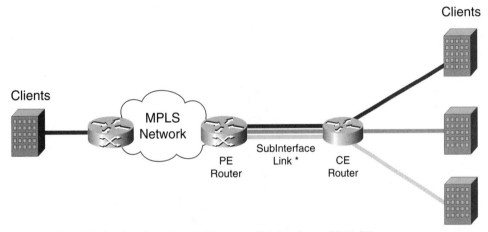

** SubInterfaceLink: Any Interface Type that Supports Sub-interfaces, FE-VLAN,
Frame Relay, ATM VCs*

The most common use for Multi-lite VRF is for Internet and VPN services via a single CE, as depicted in Figure 9-11.

We will use this scenario as a case study example in this section. Note that there is no need for policy routing when deploying this example. The premise is that all routes to and from the Internet are directed to the CE, which connects to the firewall at the central site.

Configuration Example for Internet and VPN Service Using the Same CE

A default route is applied in the global table in order to route customer traffic to the firewall. This is then advertised to the VPN, as it was for the policy routing solution.

Figure 9-11 *Application: Internet Services and VPN Services Using a Single CE*

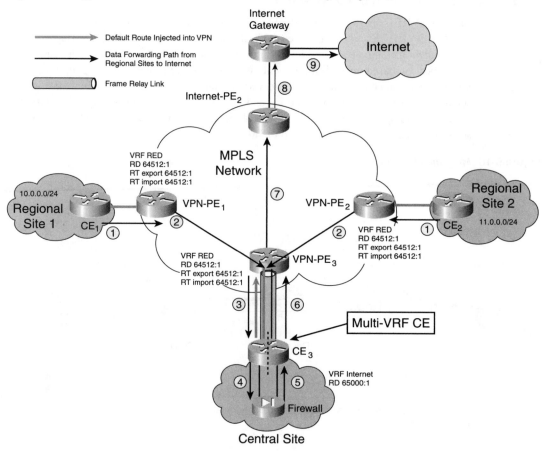

A static route is applied to the Internet VRF in order to route traffic arriving from the Internet toward the firewall. Another route is also applied to the VRF in order to provide a route back to the Internet. This can be via a default route or a dynamic routing protocol. The advantage of this solution is the ease of using a dynamic routing protocol for the Internet routes. It is possible to use the same routing protocol for both the customer/VPN and Internet routing but still keep them segregated from each other; this is done by using an address family within the routing process so that there is no leaking of routes from one environment to the other.

This solution has the same security limitations as the policy routing solution, although only the addresses within the Internet VRF are reachable directly from the Internet; other addresses on the router are routed via the firewall. If access is gained to the router, it is still possible to hop to the VPN; and if the router is the victim of a denial of service (DoS) attack, the VPN will still be affected.

The solution will work on a wide range of link encapsulation methods, but it will only work on routers supporting VRFs.

Example 9-8 is for CE$_3$ on Figure 9-11. Some of the technology used to separate different customers across the common MPLS core is used to separate the customer and Internet traffic within the CE. The CE is configured with a VPN routing and forwarding (VRF) instance that is applied to the insecure and Internet interfaces. This means that the VPN and customer interfaces are considered to be part of the router's global routing and forwarding tables, but the insecure and Internet interfaces have a different routing and forwarding table.

NOTE   This implementation example is an alternative to policy routing and having separate routers, and in Figure 9-11 we illustrate the data flow from Regional Site 1 to the Internet and the data flow from Regional Site 2 to the Internet. The flow is broken down into steps. CE$_3$ is configured for Multi-VRF/VRF-lite.

Example 9-8 *CE$_3$ in Figure 9-11*

```
ip vrf Internet
rd 65000:1
ip cef
!
interface Serial0/0
description *** Serial link to PE ***
 no ip address
 encapsulation frame-relay
!
interface Serial0/0.100 point-to-point
 description *** VPN sub-interface ***
 ip address 192.168.1.1 255.255.255.252
 frame-relay interface-dlci 100
!
interface Serial0/0.200 point-to-point
 description *** Internet sub-interface ***
 ip vrf forwarding Internet
 ip address 172.25.1.1 255.255.255.252
 frame-relay interface-dlci 200
!
interface FastEthernet1/0
 description *** Customer LAN ***
 ip address 10.0.2.1 255.255.255.0
 no ip redirects
!
interface FastEthernet1/1
 description *** Insecure LAN ***
 ip vrf forwarding Internet
 ip address 10.0.1.2 255.255.255.0
 no ip redirects
```

                                                                    continues

Example 9-8   *CE₃ in Figure 9-11 (Continued)*

```
!
ip route vrf Internet 0.0.0.0 0.0.0.0 Serial0/0.200 172.25.1.2
ip route vrf Internet 10.0.0.0 255.255.0.0 FastEthernet1/0.2 10.0.1.1
router bgp 3
 bgp log-neighbor-changes
 neighbor 192.1.3.1 remote-as 13
 neighbor 192.1.3.1 update-source Ethernet0/1.13
 !
ip classless
ip route 220.1.65.16 255.255.255.252 192.1.4.1
```

One note on Multi-lite VRF scalability factors that are limited by the platform max interfaces: memory for routes and raw processing ability and the actual performance may vary based on traffic load, number of routes, and routing processes.

Multi-VRF/VRF-lite offers the following benefits:

- Only one CE router is needed to facilitate provisioning and network management rather than a multiple CE router solution.

- A CE router has VRF functionality without full PE functionality to provide BGP routing tables.

- It overlaps customer address spaces.

- It can coexist with an MPLS-based network with no MPLS enabled on the CE.

NOTE   As we pointed out in Chapter 4, while a shared access line with the CE for Multi-lite VRF facilitates service separation, a DoS attack might affect the VPN on the PE, the single physical link between the PE and the CE, and the CE itself.

Layer 2 LAN Access

We have discussed Layer 2 access security issues in Chapter 7, particularly in the context of Ethernet over MPLS. As customers converge their services onto an MPLS-based network, Layer 2 security considerations will be even more pivotal, especially for interworking OAM constructs and interprovider pseudowire mechanisms, such as pseudowire switching, which are being discussed at the time of the writing of this book.

Some points to highlight for deployment are the following:

- Inter-As and CsC connections only in private peering relationships—Use a dedicated connection rather than a shared VLAN.

- Within VLANs, ARP spoofing (hacking tools *hunt, arpspoof*), CAM overflow (hacking tool *macof*), DoS against spanning tree, and DoS storms (a hacking tool exists) can be done. For ARP spoofing and CAM overflow prevention, look at port security. Also, disable the spanning tree on the router port by hard coding the root bridge, for example.

These are not extensive and are the most obvious best practices for Layer 2 deployments.

Summary

This chapter provided use cases, application examples, and best practice guidelines for the key principles discussed in this book.

We have also offered security notes to these use cases in order to apprise the reader of the potential risks of a deployment. One of the most important principles of this book is that an organization can certainly implement MPLS VPN networks securely.

We also provided use cases for Internet access that are commonly deployed. We have further pointed out the security considerations for some of these scenarios as explained in the previous chapters. We looked at the hybrid model for both Internet and intranet service deployments and highlighted the security considerations for this model.

Detailed Configuration Example for a PE

This configuration was made on a 7500 running 12.0(30)S. It gives a global view on a number of security features configured on a single router. As with all examples, do not enter commands with IP addresses literally into your router. Also, certain features do not work in all environments; for example, the infrastructure ACLs in this example only work because here static routing is used. Therefore, this example must be adapted specifically to every environment.

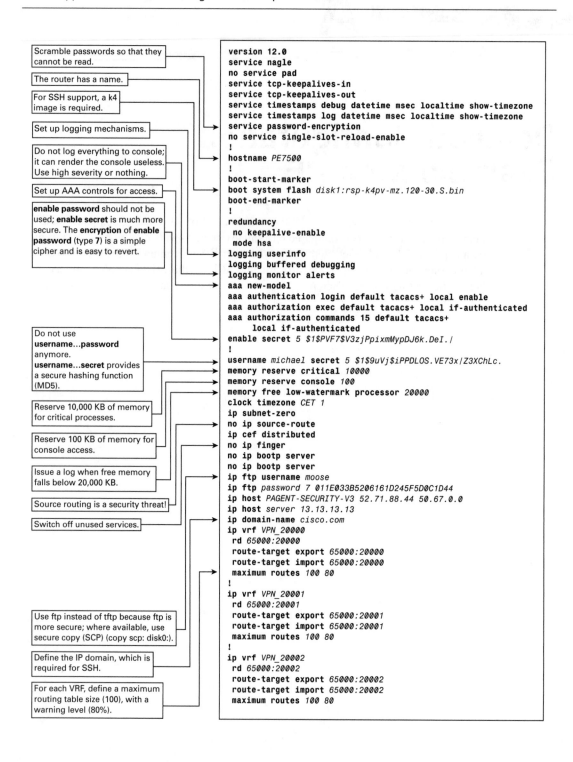

Scramble passwords so that they cannot be read.

The router has a name.

For SSH support, a k4 image is required.

Set up logging mechanisms.

Do not log everything to console; it can render the console useless. Use high severity or nothing.

Set up AAA controls for access.

enable password should not be used; **enable secret** is much more secure. The **encryption** of **enable password** (type **7**) is a simple cipher and is easy to revert.

Do not use **username...password** anymore. **username...secret** provides a secure hashing function (MD5).

Reserve 10,000 KB of memory for critical processes.

Reserve 100 KB of memory for console access.

Issue a log when free memory falls below 20,000 KB.

Source routing is a security threat!

Switch off unused services.

Use ftp instead of tftp because ftp is more secure; where available, use secure copy (SCP) (copy scp: disk0:).

Define the IP domain, which is required for SSH.

For each VRF, define a maximum routing table size (100), with a warning level (80%).

```
version 12.0
service nagle
no service pad
service tcp-keepalives-in
service tcp-keepalives-out
service timestamps debug datetime msec localtime show-timezone
service timestamps log datetime msec localtime show-timezone
service password-encryption
no service single-slot-reload-enable
!
hostname PE7500
!
boot-start-marker
boot system flash disk1:rsp-k4pv-mz.120-30.S.bin
boot-end-marker
!
redundancy
 no keepalive-enable
 mode hsa
logging userinfo
logging buffered debugging
logging monitor alerts
aaa new-model
aaa authentication login default tacacs+ local enable
aaa authorization exec default tacacs+ local if-authenticated
aaa authorization commands 15 default tacacs+
     local if-authenticated
enable secret 5 $1$PVF7$V3zjPpixmMypDJ6k.DeI./
!
username michael secret 5 $1$9uVj$iPPDLOS.VE73x/Z3XChLc.
memory reserve critical 10000
memory reserve console 100
memory free low-watermark processor 20000
clock timezone CET 1
ip subnet-zero
no ip source-route
ip cef distributed
no ip finger
no ip bootp server
no ip bootp server
ip ftp username moose
ip ftp password 7 011E033B5206161D245F5D0C1D44
ip host PAGENT-SECURITY-V3 52.71.88.44 50.67.0.0
ip host server 13.13.13.13
ip domain-name cisco.com
ip vrf VPN_20000
 rd 65000:20000
 route-target export 65000:20000
 route-target import 65000:20000
 maximum routes 100 80
!
ip vrf VPN_20001
 rd 65000:20001
 route-target export 65000:20001
 route-target import 65000:20001
 maximum routes 100 80
!
ip vrf VPN_20002
 rd 65000:20002
 route-target export 65000:20002
 route-target import 65000:20002
 maximum routes 100 80
```

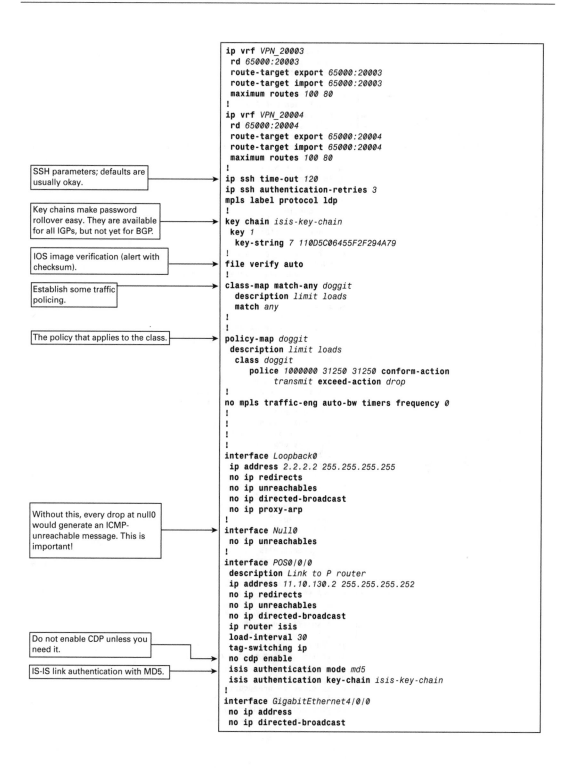

SSH parameters; defaults are usually okay.

Key chains make password rollover easy. They are available for all IGPs, but not yet for BGP.

IOS image verification (alert with checksum).

Establish some traffic policing.

The policy that applies to the class.

Without this, every drop at null0 would generate an ICMP-unreachable message. This is important!

Do not enable CDP unless you need it.

IS-IS link authentication with MD5.

```
ip vrf VPN_20003
 rd 65000:20003
 route-target export 65000:20003
 route-target import 65000:20003
 maximum routes 100 80
!
ip vrf VPN_20004
 rd 65000:20004
 route-target export 65000:20004
 route-target import 65000:20004
 maximum routes 100 80
!
ip ssh time-out 120
ip ssh authentication-retries 3
mpls label protocol ldp
!
key chain isis-key-chain
 key 1
   key-string 7 110D5C06455F2F294A79
!
file verify auto
!
class-map match-any doggit
  description limit loads
  match any
!
!
policy-map doggit
 description limit loads
  class doggit
    police 1000000 31250 31250 conform-action
          transmit exceed-action drop
!
no mpls traffic-eng auto-bw timers frequency 0
!
!
!
!
interface Loopback0
 ip address 2.2.2.2 255.255.255.255
 no ip redirects
 no ip unreachables
 no ip directed-broadcast
 no ip proxy-arp
!
interface Null0
 no ip unreachables
!
interface POS0/0/0
 description Link to P router
 ip address 11.10.130.2 255.255.255.252
 no ip redirects
 no ip unreachables
 no ip directed-broadcast
 ip router isis
 load-interval 30
 tag-switching ip
 no cdp enable
 isis authentication mode md5
 isis authentication key-chain isis-key-chain
!
interface GigabitEthernet4/0/0
 no ip address
 no ip directed-broadcast
```

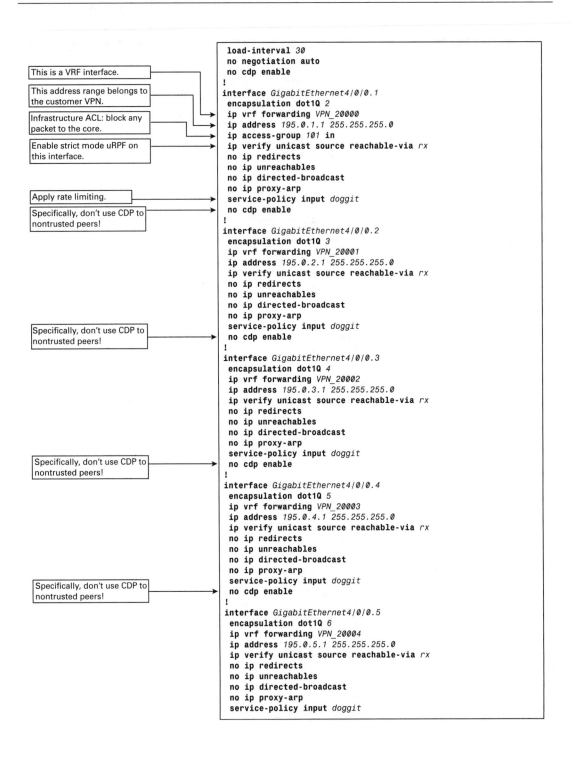

This is a VRF interface.

This address range belongs to the customer VPN.

Infrastructure ACL: block any packet to the core.

Enable strict mode uRPF on this interface.

Apply rate limiting.

Specifically, don't use CDP to nontrusted peers!

Specifically, don't use CDP to nontrusted peers!

Specifically, don't use CDP to nontrusted peers!

Specifically, don't use CDP to nontrusted peers!

```
 load-interval 30
 no negotiation auto
 no cdp enable
!
interface GigabitEthernet4/0/0.1
 encapsulation dot1Q 2
 ip vrf forwarding VPN_20000
 ip address 195.0.1.1 255.255.255.0
 ip access-group 101 in
 ip verify unicast source reachable-via rx
 no ip redirects
 no ip unreachables
 no ip directed-broadcast
 no ip proxy-arp
 service-policy input doggit
 no cdp enable
!
interface GigabitEthernet4/0/0.2
 encapsulation dot1Q 3
 ip vrf forwarding VPN_20001
 ip address 195.0.2.1 255.255.255.0
 ip verify unicast source reachable-via rx
 no ip redirects
 no ip unreachables
 no ip directed-broadcast
 no ip proxy-arp
 service-policy input doggit
 no cdp enable
!
interface GigabitEthernet4/0/0.3
 encapsulation dot1Q 4
 ip vrf forwarding VPN_20002
 ip address 195.0.3.1 255.255.255.0
 ip verify unicast source reachable-via rx
 no ip redirects
 no ip unreachables
 no ip directed-broadcast
 no ip proxy-arp
 service-policy input doggit
 no cdp enable
!
interface GigabitEthernet4/0/0.4
 encapsulation dot1Q 5
 ip vrf forwarding VPN_20003
 ip address 195.0.4.1 255.255.255.0
 ip verify unicast source reachable-via rx
 no ip redirects
 no ip unreachables
 no ip directed-broadcast
 no ip proxy-arp
 service-policy input doggit
 no cdp enable
!
interface GigabitEthernet4/0/0.5
 encapsulation dot1Q 6
 ip vrf forwarding VPN_20004
 ip address 195.0.5.1 255.255.255.0
 ip verify unicast source reachable-via rx
 no ip redirects
 no ip unreachables
 no ip directed-broadcast
 no ip proxy-arp
 service-policy input doggit
```

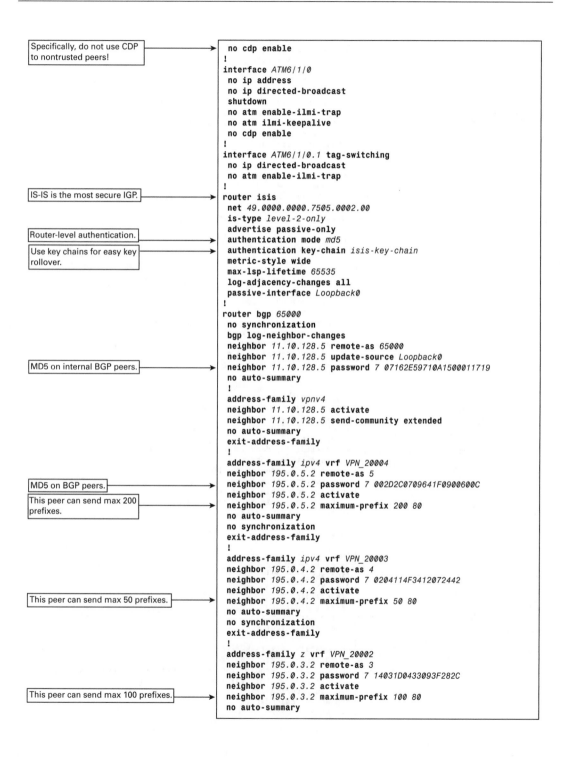

Specifically, do not use CDP to nontrusted peers!

```
 no cdp enable
!
interface ATM6/1/0
 no ip address
 no ip directed-broadcast
 shutdown
 no atm enable-ilmi-trap
 no atm ilmi-keepalive
 no cdp enable
!
interface ATM6/1/0.1 tag-switching
 no ip directed-broadcast
 no atm enable-ilmi-trap
!
```

IS-IS is the most secure IGP.

Router-level authentication.

Use key chains for easy key rollover.

```
router isis
 net 49.0000.0000.7505.0002.00
 is-type level-2-only
 advertise passive-only
 authentication mode md5
 authentication key-chain isis-key-chain
 metric-style wide
 max-lsp-lifetime 65535
 log-adjacency-changes all
 passive-interface Loopback0
!
router bgp 65000
 no synchronization
 bgp log-neighbor-changes
 neighbor 11.10.128.5 remote-as 65000
 neighbor 11.10.128.5 update-source Loopback0
```

MD5 on internal BGP peers.

```
 neighbor 11.10.128.5 password 7 07162E59710A1500011719
 no auto-summary
 !
 address-family vpnv4
 neighbor 11.10.128.5 activate
 neighbor 11.10.128.5 send-community extended
 no auto-summary
 exit-address-family
 !
 address-family ipv4 vrf VPN_20004
 neighbor 195.0.5.2 remote-as 5
```

MD5 on BGP peers.

This peer can send max 200 prefixes.

```
 neighbor 195.0.5.2 password 7 002D2C0709641F0900600C
 neighbor 195.0.5.2 activate
 neighbor 195.0.5.2 maximum-prefix 200 80
 no auto-summary
 no synchronization
 exit-address-family
 !
 address-family ipv4 vrf VPN_20003
 neighbor 195.0.4.2 remote-as 4
 neighbor 195.0.4.2 password 7 0204114F3412072442
 neighbor 195.0.4.2 activate
```

This peer can send max 50 prefixes.

```
 neighbor 195.0.4.2 maximum-prefix 50 80
 no auto-summary
 no synchronization
 exit-address-family
 !
 address-family z vrf VPN_20002
 neighbor 195.0.3.2 remote-as 3
 neighbor 195.0.3.2 password 7 14031D0433093F282C
 neighbor 195.0.3.2 activate
```

This peer can send max 100 prefixes.

```
 neighbor 195.0.3.2 maximum-prefix 100 80
 no auto-summary
```

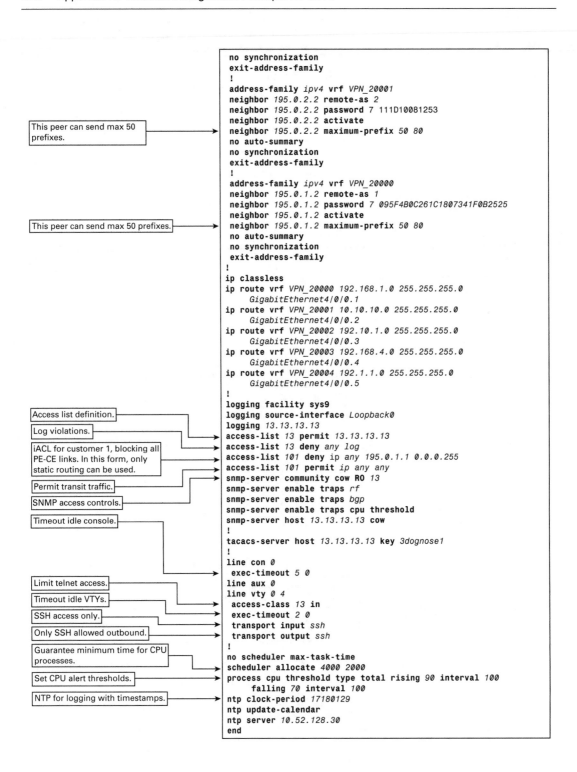

This peer can send max 50 prefixes.

This peer can send max 50 prefixes.

Access list definition.

Log violations.

iACL for customer 1, blocking all PE-CE links. In this form, only static routing can be used.

Permit transit traffic.

SNMP access controls.

Timeout idle console.

Limit telnet access.

Timeout idle VTYs.

SSH access only.

Only SSH allowed outbound.

Guarantee minimum time for CPU processes.

Set CPU alert thresholds.

NTP for logging with timestamps.

```
 no synchronization
 exit-address-family
 !
 address-family ipv4 vrf VPN_20001
 neighbor 195.0.2.2 remote-as 2
 neighbor 195.0.2.2 password 7 111D10081253
 neighbor 195.0.2.2 activate
 neighbor 195.0.2.2 maximum-prefix 50 80
 no auto-summary
 no synchronization
 exit-address-family
 !
 address-family ipv4 vrf VPN_20000
 neighbor 195.0.1.2 remote-as 1
 neighbor 195.0.1.2 password 7 095F4B0C261C1807341F0B2525
 neighbor 195.0.1.2 activate
 neighbor 195.0.1.2 maximum-prefix 50 80
 no auto-summary
 no synchronization
 exit-address-family
!
ip classless
ip route vrf VPN_20000 192.168.1.0 255.255.255.0
     GigabitEthernet4/0/0.1
ip route vrf VPN_20001 10.10.10.0 255.255.255.0
     GigabitEthernet4/0/0.2
ip route vrf VPN_20002 192.10.1.0 255.255.255.0
     GigabitEthernet4/0/0.3
ip route vrf VPN_20003 192.168.4.0 255.255.255.0
     GigabitEthernet4/0/0.4
ip route vrf VPN_20004 192.1.1.0 255.255.255.0
     GigabitEthernet4/0/0.5
!
logging facility sys9
logging source-interface Loopback0
logging 13.13.13.13
access-list 13 permit 13.13.13.13
access-list 13 deny any log
access-list 101 deny ip any 195.0.1.1 0.0.0.255
access-list 101 permit ip any any
snmp-server community cow RO 13
snmp-server enable traps rf
snmp-server enable traps bgp
snmp-server enable traps cpu threshold
snmp-server host 13.13.13.13 cow
!
tacacs-server host 13.13.13.13 key 3dognose1
!
line con 0
 exec-timeout 5 0
line aux 0
line vty 0 4
 access-class 13 in
 exec-timeout 2 0
 transport input ssh
 transport output ssh
!
no scheduler max-task-time
scheduler allocate 4000 2000
process cpu threshold type total rising 90 interval 100
     falling 70 interval 100
ntp clock-period 17180129
ntp update-calendar
ntp server 10.52.128.30
end
```

Reference List

This appendix provides a list of available sources that you can refer to for more information on MPLS VPN security.

Cisco Press Books

Abelar, Greg. *Securing Your Business Using PIX Device Manager.* Cisco Press, June 2005 (ISBN: 1587052148).

Behtash, Behzad. *CCSP Self-Study: Cisco Secure PIX Firewall Advanced (CSPFA),* Second Edition. Cisco Press, January 2004 (ISBN: 1587051494).

Bollapragada, Vijay, et al. *IPSec VPN Design.* Cisco Press, June 2005 (ISBN: 1587051117).

Carroll, Brandon. *Cisco Access Control Security: AAA Administration Services.* Cisco Press, June 2004 (ISBN: 1587051249).

Carter, Earl. *CCSP Self-Study: Cisco Secure Intrusion Detection System (CSIDS),* Second Edition. Cisco Press, February 2004 (ISBN: 1587051443).

Convery, Sean. *Network Security Architectures.* Cisco Press, April 2004 (ISBN: 158705115x).

Deal, Richard A. *Cisco Router Firewall Security.* Cisco Press, August 2004 (ISBN: 1587051753).

De Laet, Gert and Schauwers, Gert. *Network Security Fundamentals.* Cisco Press, September 2004 (ISBN: 1587051672).

Hucaby, David. *Cisco PIX Firewall Handbook.* Cisco Press, June 2005 (ISBN: 1587051583).

Kaeo, Merike. *Designing Network Security,* Second Edition. Cisco Press, November 2003 (ISBN: 1587051176).

Malik, Saadat. *Network Security Principles and Practices.* Cisco Press, November 2002 (ISBN: 1587050250).

Mason, Andrew. *CCSP Self-Study: Cisco Secure Virtual Private Networks (CSVPN),* Second Edition. Cisco Press, May 2004 (ISBN: 1587051451).

Paquet, Catherine and Saxe, Warren. *The Business Case for Network Security: Advocacy, Governance, and ROI.* Cisco Press, December 2004 (ISBN: 1587201216).

Raveendran Greene, Barry and Smith, Philip. *Cisco ISP Essentials.* Cisco Press, April 2002 (ISBN: 1587050412).

Roland, John F. *CCSP Self-Study: Securing Cisco IOS Networks (SECUR).* Cisco Press, April 2004 (ISBN: 1587051516).

Sankar, Krishna, et al. *Cisco Wireless LAN Security.* Cisco Press, November 2004 (ISBN: 1587051540).

Sullivan, Chad. *Cisco Security Agent.* Cisco Press, June 2005 (ISBN: 1587052059).

Szigeti, Tim and Hattingh, Christina. *End-to-End QoS Network Design: Quality of Service in LANs, WANs, and VPNs.* Cisco Press, November 2004 (ISBN: 1587051761).

Thomas, Tom. *Network Security First-Step.* Cisco Press, May 2004 (ISBN: 1587200996).

Vacca, John. *The Business Case for Network Disaster Recovery Planning.* Cisco Press, June 2005 (ISBN: 1587201194).

IETF

Request for Comments (RFCs) are Internet standards that you can find at http://rfc-editor.org by either entering the number or searching keywords.

Internet Drafts (IDs) are documenting work in progress. Some IDs will become RFCs in the future. You can find IDs at http://www.ietf.org/ID.html.

If you are looking for the work of a particular IETF working group, refer to the working group listing at http://www.ietf.org/html.charters/wg-dir.html. These pages contain links to all IDs and RFCs of a given working group.

The status of an ID can be checked at the ID data tracker at https://datatracker.ietf.org/public/pidtracker.cgi, as long as the ID is in the IETF. After the ID is submitted to the RFC Editor, the status can be found in the RFC Editor queue at http://rfc-editor.org/queue.html.

RFC 2547bis. draft-ietf-l3vpn-rfc2547bis-03.txt (work in progress).

Behringer, M. "Analysis of the Security of BGP/MPLS IP VPNs." draft-behringer-mpls-security-xx.txt, April 2005.

Rosen, E. "Use of PE-PE GRE or IP in BGP/MPLS IP Virtual Private Networks." draft-ietf-l3vpn-gre-ip-2547-xx.txt, April 2005.

Bonica, R., Rekhter, Y. et al. "CE-to-CE Member Verification for Layer 3 VPNs." draft-ietf-l3vpn-l3vpn-auth-xx.txt, June 2005.

Behringer, M. "Layer-3 VPN Import/Export Verification," draft-ietf-l3vpn-verification-00, March 2005.

Fang, Luyuan (ed.) and AT&T. "Security Framework for Provider Provisioned Virtual Private Networks." draft-ietf-l3vpn-security-framework-xx.txt, May 2005.

Townsley, W. M., et al. "Encapsulation of MPLS over Layer 2 Tunneling Protocol Version 3." draft-ietf-mpls-over-l2tpv3-xx.txt, February 2005.

Baugher, M., Weis, B., Hardjono, T., Harney, H. RFC 3547, "The Group Domain of Interpretation." July 2003.

Lau, J., Townsley, M., and Goyret, I. (eds.). RFC 3931, "Layer Two Tunneling Protocol—Version 3 (L2TPv3)." March 2005.

Kent, S., Atkinson, R. RFC 2401, "Security Architecture for the Internet Protocol." November 1998.

Rekhter, Y., and Li, T. RFC 1771, "A Border Gateway Protocol 4 (BGP-4)." March 1995.

ITU-T

"X.805 Security Architecture for Systems Providing End-to-End Communications." http://www.itu.int/rec/recommendation.asp?type=folders&lang=e&parent=T-REC-X.805.

INDEX

Numerics

A

B

C

D

Cisco Press

3 STEPS TO LEARNING

STEP 1   **STEP 2**   **STEP 3**

First-Step   **Fundamentals**   **Networking
Technology Guides**

STEP 1 **First-Step**—Benefit from easy-to-grasp explanations.
No experience required!

STEP 2 **Fundamentals**—Understand the purpose, application,
and management of technology.

STEP 3 **Networking Technology Guides**—Gain the knowledge
to master the challenge of the network.

NETWORK BUSINESS SERIES

The Network Business series helps professionals tackle the
business issues surrounding the network. Whether you are a
seasoned IT professional or a business manager with minimal
technical expertise, this series will help you understand the
business case for technologies.

Justify Your Network Investment.

Look for Cisco Press titles at your favorite bookseller today.

Visit **www.ciscopress.com/series** for details on each of these book series.

CISCO SYSTEMS

Cisco Press

Your **first-step** to networking starts here

Are you new to the world of networking? Whether you are beginning your networking career or simply need a better understanding of technology to gain more meaningful discussions with networking experts, Cisco Press First-Step books are right for you.

➤ **No experience required**

➤ **Includes clear and easily understood explanations**

➤ **Makes learning easy**

Check out each of these First-Step books that cover key networking topics:

- **Computer Networking First-Step**
  ISBN: 1-58720-101-1

- **LAN Switching First-Step**
  ISBN: 1-58720-100-3

- **Network Security First-Step**
  ISBN: 1-58720-099-6

- **Routing First-Step**
  ISBN: 1-58720-122-4

- **TCP/IP First-Step**
  ISBN: 1-58720-108-9

- **Wireless Networks First-Step**
  ISBN: 1-58720-111-9

Visit **www.ciscopress.com/firststep** to learn more.

What's your next step?

Eager to dig deeper into networking technology? Cisco Press has the books that will help you move to the next level. Learn more at **www.ciscopress.com/series**.

ciscopress.com   **Learning begins with a first step.**

Cisco Press

SAVE UP TO 30%

Become a member and save at **ciscopress.com**!

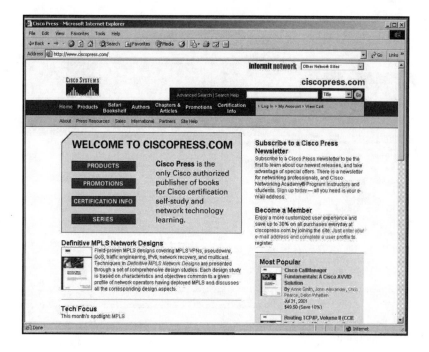

Complete a **user profile** at ciscopress.com today to become a member and benefit from **discounts up to 30% on every purchase** at ciscopress.com, as well as a more customized user experience. Your membership will also allow you access to the entire Informit network of sites.

Don't forget to subscribe to the monthly Cisco Press newsletter to be the first to learn about new releases and special promotions. You can also sign up to get your first **30 days FREE on Safari Bookshelf** and preview Cisco Press content. Safari Bookshelf lets you access Cisco Press books online and build your own customized, searchable electronic reference library.

Visit **www.ciscopress.com/register** to sign up and start saving today!

The profile information we collect is used in aggregate to provide us with better insight into your technology interests and to create a better user experience for you. You must be logged into ciscopress.com to receive your discount. Discount is on Cisco Press products only; shipping and handling are not included.

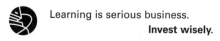

Learning is serious business.
Invest wisely.

SEARCH THOUSANDS OF BOOKS FROM LEADING PUBLISHERS

Safari® Bookshelf is a searchable electronic reference library for IT professionals that features thousands of titles from technical publishers, including Cisco Press.

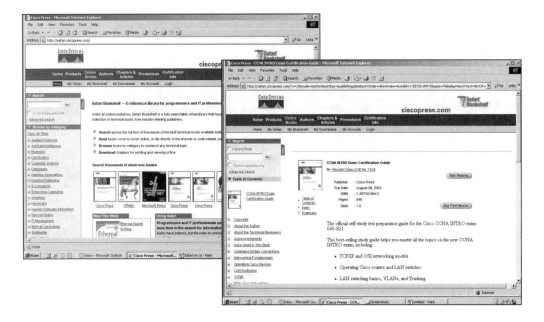

With Safari Bookshelf you can

- **Search** the full text of thousands of technical books, including more than 130 Cisco Press titles from authors such as Wendell Odom, Jeff Doyle, Bill Parkhurst, Sam Halabi, and Dave Hucaby.

- **Read** the books on My Bookshelf from cover to cover, or just flip to the information you need.

- **Browse** books by category to research any technical topic.

- **Download** chapters for printing and viewing offline.

With a customized library, you'll have access to your books when and where you need them—and all you need is a user name and password.

TRY SAFARI BOOKSHELF FREE FOR 14 DAYS!

You can sign up to get a 10-slot Bookshelf free for the first 14 days.
Visit **http://safari.ciscopress.com** to register.